Cultivating the Sociological Imagination

Concepts and Models

for Service-Learning

in **Sociology**

James Ostrow, Garry Hesser, and Sandra Enos, volume editors

Edward Zlotkowski, series editor

STERLING, VIRGINIA

Originally published by AAHE

Published in cooperation with American Sociological Association

This monograph was published in cooperation with:

American Sociological Association
1307 New York Avenue NW, #700
Washington, DC 20005
ph 202/383-9005
fax 202/638-0882
www.asanet.org

Cultivating the Sociological Imagination: Concepts and Models for Service-Learning in Sociology (AAHE's Series on Service-Learning in the Disciplines)
James Ostrow, Garry Hesser, and Sandra Enos, *volume editors*
Edward Zlotkowski, *series editor*

About This Publication

This volume is part of AAHE's Series on Service-Learning in the Disciplines. Copyright © 1999 American Association for Higher Education. Copyright © 2005 Stylus Publishing, LLC. All rights reserved. Printed in the United States of America. For information about additional copies of this publication or other AAHE or Stylus publications, contact:

Stylus Publishing, LLC.
22883 Quicksilver Drive
Sterling, VA 20166-2102
Tel.: 1-800-232-0223 / Fax: 703-661-1547
www.Styluspub.com

ISBN 1-56377-017-2
ISBN (set) 1-56377-005-9

Contents

Part 3
Action Research

Action Research: The Highest Stage of Service-Learning?

Examining Communities and Urban Change:
Service-Learning as Collaborative Research

Afterword

Sociology, Service, and Learning, For a Stronger Discipline

Appendix

About This Series

by Edward Zlotkowski

The following volume, *Cultivating the Sociological Imagination: Concepts and Models for Service-Learning in Sociology*, represents the seventh in a series of monographs on service-learning and academic disciplinary areas. Ever since the early 1990s, educators interested in reconnecting higher education not only with neighboring communities but also with the American tradition of education for service have recognized the critical importance of winning faculty support for this work. Faculty, however, tend to define themselves and their responsibilities largely in terms of the academic disciplines/interdisciplinary areas in which they have been trained. Hence, the logic of the present series.

The idea for this series first surfaced late in 1994 at a meeting convened by Campus Compact to explore the feasibility of developing a national network of service-learning educators. At that meeting, it quickly became clear that some of those assembled saw the primary value of such a network in its ability to provide concrete resources to faculty working in or wishing to explore service-learning. Out of that meeting there developed, under the auspices of Campus Compact, a new national group of educators called the Invisible College, and it was within the Invisible College that the monograph project was first conceived. Indeed, a review of both the editors and contributors responsible for many of the volumes in this series would reveal significant representation by faculty associated with the Invisible College.

If Campus Compact helped supply the initial financial backing and impulse for the Invisible College and for this series, it was the American Association for Higher Education (AAHE) that made completion of the project feasible. Thanks to its reputation for innovative work, AAHE was not only able to obtain the funding needed to support the project up through actual publication, it was also able to assist in attracting many of the teacher-scholars who participated as writers and editors.

Three individuals in particular deserve to be singled out for their contributions. Sandra Enos, former Campus Compact project director for Integrating Service With Academic Study, was shepherd to the Invisible College project. John Wallace, professor of philosophy at the University of Minnesota, was the driving force behind the creation of the Invisible College. Without his vision and faith in the possibility of such an undertaking, assembling the human resources needed for this series would have been very difficult. Third, AAHE's endorsement — and all that followed in its wake — was due largely to then AAHE vice president Lou Albert. Lou's enthusiasm for the monograph project and his determination to see it adequately supported have been critical to its success. It is to Sandra, John, and Lou that the monograph series as a whole must be dedicated.

Another individual to whom the series owes a special note of thanks is Teresa E. Antonucci, who, as program manager for AAHE's Service-Learning Project, has helped facilitate much of the communication that has allowed the project to move forward.

The Rationale Behind the Series

A few words should be said at this point about the makeup of both the general series and the individual volumes. At first glance, sociology may seem a natural choice of disciplines with which to link service-learning. However, "natural fit" has not, in fact, been a determinant factor in deciding which disciplines/interdisciplinary areas the series should include. Far more important have been considerations related to the overall range of disciplines represented. Since experience has shown that there is probably no disciplinary area — from architecture to zoology — where service-learning cannot be fruitfully employed to strengthen students' abilities to become active learners as well as responsible citizens, a primary goal in putting the series together has been to demonstrate this fact. Thus, some rather natural choices for inclusion — disciplines such as anthropology, geography, and religious studies — have been passed over in favor of other, sometimes less obvious selections from the business disciplines and natural sciences as well as several important interdisciplinary areas. Should the present series of volumes prove useful and well received, we can then consider filling in the many gaps we have left this first time around.

If a concern for variety has helped shape the series as a whole, a concern for legitimacy has been central to the design of the individual volumes. To this end, each volume has been both written by and aimed primarily at academics working in a particular disciplinary/interdisciplinary area. Many individual volumes have, in fact, been produced with the encouragement and active support of relevant discipline-specific national societies. For this volume, in fact, we owe thanks to the American Sociological Association.

Furthermore, each volume has been designed to include its own appropriate theoretical, pedagogical, and bibliographical material. Especially with regard to theoretical and bibliographical material, this design has resulted in considerable variation both in quantity and in level of discourse. Thus, for example, a volume such as Accounting contains more introductory and less bibliographical material than does Composition — simply because there is less written on and less familiarity with service-learning in accounting. However, no volume is meant to provide an extended introduction to service-learning *as a generic concept.* For material of this nature, the reader is referred to such texts as Kendall's *Combining Service and Learning: A Resource Book for Community and Public Service* (NSIEE, 1990) and Jacoby's *Service-Learning in Higher Education* (Jossey-Bass, 1996).

I would like to conclude with a special note of thanks to Jim Ostrow, Garry Hesser, and Sandra Enos, coeditors of this volume. The care they have taken to build on other, related efforts in sociology has helped ensure the special value of this volume. I would also like to acknowledge the generous assistance of Michelle Loyd-Paige of Calvin College, who provided feedback on the manuscript.

March 1999

Preface

Service-Learning:
Not Charity, But a Two-Way Street

by Judith R. Blau

Volunteering is arguably one of America's most distinctive social practices. Its organizational base, participants, and source of legitimacy have greatly varied over time, and it reveals important aspects of changes in American society as it implicates other important social institutions. The purpose of my prefatory piece is to examine this assumption more carefully, because I will contend that significant recent trends in higher education have been accompanied by developments in service-learning programs. I also suggest that the motivations that students bring to a service-learning course are different today from what they were 20, or even 10, years ago. As a result, the instructor may gain more than she or he ever anticipated. Service-learning may lie in the direct historical path of "charity" and welfare, but it is based on very different assumptions, namely, that it is quid pro quo: It is difficult to know in which direction the services are flowing, and whether the students are helping to empower the clients or the other way around. A historical and interpretive overview sheds some light on recent changes in volunteering as a social institution, and also, I believe, on our own and our students' conceptions of citizenship in the classroom and in the worlds outside of it.

From Volunteering to Charity

Tocqueville (1991) described American volunteering in around 1830 in these terms: "Among democratic nations . . . citizens are independent and feeble; they can do hardly anything by themselves. . . . They all, therefore, become powerless if they do not learn voluntarily to help one another" (109). Volunteering as a democratic activity among equals made particular sense from early colonial times into the 19th century. There were high rates of immigration and geographical mobility, and this encouraged cooperation as communities needed to quickly absorb newcomers and to maintain stability. Both in sparsely populated rural hinterlands and in densely populated cities, residents were mutually dependent on one another. Given the absence of class traditions associated with an aristocracy and the ritualized patterns of aristocratic etiquette (noblesse oblige), a fairly distinctive American egalitarian ethos encouraged a free and easy pattern of giving and receiving.

From the beginning, a weak state was another condition that promoted informal patterns of volunteering. Through informal, but nonetheless elaborate and complex, norms of reciprocity, rural Americans learned that when their barn needed raising or their harvests needed extra hands, they could turn to neighbors miles away who would help. Urbanites relied on co-nationals or co-religionists to provide help with children or to share food and other resources.

Nonurban and urban volunteering alike provided practical assistance but also helped to create invisible bonds of social solidarity and community. These patterns were well established in the antebellum period when Tocqueville wrote, and they were based, according to him, on a deep egalitarianism that helped to foster a civic order of decency and mutual regard. But volunteering was consistent with other social institutions that lightly bore the Protestant and democratic stamp of the new nation. The Great Awakenings of the late 18th and early 19th centuries gave rise to the common school, and also to important social movements, notably abolitionism and suffrage. Popular religious traditions accompanied Americans' rejection of European literary and artistic traditions in favor of a homespun piety about our humble place in nature (expressed so well in Transcendentalism) and, at times, about the virtues of communitarian values over those of individualism (as evident in the utopian communal experiments).

This is not to imply that popular religion and traditions of voluntarism obliterated social and moral boundaries. One emergent ethos of mid 19th-century America was a shift away from the strictest strains of Puritanism — in which one helped others to prove one's own worthiness to God and thus save one's *own* soul — to evangelicalism — in which one helped others to save *their* souls. Not all were worthy participants in community life or recipients of community largesse, and some groups chose exclusion. Catholics, Mormons, blacks, Native Americans, Appalachian whites, and Chinese — to give a few notable examples — were largely left to their own devices. This helps to explain the divergence of social institutions later in the 19th century devoted to schooling, medical care, and social welfare. On the one hand, there were the relatively secularized congeries of charitable organizations and schools that trace their origins to evangelical traditions, many of which were later co-opted by government agencies. However, distinctly parochial schools and charitable institutions retained a greater autonomy. To a considerable extent, black communities and churches were also allowed to develop their own means for the care of children, the aged, and the poor.

At the end of the century, large waves of immigrants from southern, eastern, and central Europe accompanied major changes in American society — notably, an unprecedented concentration of economic power and the growth of a middle class composed of white natives. Social Darwinism emerged as a popular and widespread view among Americans about the superiority of Western democratic nations among the world, while also justifying the capitalist system and the privileges and dominance of white Anglo-Saxon Protestants. Immigrants posed a growing threat to elites as well as to the middle and working classes. Charity became a major defense that accompanied fears of social upheaval. Benign social tool that it is, the social institution of charity reified multiple distinctions — between income and wages, native and foreign, whites and others, Protestants and non-Protestants, and between "us" and "them." Charity was a significant component of a moral crusade that included zealous attempts to regulate "vice" and, along with immigration reforms, was intended to restore the social health of American society.

Thus, from about 1800 to about 1920, there was a shift from reciprocity that underlay community norms of volunteering, to an emphasis on the religious worth of voluntarism, and then to an emphasis on social control and conformity. The latter pattern was quite consistent with modernism. That is, accompanying Americans' conviction that there was a universal model of national development was the idea that there was a singular model of medicine, of education, of marriage and socializing children, and of community. With only slight exaggeration, it can be said that there was a widespread conception that some people "suffered" from a culture of poverty, from the social deprivations of a rural upbringing, or from the deprivations of ethnic origins.

Pedagogy and Service-Learning

In the 1980s, community service programs, at least as I experienced them, mainly attracted undergraduates because they provided opportunities for career internships. By the 1990s, however, a new conception of service-learning had evolved, as described especially well in subsequent chapters of this volume. In a sense, it provides a pedagogical alternative to undergraduates' working on an original research project. The main difference is that the students are expected to learn "from" their subjects, not "about" them. Under the best of conditions, the student participants in a service-learning class feel that both they and the clients gain from the experience. Middle-class students are not unaware that while the dismantling of our modest welfare programs has chiefly affected the poor, their own lives and futures are not that secure either. Educational subsidies are being reduced as tuitions rise faster than families' ability to pay, affirmative action for women and minorities is threatened, and returns to education are not that certain as the economy is in a state of flux. Perhaps, reminiscent of antebellum America, there is a sense of all possibly being in the same boat.

A notable feature of contemporary higher education is that the college-age population is more diverse than it has ever been. In most four-year colleges, the ratio of males to females is about one to one; the proportion of black students is nearly the proportion in the general population; and there has been a dramatic increase in the numbers of foreign students, some of whom notably outperform native-born students. One response of universities has been to introduce courses in multiculturalism or cultural diversity (see Taylor 1994; West 1993), which students at my own university take through a "perspectives" requirement. These courses sensitize students to the social, economic, and cultural complexities of the contemporary world, and they provide undergraduates with a sense that there is a core human experience but also great variation in values, priorities, and group beliefs.

Discussing this in the abstract can be difficult, but the issues lend themselves to my service-learning courses Urban Sociology and Immigration. I can parenthetically note here that I am often not prepared for understanding students' ideas about cultural differences and cultural diversity. Once, in a bond of explicit solidarity, black and white students united linguistically against me, the Northern instructor, and in one voice "spoke Southern." Many Southerners can speak ⸍a variety of dialects as well as "standard English." The "New South" has posed challenges for young adults, many of whom grew up in highly segregated communities and attended schools for which the correlation between track and race was perfect. Interracial relations on campus are relatively casual, certainly not inappropriate to discuss, and the emphasis is on "choice," not convention. This changing student culture is an important context for the service-learning courses.

At the University of North Carolina, a student-initiated program, APPLES (Assisting People in Planning Learning Experiences in Service), is the vehicle by which I gain access to local agencies. Advanced students who work with APPLES provide supplementary group sessions for my students, and the staff provides assistance if things go wrong. There are two pedagogical problems. The first is to clarify for oneself and one's students how the theories, concepts, substantive problems, and methodologies discussed in class are related to the service component. The second is to help students reflect on their own social worlds and how those worlds contrast with those of agency clients. Because there is insufficient time in class to devote much discussion to the ethics of dealing with clients, I have devised a few hard and fast rules that tend to trigger responsible and respectful relationships with clients. For example, students must never disclose the name of a client either in class discussions or in written papers.

An unexpected benefit of these classes is that students become aware of the differences among themselves with respect to their own upbringings and develop a richer appreciation of these differences. For example, when a white and a black student worked together in the same Head Start class, it became clear to them that their own cultural backgrounds affected their perceptions of the roles they played in the class. The white student thought the children were "starving for affection" and used her time at the agency "holding and cuddling the children." The black student worked with the teacher to enforce ideas about "high expectations" and used her time helping to plan programs in nutrition and hygiene.

For one student, a math major and serious chess player, the experience led to a summer job and, by his own account, had a transformative effect on his life. He volunteered at the local YMCA to teach chess to youngsters. This went well. His chess students were more or less like himself — middle class and largely the sons and daughters of university staff and faculty. It was sheer coincidence that he visited a friend in Washington, DC, who was working in inner-city neighborhoods. My student discovered timed ("street") chess in the park at Dupont Circle, lost mostly to the much faster black youths, and then imported timed chess back to North Carolina, where he taught it in a local recreational center. By the end of the fall semester, he had gained considerable confidence and intellectual self-esteem. There were other successes that semester, including the experiences of students who worked with the community police, a female basketball player and a football player who volunteered in after-school athletic programs in a public school, and a Vietnamese student who worked in a local homeless shelter and then wrote a paper comparing rural Vietnam homelessness with Southern urban U.S. homelessness.

Besides these experiences in Urban Sociology with APPLES, I have taught a course on ethnicity and immigrants, and the APPLES staff helped to identify a variety of agencies that work with immigrants, farmworkers, and refugees. Virtually all of the texts and monographs that lend themselves to an undergraduate class on this topic deal with urban immigrants, not rural, and there is little written on immigrants in the South (except for Florida), so that the students had an opportunity to think comparatively about their own experiences and the case studies of urban immigrants that they were reading. In this course on ethnicity and immigration, students worked with Bosnian and Cuban families, Mexican agricultural workers, and with employees of the local poultry factories. Such experiences as these became vehicles for the easy introduction of other sociological topics — such as labor markets and stratification — that I had not anticipated, but, far more important, the class easily became a casual and noncontrived democracy in the best sense of the word. In an atmosphere of civic trust, they could discuss barriers to opportunity just as easily as they could debate fairly volatile issues, such as the antiimmigrant "English First" movement. Such discussions as these were informed by students' firsthand experiences with the coping abilities of Mexican migrant workers and with the exploitation of Latino and African-American workers in the poultry industry.

The APPLES office has evolved a formal blueprint that helps instructors with the organizational and strategic issues of service-learning. It includes the following: (1) students' contracts that spell out the responsibility of the agency to the students, and the responsibilities of the student; (2) an inservice training session that the agencies provide; (3) monthly or bimonthly meetings with session leaders held outside of class and outside of the agencies. In addition, I distribute a set of questions that is designed to link the substantive content of the course with student experiences.

Not Charity, But a Two-Way Street

There are multiple benefits of service-learning. I have found that relating course materials to real-life experiences enhances the challenges for students to think in original ways about substantive problems in sociology. Because we sociologists can tacitly hang so much literature and empirical detail on such concepts as "social inequality" and "industrialization," these hardly appear to be abstractions to us when we discuss them in class. This is not the case for typical American undergraduates, for whom such concepts are really difficult to understand unless they can link the concepts up with experiences in their daily lives. Furthermore, service-learning courses can help to level the playing field for students (something, in fact, earlier and perhaps surprisingly advocated by Durkheim [1973: 97]). Some students who lack superior high school backgrounds but are highly motivated can do especially well, because these courses rely in part on maturity in worlds outside of the classroom (see Griffith and Connor 1994).

I have written elsewhere that social life in this era depends on structures of interdependence that are inimical to hierarchies and traditional authority (Blau 1993) but also inimical to structures that promote competition that erodes the frameworks of cooperation and empathy. I suggested that in order to sustain these interdependencies, it is useful to distinguish "morality," which asserts the superiority of a particular group over others, from an ethic of difference, which privileges no group. It is consistent with that point of view to challenge students to consider their own cherished beliefs as they work with children and adults who come from Mexico, Bosnia, Laos, and Vietnam and also with Americans who have had life experiences different from their own. I confess that when black and white Southern students ganged up in jest against me, the Northerner, I felt mighty pleased with my efforts in that class.

The publication of this volume represents an important milestone in higher education. Service-learning classes are so tied to particular communities that it is a challenge to distill curricula and class exercises that can be of general use. Its editors and authors bring their sociological wisdom and imagination to this difficult task. Discussions in the introduction and following chapters, along with the appended syllabi, provide ways in which such programs can be adopted in most undergraduate curricula in sociology. One assumes that this is not the last word on this project. Infinite possibilities exist for linking the community with the classroom, and this is a significant beginning for further innovation.

References

Blau, Judith R. (1993). *Social Contracts and Economic Markets*. New York, NY: Plenum Press.

Durkheim, Emile. (1973, orig. 1925). *Moral Education: A Study in the Theory and Application of the Sociology of Education*. New York, NY: Free Press.

Griffith, Marlene, and Ann Connor. (1994). *Democracy's Open Door: The Community College in America's Future*. Portsmouth, NH: Boynton/Cook.

Taylor, Charles. (1994). *Multiculturalism: Examining the Politics of Recognition*. Princeton, NJ: Princeton University Press.

Tocqueville, Alexis de. (1991, orig. 1840). *Democracy in America*. Vol. 2. New York, NY: Alfred A. Knopf.

West, Cornel. (1993). *Beyond Eurocentrism and Multiculturalism*. Monroe, ME: Common Courage Press.

Introduction

Service-Learning and the Teachability of Sociology

by James Ostrow

By definition, no practicing sociologist believes that the meaning of social existence is reducible to an existing "body of knowledge," as if analytical reflection were simply a recapitulation. Unfortunately, this tautological remark is necessary when considering the sociology curriculum, where too often the mysteriousness of social life is obfuscated by presented "facts," "concepts," and "methods." The following essays on service-learning make the deceptively simple claim that sociology can be taught. I refer to the teachability of "sociology" in its pure form, as a practice, rather than as a set of items that are detached and isolated from practice *in order to* teach. This book suggests, in other words, that we can and should teach sociology rather than a mock-up of it, and that the service-learning course assignment is an extremely useful vehicle for doing so.

This book argues the merits of service-learning in sociology, or students engaging in sociological analysis through projects that are designed to make a positive impact in communities. In making this argument, we recognize that a form of teaching is being discussed that has been employed under various names by sociology instructors long before the idea of "service-learning" took hold in higher education. Our intention is only to provide a forum for discussing community-based learning under the auspices of this new rubric. In this sense, we use the emergence of a powerful and exciting cross-disciplinary movement in higher education as a foil for endorsing what many in our discipline have known for a long time: that involving students in local community projects provides an excellent vehicle for exercising their sociological imagination.

Skeptics within the discipline will contend that engaging students' interests in the empirical and theoretical process of discovery is a realistic objective only subsequent to the introductory-level course experience. On the one hand, doing actual sociological work presupposes understanding a body of basic principles that it is the business of lower-level courses to teach; on the other hand, expecting students to be interested in conducting and motivated to conduct actual investigations ignores the reality of why most students — certainly most nonmajors — take introductory courses. Since it is only one or two *courses* with which many students are concerned, covering established wisdom *in the discipline* must be the instructor's main pedagogical responsibility. Textbooks and examinations that are tailored to this purpose are thus employed.

The above argument presumes that "sociology" as a *performed phenomenon* is fundamentally different from "sociology" as a *taught phenomenon*. But with this presumption we lose sight of the *value* of established sociological wisdom and its transferability. It is only insofar as available sociological principles or techniques are convertible into the operative, embodied dispositions of an inquiring mind that they exist as "part of the discipline." We should not pretend that all students will become practicing scholars in the discipline, yet why not teach *sociology* instead of a pedagogically induced fabrication?

In order to do the work of sociology — which is to say, in order to inquire into and acquire understanding of a changing social world — one must make a beginning with acquired methodological and analytical skills. It is precisely in that sense that such skills can be introduced in the classroom: for the purpose of and in and through the activity of sociological inquiry. It is in this way that these skills have the best chance of developing and being exercised as John Dewey's "habits of mind" (Dewey 1929) — ways of being sensitive to the world that, in this case, enable sociological discovery.

Hence, the instructor's task is to provide the sort of experience through which the sociological habit of mind can develop. Fieldwork projects that have community service as their frame are excellent vehicles for accomplishing this objective. It is true that the sociology student needs to see that observation and analytical discovery are possible anywhere, with no one type of setting being "better" than another for sociological exploration. The pedagogical advantage of community service projects may hold for other types of settings as well; my point is only that this advantage for community service projects holds consistently, making service-learning a sound pedagogical choice.

One good reason for this choice is access: Community service projects provide entry into sites that lend themselves nicely, through observation and conversation, to analyzing the structure and dynamics of social life. It could be argued that in any academic discipline "service-learning" requires the student to view the community service setting as a *field site* for making *analytical discoveries*. In this sense, the point about access can be made across the curriculum. A further key for sociology is that service projects place students typically in direct contact with socially and economically disadvantaged members of the community. Moreover, the students frequently have this contact within organizations that are designed to address these disadvantages (with varying degrees of effectiveness). That organizational design is, of course, precisely what renders these sites accessible, as students are assigned tasks or work on projects that are defined by this design.

Students are participant observers who access their sites under a quid pro quo: They are there to engage in the organization's practice of offering assistance to the individuals who are served by it. Students thereby engage in fieldwork with the ethical constraint of returning something in exchange; at the same time, by operating under this constraint the kinds of rapport that yield richer information from a setting's members are established more quickly. This is particularly the case where, beyond fitting into a preexisting volunteer track, students work on projects or perform service that produces something new for an organization and those served by it.

Beyond the fact of field-site access, the community service experience provides for the possibility of a particularly rich awareness of the social circumstances that situate individual involvement. An excellent example of this is community service or projects where students encounter homeless adults. Students are often confronted with their own economic and cultural positioning as a distancing force between themselves and the homeless. This often manifests itself as an intense self-consciousness, where students become acutely apprehensive about how they are seen by the setting's inhabitants. Suddenly all sorts of markers of students' own social positioning that are typically taken for granted bubble up into their awareness — how they are dressed, how they talk, where they come from. Hence, one student visiting a homeless shelter yearns to dissociate herself from her friend's car:

> I felt as if [I were] somehow flaunting my privileges in front of them, even though it was not my car and I have never even owned a car. I felt an almost uncontrollable urge to tell them that it was my friend's car and that I had wanted to walk here, but she wouldn't let me.

I have argued elsewhere that this sort of experience can be the ground for a deeper understanding of phenomena such as stigma and class, as well as the interplay between them (Ostrow 1995). I say "deeper" for two reasons: (1) because the terms now become operative concepts for grasping the meaning of *discovered* phenomena, and (2) because the felt intensity of the community service experience can lead to a more enduring sensitivity to and concern about cultural and economic inequality than would otherwise occur.

This is not to say that the community service experience is necessarily a ground for sociological understanding. As Kerry Strand argues in this volume, community service could lead in the opposite direction; that is, students might experience a reinforcement of their own negative stereotypes of members of socially marginalized groups. It would be a facile response to say that students must therefore "reflect." In a certain sense, their engaging in reflection is unavoidable; service-learning is involving students in circumstances that are new to them and that they will be compelled to make sense of in some way. In short, students will be *reflecting* whether or not we pay pedagogical attention to them, whether or not we structure how they do so. The task pedagogically is not merely to "ride out" the experience through reflection with the student; it is often necessary to urge twists and turns on original reflective moments — preserving that invaluable anchorage of reflection in the felt intensity of the service experience.

Consider the following case, where a student asks a client of a drug and alcohol detoxification program if he dislikes the students' being there:

> The first time we went, we were watching a movie and he took every opportunity to turn around and glare at us. Finally, after we had gone a few times, I summoned up the courage to ask him if our presence had in any way offended him. He looked at me straight in the eye for a second and then said, "Yeah, but I'll get used to it." I asked him why and he told me that he was unused to being observed, but he knows that it's part of being there. I apologized to him, because I felt I had to. He stopped me mid-apology and apologized to me. He said he was just grouchy because his life wasn't going the way he had planned and he was discouraged. This same man greets me with a smile when I now walk into the center.

The student goes on to produce a clever analysis of a transformed social relationship, focusing on this man's change in persona. But along with this beautiful experience and its accompanying initial reflections, the sociology instructor may wish to push for a more thoroughgoing inquiry. Why was the student's observing presence initially offensive to this man? And if it was offensive, how can we understand the man's silence? What precisely are the social dynamics of a setting within which "getting used to being observed" is "part of being there"? Beyond the standpoint of performing "community service," many students do in fact experience themselves in positions of power and privilege analogous to the staff's. Not only can they come and go as they please, but their responsibilities are often similar to the staff's. Hence, this student's experience may serve as a participant observer's window into the social structure of the human services staff-client relationship or, more generally, into the institutional structure of "emergency care" or, even more broadly than this, into the socioeconomic and sociopolitical conditions of problem-targeted social services.

The next example comes from a student who helped to serve dinner in a local church food program:

> I heard one of the children say, "Mom, where are we going to sleep tonight?" The mother's voice was quiet, but as I walked I strained to hear her response: "We'll find somewhere; we always do." I clenched my grip around the apple carton. I became so angry, I felt like throwing the box on the floor. . . . I wanted to invite all of these people back to [college] and give them a place to stay. I wanted to do so much, but in reality all I could do was pass

out apples and try to get to know and understand them. I was starting to understand.

Here we have an intense moment for a student captured by written interpretation. It is also a base for what the sociology course should provide: the motivation and the tools for investigating the larger meaning of this experience. Homelessness is perceived as being unshakable by individual community service — an important insight, but what then is homelessness and what are the forces that perpetuate it? Homeless individuals are perceived as being underserved, disadvantaged, as opposed to being necessarily lazy or in some other way flawed characterologically. What, then, leads to the latter prevailing views of the homeless, and what do these views mean for homeless persons in their everyday lives? There is, in short, more for the student to do than pass out apples: Sociology provides the vehicle for broader and deeper understanding, for inquiries that might lead to solutions.

This book explores some of the pedagogical opportunities for sociology that present themselves through the service-learning experience. Some of the discussion may frustrate those who believe that the engagement of students in community service within the college curriculum must be endorsed at any cost, without reservation — that is, proselytized for the sake of the "service-learning cause." A vigorous endorsement of service-learning is provided in these essays, but we hope that it is done so with the kind of sociological sensitivity that forces careful consideration of the forms, risks, and benefits of service-learning projects within the curriculum.

Service-Learning and the Critical Examination of Social Life

We need to place the idea of service-learning under the lens of critical sociology. Service-learning has the potential to enhance students' understanding of the critical and systemic focus of sociology, but this potential is realized only through careful course design as well as historical sensitivity to the meaning of service during the 19th and 20th centuries.

Part 1 of this book explores the advantages, the pitfalls, and the variety of approaches to engaging students in critical, sociological inquiry through service-learning. Sam Marullo's essay develops the idea of the potential contribution of service-learning to engaging students in critical, structural investigations of social problems. He discusses seven educational benefits of service-learning in higher education, and he focuses on how the sociology course provides particularly fertile ground for realizing these benefits. Marullo argues that service-learning has revolutionary potential for student development as well as for the role of colleges and universities in promoting and advancing positive social change. He cautions that "this revolutionary potential can be realized . . . only if we establish service-learning programs that are truly challenging of the status quo." For Marullo, this means that it is crucial for the discipline of sociology to play a central role in defining the role of service-learning in higher education.

Kerry Strand is more cautious in her advocacy for service-learning, as she wonders about its compatibility with a discipline that seeks to engage students in alternatives to conventional thinking about social issues and problems. She believes that service-learning can enhance this pedagogical effort, but only by avoiding certain pitfalls that can dismantle the critical essence of sociological teaching. Strand cites several such pitfalls; one is the possibility of prioritizing individual experience over systemic analysis in understanding social life. This hardly "[jibes] well with social scientists' efforts to have students recognize that personal experience is only one source — and not a terribly valid or reliable one — for understanding the world." Strand argues for the advantages of dissolving the obstacles to effective pedagogical linkages between service-learning and sociological investigation, suggesting that "the benefits for teaching and learning can be far-reaching."

J. Richard Kendrick's essay provides a detailed typology of the variety of approaches to incorporating service-learning into a sociology course. The care with which the sociology instructor makes choices along the nine dimensions identified by Kendrick will certainly go a long way toward avoiding the pitfalls and realizing the benefits of service-learning discussed in the prior essays. As Kendrick notes, the key to success is not rigid adherence to one right way to structure a course around service-learning; the key is to "continually refine our methods and move toward even more effective ways to integrate service with learning in our courses." Kendrick also advises the instructor to draw upon existing models of service-learning, and here I alert the reader to the superb volume edited by Morton Ender et al., *Service-Learning and Undergraduate Sociology: Syllabi and Instructional Materials* (ASA, 1996). This book includes a comprehensive set of syllabi and assignments from various sociology courses that incorporate service-learning projects.

Pedagogical Advantages of Service-Learning

What, precisely, are the pedagogical benefits of service-learning for sociology? How can service-learning advance student understanding of issues that are of central theoretical concern in the discipline? Sandra Enos's discussions with Calderon and Furstenberg, as well as the essays by Barbara Vann, Martha Bergin and Susan McAleavey, and Hugh Lena, cite individual approaches to implementing service-learning in the sociology curriculum.

Calderon's is the perspective of the social activist, or more specifically of the sociologist committed to working toward social change in and through his teaching and research. Drawing upon his experiences as farmworker, community organizer, and sociological researcher, Calderon discusses the challenges and opportunities that are inherent in an innovative service-learning pedagogy. Service-learning becomes simultaneously a vehicle for a richly critical engagement with sociological theory but also a foundation for a commitment to engaging social issues throughout one's personal life. As a consequence, students may well develop enduring dispositions "to use their lives, their knowledge, and their values to build a better community."

Frank Furstenberg describes his experiences with a year-long seminar involving students in collaborative community research in the West Philadelphia public schools. Students work with high school youth in West Philadelphia on various action-research projects — including the development of school-based service-learning and the prevention of teen pregnancies. Furstenberg emphasizes the richer sociological understanding that students acquire when they are actually situated within the urban school. In working with inner-city youth, University of Pennsylvania students acquire a deeper sensitivity than could be conveyed in the college classroom to the "despair that the high school students feel and the disparity between what they would like to have and what they're getting." Furstenberg also notes the extent to which this form of teaching engages him more deeply in urban education research — action research that can make a positive difference in the Philadelphia schools. Indeed, he emphasizes that his teaching and research are inseparable from the linking of Penn and its surrounding community — work that "signifies a small measure of balance and exchange."

Vann explores connections between service-learning and symbolic interactionism, focusing on how the service-learning experience compels students to recognize the usefulness of the interactionist perspective for understanding the social world. One important reason for this is the initial uncertainty that students often have about how they should relate to others at a community site. In Vann's view, the symbolic interactionist idea of "role taking" and its various components is an important foundation for students' reflections on their uncertainty, as well as for students' critically examining their views of others in the setting. The students "get at the meaning behind their own and others' actions within the interactional setting of the service site."

Bergin and McAleavey's chapter is a "meta-reflection"; that is, they examine how the pedagogy of service-learning can enrich our understanding of the processes of reflection that students undergo as they "learn sociology." The authors' careful delineation of phases of the reflective process is designed to focus our attention on the advantages of such an understanding for, in turn, tapping the service-learning experience for its maximum potential in the sociology classroom. Reflection is the "process through which humans develop and retain awareness of themselves and their environments, grow and change, review and expand, create analogies, and consider new contexts for experience." Bergin and McAleavey demonstrate that we must understand the structure and dynamics of this process if we are to grasp the power of service-learning.

Lena is interested in meta-reflection as well — but his meta-reflection is the student's, not the professor's. Lena describes a course that is designed as its own service-learning site; that is to say, students work together as a group and serve the group by actually constructing the content and organizational structure of the class. Lena argues that this kind of academic experience provides critical organizational understanding that prepares students to participate productively in service projects sponsored by Providence College's Public and Community Service Studies Program. At the same time, the course forces students to critically assess the purposes of service-learning and their roles within the larger community. In discussing this course initiative, Lena argues that service-learning has the potential to mount an effective challenge to the "number of structural elements in higher education that . . . reinforce passivity and discourage active learning."

Course-Based Community Research

Service-learning can also engage students in a deeper appreciation of the value of sociological research. It can be a vehicle through which students are immersed in "the field" and, through this immersion, discover the need for research-based inquiry. Douglas Porpora and Garry Hesser argue that the most direct approach to integrating service-learning and sociological research is course-based action research, or service-learning projects that research issues and problems of direct importance to local communities. Both authors are interested particularly in the scholarly possibilities existing for both students and faculty in *participatory* action research projects — research that is designed and implemented collaboratively with community partners.

Porpora develops the idea of service-learning as a framework for research. Taking his departure from Robert Lynd's famous query, "knowledge for what?," Porpora explores the possibilities and difficulties in linking scholarly research, community service, and teaching. How can sociological research matter to a nonacademic public? Porpora's answer is action research — sociologists collaborating with local communities in their research. He notes obstacles within the academy to recognizing the importance of contributing to the community as a criterion in the assessment of scholarly research. This is a crucial problem: "If action research is not to be ghettoized as just another sectional interest within sociology, its scholarly results will have to speak to the broader discipline." Porpora also explores the effort — a rarely fulfilled but worthwhile struggle — to engage students in research-based service at a level that, beyond the community contribution, contributes to scholarly understanding within the discipline.

In Hesser's view, service-learning should function as the vehicle through which there exists a working "conversation and dialogue with the cities and neighborhoods where our colleges and universities are located." Hesser elaborates on the importance of collaborative, community-based — or "participatory action" — research as a model for service-learning in sociology by comparing examples from the University of Dayton, Loyola University, and a consortium of eight colleges in Minnesota. Students acquire the sociological imagination through service-learning framed by an essential principle: "sustained collaboration and reciprocity [that enhances] the capacities of communities and students alike."

Service-Learning and the Sociological Imagination

What, finally, is the role of service-learning in the discipline — or, more specifically, how does service-learning enhance our conception of sociology as a teachable field of methods and ideas? William Heard Kilpatrick argued that student learning is most valued and enduring when grounded within "wholehearted, purposeful activity in a social environment" (1918: 330). We may couple that pedagogical principle with what is surely the ethical imperative implicit in the sociological effort: that human beings should in their thoughts and conduct be disposed to the welfare of others. Service-learning provides students a chance to catch hold of the intellectual and ethical importance of the sociological imagination. We believe that the reader of this volume will conclude that when the community project in the sociology curriculum is thought through and constructed carefully, the principle of "teaching the real thing" and service-learning complement each other extremely well.

References

Dewey, J. (1929). *Experience and Nature*. 2nd ed. Chicago, IL: Open Court.

Ender, M., B. Kowalewski, D.A. Cotter, L. Martin, and J. DeFiore, eds. (1996). *Service-Learning and Undergraduate Sociology: Syllabi and Instructional Materials*. Washington, DC: American Sociological Association.

Kilpatrick, W.H. (1918). "The Project Method." *Teachers College Record* 19: 319-335.

Ostrow, J. (1995). "Self-Consciousness and Social Position: On College Students Changing Their Minds About the Homeless." *Qualitative Sociology* 18(3): 357-375.

Sociology's Essential Role:
Promoting Critical Analysis in Service-Learning

by Sam Marullo

There has been enormous growth in the number of service-learning cours-es and programs across the United States over the past dozen or so years. Although the development of service-learning can be seen as an outgrowth of or successor to experiential education programs, there is a distinctive emphasis of service-learning on critical analysis that distinguishes it from experiential education programs such as internships or apprenticeships, which have focused more on preprofessional training and/or the acquisition of occupational skills by the student. Service-learning programs — at least the type on which I will focus here — are designed as part of a liberal arts program with an emphasis on critical thinking and commitment to civic involvement that may be independent of the student's intended profession.[1]

Sociology as a discipline has an essential contribution to make to such service-learning programs in that it provides the student participants with the ability to undertake structural analyses of the causes of social problems around which their service is based. By incorporating sociology into service-learning programs, students are able to make systematic observations of how social ills are structured through institutional operations and a culture that reinforces them. Sociology can also assist them in undertaking analy-ses of various means of addressing social problems. Because of this key intellectual contribution — of teaching students how to undertake structur-al analysis as a type of critical thinking — I would argue that sociologists must take a prominent role in developing service-learning programs at the institutional level in order to ensure that students develop the critical-think-ing skills that enable them to move from an intellectual framework of char-ity to social justice.

Service-Learning Goals, Sociology's Essential Contributions

Although limited, there is an emerging body of literature that demonstrates the beneficial educational outcomes of service-learning. For sociology as a discipline, service-learning provides a mechanism for getting our students

The author would like to thank the following for their helpful comments and sugges-tions on this article: Sandra Enos, Garry Hesser, Christopher Koliba, Keith Morton, Patricia O'Connor, James Ostrow, Penny Rue, Randy Stoecker, and Lee Williams.

into the community to study community life and social problems firsthand. The historical roots of American sociology, found in the Chicago School tradition, placed a heavy emphasis on students' venturing into the community to undertake systematic studies of social life, often with an emphasis on the social problems of the times. Service-learning renews this interest and captures this appeal and excitement for our students.[2] For sociology, then, service-learning offers the opportunity for our students to acquire a better theoretical and conceptual understanding of the discipline because the problem areas in which they work have been and continue to be the core issues of our discipline.

The academic work required of students should include an analysis of their service that seeks to understand a problem's causes, operations, and consequences. It is this analytical component that necessitates that sociological theories, concepts, and/or research methods be incorporated into the program. We must provide students with the sociological imagination that enables them to link the individual biographies of the people with whom they work with the larger social forces that have affected them (Mills 1959: 4-5). In the course of this analysis, students should become aware of the systemic, social nature of inequality, injustice, and oppression. This may then become a further impetus for them to reflect on how it is that their future work and living arrangements may in fact contribute to the problems they see.

In addition to the conceptual and theoretical enrichment provided by service-learning, there are several other educational and developmental benefits provided by service-learning that are essentially linked to sociology. Students' cognitive skills are enhanced through the problem-solving and social interaction dynamics they face in the course of undertaking their community service work. Their values development is promoted by their exposure to people who face greater problems than they do and by working with people who are committed to ameliorating these problems. They learn citizenship and political participation skills by contributing to their communities and developing the social impulse to do so later in life (Putnam 1995). In most cases, they are exposed to greater diversity in terms of race, class, ethnicity, gender, religion, nationality, or sexual preference because the community-based organizations with which they work are either more heterogeneous or simply different from the campus student body. Students come to see service as a part of their civic responsibility, and they learn that corporate bodies, as modeled by the university, have an obligation to serve the communities in which they are located. And finally, students acquire the skills to become active agents of social change through an empowerment process that starts with their becoming responsible for their own education and leads them to becoming advocates for change on behalf of those with fewer resources than themselves. Each of these seven benefits of service-learning will be examined in more detail below, paying special attention to the essential role sociology has with respect to that area.

Conceptual and Theoretical Understanding

In his review of the literature on student learning, Hesser (1995:33) points out the paucity of studies that attempt to measure student learning outcomes based on learning outside the classroom. This is due, in part, to the enormous range of variables that need to be considered as possible influences and the difficulty in measuring learning outcomes. As a means of short-circuiting this challenge — while larger, national-scale studies are under way — Hesser undertook a study of university and college faculty to acquire information on their assessment of students' learning as enhanced by the students' community service experience. On a number of indicators, he found that three-fourths to four-fifths of the faculty respondents believed that students' learning was enhanced in areas such as improving their critical-thinking/analytical skills and understanding key concepts in the course. They also felt that overall student learning was better (48 percent) or much better (35 percent) in courses with a community service component as compared with the same courses without it (Hesser 1995: 34-36). Thus, assuming the substantial reliability and credibility of faculty members as judges of students' learning, Hesser concludes that community service does in fact improve students' learning as it simultaneously makes faculty into better, more self-reflective teachers (1995: 37, 40).

As sociology is the science of social interactions, group dynamics, and institutional and structural relations, it is quite logical that students learn theories and concepts about social life better when they observe them first-hand (Chesler 1993; Miller 1994; Porter and Schwartz 1993; Shumer 1994). In contrast to the natural sciences, the social sciences have no formal educational methodology for applying their claims or findings to "real-life" circumstances. The laboratory for applying, testing, and evaluating claims about social relations is the larger society. As Schall (1995) pointed out in her presidential address to the Association for Public Policy Analysis and Management, this process is often swamp-like, forcing us to deal with messy problems and all their complexities and uncertainties. However, it enables us to avoid the "high ground" of overly neat and clear descriptions of social problems that might appear easily remediable through simple solutions. Our best leaders and professionals of the future have to be prepared to navigate among the swamps as well as the high ground. Schall concludes that reflective swamp learning — through service-learning — is a necessary component for training for all policy and management professionals (1995: 216).

Because of the nature of our discipline, sociologists are particularly well suited to see the value of service-learning. Dating back to the earliest

Chicago School studies, the city and the community have served as the laboratory for our research. For as long as there has been a discipline, sociology faculty have sent students into the field to do ethnographies and participant research, so the service-learning pedagogical claim that "the real world is a crucible to test our theories" is second nature to us (Daly 1993). Evaluation studies, community power studies, organizational studies, and studies of social movements and community organizing — with their large bodies of knowledge and long-standing research traditions — can be carried over directly to service-learning initiatives.

Service-learning assignments enable students to take the claims they read and hear in their sociology courses and test those claims against the reality they observe in their service site. This experience not only enables them to understand better the material they are reading but also helps them to place their own life experience in a broader context by providing a comparative base of a different reality (Cohen and Kinsey 1994; Miller 1994). Especially for the typically more affluent students at a private liberal arts college, but also for university students in general, exposure to the living conditions of the poor is a very educational experience.[3] It is not merely exposure, however, that brings to life the concepts and theories that we teach about in our lectures and that the students read about in their texts. In addition, the students must be consciously aware of their observer status, and, like any good field researcher, they must try to be systematic and deliberate in making their observations. Through the reflection exercises (papers, journals, guided writing, etc.), we challenge them to apply the theories and concepts to the social interactions at their site. To paraphrase Shulman (1991), we learn not merely by doing but by *thinking* about what we are doing.

The Joint Education Project (JEP) at the University of Southern California provides a wonderful example of how students' community service is integrated into a number of sociology courses. The JEP staff and sociology faculty have developed a wide range of "thought" questions that ask students to apply concepts and theories to the service sites at which they are working. Sometimes, the questions solicit a rather straightforward conceptual illustration, such as the following question on deviance:

> *Describe one example of deviant behavior (or evidence from such behavior) that you notice either during or en route to your assignment. Do you believe your example is a common occurrence or a more rare phenomenon? What social factors might contribute to this deviant behavior? (JEP n.d.)*

On a more sophisticated level, the questions ask students to apply theories or perspectives to an actual situation that they have encountered in their volunteer work as a means of better understanding it. For example:

Select a social problem or situation in your JEP assignment. Choose one of the major theoretical perspectives in sociology (functionalism, conflict theory, interactionism, human ecology, dramaturgy, or any subarea) and discuss how using this perspective can help to explain that social problem/situation. (JEP n.d.)

At a yet more conceptually sophisticated level, students could be asked to compare and contrast multiple theoretical perspectives as they apply to the problem area in which the students are working, or to provide a critique of the theory as it applies to their site.

Over time, the staff and faculty have worked to refine and apply these questions to the service sites that students typically encounter in Los Angeles. They have indexed and cross-referenced the questions much like a study guide for an introductory sociology text, so that regardless of what course or text the professor is using, appropriate questions can be located easily by the professor. This helps to lower the initial costs of developing applications for faculty members who are themselves unfamiliar with all of the sites at which the students are likely to be working. The Joint Education Project also has the resources, in the form of professional staff and teaching assistants, to help the faculty members read and evaluate the students' journals. In this way, the burden of additional ongoing as well as start-up time commitment on the part of faculty members to develop and implement service-learning courses is limited.

Cognitive-Skills Development

Quasi-experimental research on service-learning courses shows that several cognitive skills, such as critical thinking, problem solving, leadership, and conflict resolution, are learned better through the real-life experiences attained in service-learning courses as compared with reading and lecture courses (Conrad and Hedin 1991; Miller 1994). Evidence from experiential learning and internship programs finds greater cognitive-skills development when these programs are compared with traditional classroom experiences (Batchelder and Root 1994; Conrad and Hedin 1990; Couto 1993; Fullinwider 1990; Stanton 1990). Critical-thinking skills are enhanced because students are forced to confront simplistic and individualistic explanations of social problems with the complex realities they see in their volunteer work. Readings, class discussions, faculty-student dialogue, and interactions of community partner with student force them to see institutional, structural, and systemic factors contributing to the problems the students observe (Batchelder and Root 1994; Hedin 1989).

As they begin to try to help the clients they are serving, students invariably confront problems and constraints. Often these are due to bureaucratic regulations, limited resources, or disempowering situational contexts — conditions with which many university students might be somewhat unfamiliar. These real-world challenges provide rich opportunities for analysis and reflection on the social structuring of opportunities (Miller 1994: 33-35). They challenge our students to develop their problem-solving skills by taking their higher-ground knowledge and classroom learning into the swamps of reality and challenging them to make a difference (Schall 1995).

Students' conflict-resolution skills are developed because the situations in which they operate are rife with conflict. Social welfare bureaucracies and nonprofit service agencies never have sufficient resources to address the needs confronting them, which leads to conflicting interests and demands between and among staff and clients. Students empathize with their clients and possibly become agents on their behalf (Hedin 1989). Students must then face the same challenge of resolving such conflicts, even if only vicariously, and develop their repertoire of methods to do so (Batchelder and Root 1994). In each area — critical thinking, problem solving, and conflict resolution — readings, class discussions, and faculty-student conversations need to be designed to help the students develop their cognitive skills.

The discipline of sociology offers several distinctive analytical tools that facilitate this cognitive-skills development among our students. Our disciplinary habit of examining unintended as well as intended consequences, latent and dysfunctional outcomes as well as manifest and functional ones (Merton 1968), prepares our students for the complex reality that social interventions do not always, or only, work as envisioned. Similarly, as we explain the social construction of reality and the structuring of interests, students are better able to understand how power and conflict are played out in everyday life. The sociological imagination helps students to simultaneously place social interactions in their larger context as well as trace the effects of larger social forces on the individual — finding the strange in the familiar and the general in the particular, as C. Wright Mills (1959) would say. And when students are working at service sites where they are addressing social problems, the sociological perspective forces them to examine the structural causes of problems rather than allowing those problems to be reduced to psychological or idiosyncratic explanations. Consequently, they are less likely to blame the victim for his or her problems than if the students were left on their own to come to an understanding of the people with whom they work. Although there are numerous other sociological insights, just these four applications illustrate the essential role sociology has to play in the operation of a service-learning program.

Values Education

Researchers have found that values formation and the moral development of students is enhanced when they are forced to confront social problems (Fullinwider 1990; Hamilton and Fenzel 1988; Kirby et al. 1991). Such moral development occurs through a series of steps, largely following Kohlberg's (1975) model of moral reasoning. In taking adolescents who may have never been exposed to social problems and who may have experienced few challenges to having their own needs and desires fulfilled, service-learning experiences expose students to such challenges (Delve, Mintz, and Stewart 1990; Olney and Grande 1995). By providing support, encouragement, and explanations to student participants, service-learning educators help students begin to identify the needs and challenges faced by others, explore various explanations of such problems, and begin to empathize with the victims of injustice, oppression, and structured inequities. Ultimately, this moral development leads to internalized values regarding social justice as well as to respect for human life and dignity (Eisenberg, Lennon, and Roth 1983; Hamilton and Fenzel 1988; Keen 1990; Stanley 1993). In their study of students' development of social responsibility, Olney and Grande found support for this exploration-realization-internalization model as students increased their community service activities. Students with the highest level of commitment to community service scored highest on the scale of internalization of social justice (1995: 46-48).

The sites at which students in a service-learning program undertake their work are likely to differ from those selected for experiential education internships with regard to both the type of people with whom the students work and the type of organization in which the students undertake that work. In experiential education programs, students are more likely to be placed in positions where they carry out activities with the expectation that they will acquire skills or training enabling them to undertake a particular type of work after completion of the program. Hence, many internships are located in work settings where there are considerable resources and the site supervisors and clients with whom the students work are not needy. Such placements may include for-profit corporations, government agencies, and legislative bodies. In service-learning programs, the subpopulations with whom students work are defined by some type of need, oppression, discrimination, disenfranchisement, or some other characteristic that limits their life chances. Students typically work in nonprofit agencies or advocacy organizations. The nonprofit organizations in which they work often have resources that are inadequate to the task of serving the needs they must address. For sociology students, this experience itself is likely to make real the concepts they learn about stratification and the unequal distribution of resources and opportunities.

The sociological perspective comes in handy with respect to values education and thus should be an integral part of a service-learning program. As a discipline, we explicitly study values and pay particular attention to values conflicts. Our explicit elaboration of values helps our students with their own values clarification as young adults in the process of identity formation. Our theoretical discussion of how values conflicts can be resolved — through prioritization, compromise, cognitive dissonance, contextualizing, and negation — comes to life when we challenge students to illustrate these with examples from their service-learning sites. The sociological imagination further assists in their values development as we enable and encourage our students to take on the role of others. By placing themselves in the shoes of others, they in turn come to understand better the concept of the social structuring of choices (Ringuette 1983). In discussions of the looking glass self, students see themselves reflected differently through the eyes of the clients whom they serve, further developing their own sense of worth. Finally, the autonomy of our students is further developed as we challenge them with more complex role sets and with juggling more, and more-diverse, demands and role partners in the course of undertaking their service work (Coser 1975).

Citizenship

A fair amount of the limited research on service-learning has focused on its effects on students' attitudes about citizenship and civic participation, their anticipated forms of future participation, and their current levels of civic involvement. The evidence indicates that students are indeed impacted in such a way as to increase their commitment to and actual involvement in civic participation. The explanation offered for this finding is that individuals learn about their obligation to the community and to the nation by working for and with others toward a collective good. Proponents of explicit civic education see service-learning as a vehicle for teaching the skills and perspectives needed for responsible citizenry in a democracy (Barber and Battistoni 1993; Newmann 1990; O'Neil 1990). According to Barber (1991), service-learning fulfills these needs by promoting collective activity that is empowering; students must work in groups or teams to achieve their goals, and they must have some input into the decision making about what is to be done. Furthermore, Barber argues that such activity should be defined or set up not as altruism or charity work but rather as constituting the greater public interest (1991: 51). This means that the students are serving a greater public good that is also their own, rather than serving merely their own or another's private interests.

At its best, sociology is the discipline of the committed public citizen and servant. Prominent sociologists have often played the role of social critic and statesman. Assuming that the social world is knowable through empirical observation and seeking to find pragmatic solutions to social problems, sociology is the key social science discipline suited to meet this challenge. It can be used to inform both citizen and policymaker of causes and consequences of particular social problems and to evaluate the impact of various alternative interventions. In this manner, students learn not only about research and evaluation methods but also about group dynamics, emergent norms, and organizational analysis (Grzelkowski 1986). In addition, knowledge of sociology enhances the social capital of the public, whether it is through the increased awareness of the extent of social problems or through its impact on enhancing citizens' ability to intervene in and address them (Barkan, Cohn, and Whitaker 1995; Hirsch 1990). Sociological studies of political participation and social organization can inform and guide students regarding their options for civic participation. Theory and research on social movements and community organizing increase the opportunities for and effectiveness of citizens' collective action to shape and create their civic life.

Diversity

Service-learning programs expose students to differences among people across class, race, ethnicity, gender, age, sexual preference, religion, nationality, and other social criteria. This exposure has the potential of simply reinforcing stereotypes and prejudices, and perhaps even sparking conflict across these divisions. However, we also know from the classical social psychological research on race relations that positive intergroup relations are most likely to emerge when people are placed in contexts in which they can work together for a common good (Allport 1954). Service-learning programs promote such positive interactions and provide a supportive context for their development and interpretation (Berry 1990; Permaul 1993).

Many college students grow up in fairly homogeneous neighborhoods — typically segregated by race, with little class variation. Service-learning experiences are likely to expose students to a wide range of class, race and ethnic, and other social categories in the community with which they are likely to have had little previous contact. Similarly, through work in groups, the diversity of the student body can play a role in helping our students to appreciate and become familiar with differences. Working toward a common goal is the best way to create mutually respectful and egalitarian views (Barber 1991). Furthermore, most college students are still experiencing the challenge of discovering and defining their own identity, so exposure to different types of people helps in this identity formation as well as in teaching respect for others.

Most educational institutions have made a commitment to educating about and for a culturally diverse society and world. In his study of a cross-cultural service-learning program, Pyle (1981) found that service-learning conducted while studying overseas led to students' increased development in autonomy, maturity, and sense of interdependence. Aparicio and Jose-

Kampfner (1995) discuss the effectiveness and value of service-learning in preparing teachers for teaching in a multicultural classroom. From the university's point of view, having students and faculty working with community partners is not only a good way to diversify the educators and role models with whom our students work but also an effective mechanism for minimizing university-community conflict.

Although diversity and its virtues are currently something of a fad in higher education, sociology has long been a discipline that has studied diversity, encouraged understanding of differences, and promoted respect for other cultures. Clearly, we have much to offer to our colleagues in the design of service-learning programs and to our students in the way that we teach our courses on race and ethnicity, social class and inequality, gender, and other social distinctions. In addition to teaching the theories and research on social differences, we are in a position to demonstrate them through service-learning. We can also model our findings in the way in which we set up our group projects, both in terms of the students' internal group dynamics and externally in the way in which we deal with our community partners. Harkavy and his colleagues involved in the West Philadelphia Improvement Corps stress the importance of learning from and conducting research with the community partner as a way of diversifying and triangulating our ways of knowing (Benson and Harkavy 1994; Greenwood, Whyte, and Harkavy 1993; Harkavy and Puckett 1991). In my own Race and Ethnic Relations classes, I have students work on group service or research projects that are built first of all on having a diversity of students in each group and setting up group incentives and reward structures that encourage cooperation. In addition, students work with community organization leaders — disproportionately likely to be women and/or people of color — in developing the projects and learning about an organization's and a community's goals. This design helps students to have a greater awareness of diversity, to overcome some of their preconceived notions about others, and to practice the skills of communicating and interacting in a diverse context.[4] In their report on teaching a class about HIV/AIDS, Porter and Schwartz (1993) report that students' anxieties about working with people with HIV/AIDS and with organizations based in the gay and lesbian community dissipated throughout the semester.

Service

Universities have claimed a role in providing service to the community through utilizing their ability to create new knowledge and in training the future leaders of communities and the nation. Service-learning is an extension of the university's service commitment in three ways: It provides services directly to those who are most in need; it can provide basic or applied research on the nature of the problems confronting a community; and it can evaluate and assess the efficacy of service-delivery alternatives. The first refers to the obligation of the university as a corporate entity and acknowledges that in exchange for the benefits it receives from the community, the university should provide tangible services that it is especially well qualified to offer (Boyer 1994).[5] The second, often under the rubric of participatory action research (see Porpora in this volume; Whyte 1991), entails university researchers' working with community members or representatives to define questions for which the community needs answers and to undertake the research to find those answers (see Hesser in this volume; Reardon 1994). The third involves the researcher in making an assessment of how effectively the services are being provided, with what costs, and in comparison with other alternatives. In each case, the university brings to the community its ability to mobilize intellectual or knowledge-based resources, skilled professionals, and its students in the process of delivering services. However, one important lesson that participatory action researchers have learned must be kept in mind — namely, that the community partner must be a real partner in the delivery, research, and evaluation processes and that the community's perspective needs a voice in validating the results of such research (Bartunek 1993).

Here again, the history of applied sociological research in social problems, community studies, and evaluation research demonstrates the applicability of sociology to service-learning. On an entry level, sociology students (like other college students) provide an extra pair of hands, energy and enthusiasm, and perhaps some organizational or technological expertise when they first begin to work in the community. However, on a second level of sociology courses, those dealing with urban issues, social problems, and various forms of inequality, we can have students read some of the studies in the literature relevant to the service site and think about how they can undertake research that would be useful for the community. In research methods courses, we can have students conduct research projects with community organizations, gathering and analyzing the data the communities have great need for but too few resources and expertise to acquire. We can also have our students undertake program evaluations and focus groups to assess the operations of a particular program. If there is an ongoing relationship among the faculty, university staff, and community members, there is likely to be a long list of questions that need some type of research. Such applied projects can turn out to be especially exciting for the students to work on, as they see the need for and value of their sociological research.

Social Change Advocacy

Perhaps the most revolutionary and controversial element of service-learning is its potential for social change. Service-learning is a relatively new academic social movement that has emerged in response to U.S. society's deepening urban, social, and economic problems. The university's unfortunate response has been to limit its role to the economic socialization (and preprofessionalization) of students. I have described the movement as being more potential than actual, since the potential has not been well developed or articulated. Service-learning programs, if implemented properly, should be critical of the status quo and should ultimately challenge unjust structures and oppressive institutional operations (Marullo 1996). It is the analytical component of service-learning that gives it revolutionary potential, because it is precisely this component that will reveal the systemic, social nature of inequality, injustice, and oppression. Service-learning is also revolutionary to the extent that it creates a partnership for change among community and university actors. Once the sources of social problems are seen to reside in the social and political systems that so lavishly reward the few at the expense of the many, it becomes obvious that such systems require change. It is in the ensuing step, advocating for change and assisting students to acquire the knowledge and skills to become agents of change, that the revolutionary potential becomes real. In this sense, service-learning provides an opportunity for institutionalizing on college campuses activism committed to social justice.

Service-learning has the potential to revolutionize the university's operations, pedagogy, curriculum, rank and tenure procedures, and resource allocations. Faculty life can also be fundamentally changed, as service-learning may enable individual faculty members to fully integrate their research, teaching, and service commitments and link them to their immediate community. Finally, service-learning represents a potentially revolutionary force for the society at large. It can alter the university-community relationship, creating a partnership committed to the well-being of surrounding neighbors and the larger community. Even larger than this is the revolutionary potential of service-learning as a means of educating our youth in preparation for how they will interact with the larger society. This potential goes beyond the mere provision of services by young, talented, and energetic college students to communities in need. It includes the critical-thinking skills that students acquire as they are forced to confront the question of why these problems persist. It includes the empowerment that students experience as they learn how to challenge dysfunctional institutional operations. It lies in the lifelong commitments that students create for themselves as engaged civic actors. All this revolutionary potential can be realized, however, only if we establish service-learning programs that are truly challenging of the status quo.

In Sum

It is up to sociologists to fulfill the role of teaching students how to undertake critical structural analysis. Being able to trace structural and institutional effects is a crucial analytical skill needed by today's youth. As a discipline, sociology has always attempted to debunk popular myths, move beyond psychological reductionism, and prevent blaming the victim. Prominent sociologists from Edgar Burgess to W.E.B. DuBois to C. Wright Mills to James Coleman to Elliot Leibow to Lillian Rubin to William Julius Wilson have played the role of social critic, undermining half-truths and simplistic explanations of social problems. Service-learning can be a vehicle for creating generations of students who can understand and appreciate the complexity of current social problems. In all likelihood, our next generation of activists and leaders will come out of this movement. If we fulfill well our role as teachers, we will have produced adults who have good conceptual, analytical, and cognitive skills; who have clarified their values and developed their social skills in the crucible of real-life applications; who are committed and active citizens; and who are committed activists for social justice. I hope sociologists are up to this challenge.

Notes

1. Indeed, the intention is to have students incorporate civic and social responsibility into any profession they may enter.

2. Especially for students attending urban universities who have grown up in the suburbs, this exposure to urban life and the social problems concentrated there is an educational experience. Similarly, for service-learning programs at rural universities, the continued existence of rural poverty is likely to be an eye-opening experience. In both cases, the education consists, in part, of exposing students to social interactions different from those with which they are accustomed due to the high levels of racial, ethnic, and class segregation of U.S. society.

3. It also poses a new challenge, to move the students beyond the initial shock, anger, and guilt reactions they are likely to experience in observing such desperate conditions, and to move them to a point where they believe they can become agents of change.

4. Some of this is quite subconscious. In students' journals at the beginning of the semester, they often write about their anxieties about being unfamiliar with "others" and about whether or not they will be accepted. By the end of the semester, this is no longer an issue for them, and they often comment on their new familiarity with the environment they once perceived as foreign and the ease with which they acquired this familiarity.

5. As a result of their nonprofit status, universities pay lower or no property and sales taxes, receive tax support directly and indirectly through federal, state, and locally

funded programs, and are subsidized through federal and state tuition-assistance programs.

References

Allport, Gordon. (1954). *The Nature of Prejudice*. Cambridge, MA: Addison-Wesley.

Aparicio, Frances, and Christina Jose-Kampfner. (Fall 1995). "Language, Culture, and Violence in the Educational Crisis of U.S. Latino/as: Two Courses for Intervention." *Michigan Journal of Community Service-Learning* 2: 95-104.

Barber, Benjamin. (Spring 1991). "A Mandate for Liberty: Requiring Education-Based Community Service." *The Responsive Community* 1: 46-55.

————, and Richard Battistoni. (June 1993). "A Season of Service: Introducing Service-Learning Into the Liberal Arts Curriculum." *PS: Political Science & Politics* 16(2): 235-240, 262.

Barkan, Steven, Steven Cohn, and William Whitaker. (1995). "Beyond Recruitment: Predictors of Differential Participation in a National Antihunger Organization." *Sociological Forum* 10(1): 113-134.

Bartunek, Jean. (1993). "Scholarly Dialogues and Participatory Action Research." *Human Relations* 46(10): 1221-1233.

Batchelder, Thomas, and Susan Root. (1994). "Effects of an Undergraduate Program to Integrate Academic Learning and Service: Cognitive, Prosocial Cognitive, and Identity Outcomes." *Journal of Adolescence* 17: 341-355.

Benson, Lee, and Ira Harkavy. (Fall/Winter 1994). "1994 as Turning Point: The University-Assisted Community School Idea Becomes a Movement." *Universities and Community Schools* 4: 5-8.

Berry, Howard. (1990). "Service-Learning in International and Intercultural Settings." In *Combining Service and Learning: A Resource Book for Community and Public Service*, edited by Jane Kendall and Associates, pp. 311-313. Raleigh, NC: National Society for Experiential Education.

Boyer, Ernest. (March 9, 1994). "Creating the New American College." *Chronicle of Higher Education*: A48.

Chesler, Mark. (1993). "Community Service-Learning as Innovation in the University." In *Praxis I: A Faculty Casebook on Community Service-Learning*, edited by Jeffrey Howard, pp. 27-40. Ann Arbor, MI: OCSL Press, University of Michigan.

Cohen, Jeremy, and Dennis Kinsey. (1994). "'Doing Good' and Scholarship: A Service-Learning Study." *Journalism Educator* 48(4): 4-14.

Conrad, Dan, and Diane Hedin. (1990). "Service: A Pathway to Knowledge." In *Combining Service and Learning: A Resource Book for Community and Public Service*, edited by Jane Kendall and Associates, pp. 245-256. Raleigh, NC: National Society for Experiential Education.

————. (June 1991). "School-Based Community Service: What We Know From Research and Theory." *Phi Delta Kappan* 72: 743-749.

Coser, Rose. (1975). "The Complexity of Roles as a Seedbed of Individual Autonomy." In *The Idea of Social Structure*, edited by Lewis Coser, pp. 237-263. New York, NY: Harcourt Brace Jovanovich.

Couto, Richard. (1993). "Service-Learning in Leadership Development." In *Rethinking Tradition: Integrating Service With Academic Study on College Campuses*, edited by T. Kupiec, pp. 67-72. Denver, CO: Education Commission of the States and Campus Compact.

Daly, Kathleen. (1993). "Field Research: A Complement for Service-Learning." In *Praxis I: A Faculty Casebook on Community Service-Learning*, edited by J. Howard, pp. 85-95. Ann Arbor, MI: OCSL Press, University of Michigan.

Delve, Cecelia, Suzanne Mintz, and Greig Stewart. (1990). "Promoting Values Development Through Community Service: A Design." In *Community Service as Values Education*, edited by C. Delve, S. Mintz, and G. Stewart, pp. 7-30. New Directions for Student Services, No. 50. San Francisco, CA: Jossey-Bass.

Eisenberg, N., R. Lennon, and K. Roth. (1983). "Prosocial Development: A Longitudinal Study." *Developmental Psychology* 19: 846-855.

Fullinwider, Robert. (1990). "Learning Morality." In *Combining Service and Learning: A Resource Book for Community and Public Service*, edited by Jane Kendall and Associates, pp. 405-406. Raleigh, NC: National Society for Experiential Education.

Greenwood, Davydd, William Foote Whyte, and Ira Harkavy. (1993). "Participatory Action Research as a Process and as a Goal." *Human Relations* 4(2): 175-192.

Grzelkowski, Kathryn. (April 1986). "Merging the Theoretical and the Practical: A Community Action Learning Model." *Teaching Sociology* 14: 110-118.

Hamilton, Stephen, and L. Mickey Fenzel. (1988). "The Impact of Volunteer Experience on Adolescent Social Development: Evidence of Program Effects." *Journal of Adolescent Research* 1(1): 65-80.

Harkavy, Ira, and John Puckett. (1991). "Toward Effective University-Public School Partnerships: An Analysis of a Contemporary Model." *Teachers College Record* 92: 556-581.

Hedin, Diane. (1989). "The Power of Community Service." *Proceedings of the Academy of Political Science* 37: 201-213.

Hesser, Garry. (Fall 1995). "Faculty Assessment of Student Learning: Outcomes Attributed to Service-Learning and Evidence of Changes in Faculty Attitudes About Experiential Education." *Michigan Journal of Community Service-Learning* 2: 33-42.

Hirsch, Eric. (1990). "Sacrifice for the Cause: Group Processes, Recruitment, and Commitment in a Student Social Movement." *American Sociological Review* 55: 243-254.

Joint Education Project. (n.d.). "Questions and Concepts for Sociology Courses." Los Angeles, CA: University of Southern California.

Keen, Cheryl. (1990). "Effects of a Public Issues Program on Adolescents' Moral and Intellectual Development." In *Combining Service and Learning: A Resource Book for*

Community and Public Service, edited by Jane Kendall and Associates, pp. 393-404. Raleigh, NC: National Society for Experiential Education.

Kirby, Donald, et al. (1991). *Ambitious Dreams: The Values Program at LeMoyne College.* New York, NY: Sheed & Ward.

Kohlberg, Lawrence. (1975). "The Cognitive-Developmental Approach to Moral Education." *Phi Delta Kappan* 56: 670-677.

Marullo, Sam. (1996). "The Service-Learning Movement in Higher Education: An Academic Response to Troubled Times." *Sociological Imagination* 33(2): 117-137.

Merton, Robert. (1968, orig. 1957). "Manifest and Latent Functions." In *Social Theory and Social Structure,* pp. 73-138. New York, NY: Free Press.

Miller, Jerry. (Fall 1994). "Linking Traditional and Service-Learning Courses: Outcome Evaluations Utilizing Two Pedagogically Distinct Models." *Michigan Journal of Community Service-Learning* 1: 29-36.

Mills, C. Wright. (1959). *The Sociological Imagination.* New York, NY: Oxford University Press.

Newmann, Fred. (1990). "Learning Citizenship Through Practice." In *Combining Service and Learning: A Resource Book for Community and Public Service,* edited by Jane Kendall and Associates, pp. 234-236. Raleigh, NC: National Society for Experiential Education.

Olney, Cynthia, and Steve Grande. (Fall 1995). "Validation of a Scale to Measure Development of Social Responsibility." *Michigan Journal of Community Service-Learning* 2: 43-53.

O'Neil, Edward. (1990). "The Liberal Tradition of Civic Education." In *Combining Service and Learning: A Resource Book for Community and Public Service,* edited by Jane Kendall and Associates, pp. 190-200. Raleigh, NC: National Society for Experiential Education.

Permaul, Jane S. (1993). "Community Service and Intercultural Education." In *Rethinking Tradition: Integrating Service With Academic Study on College Campuses,* edited by T. Kupiec, pp. 83-88. Denver, CO: Education Commission of the States and Campus Compact.

Porter, Judith, and Lisa Schwartz. (1993). "Experiential Service-Based Learning: An Integrated HIV/AIDS Education Model for College Campuses." *Teaching Sociology* 21: 409-415.

Putnam, Robert. (January 1995). "Bowling Alone: America's Declining Social Capital." *Journal of Democracy* 6: 65-78.

Pyle, K. Richard. (November 1981). "International Cross-Cultural Service/Learning: Impact on Student Development." *Journal of College Student Personnel:* 509-514.

Reardon, Kenneth. (Fall 1994). "Undergraduate Research in Distressed Urban Communities: An Undervalued Form of Service-Learning." *Michigan Journal of Community Service-Learning* 1: 44-54.

Ringuette, Eugene. (1983). "A Note on Experiential Learning in Professional Training." *Journal of Clinical Psychology* 39(2): 302-304.

Schall, Ellen. (1995). "Learning to Love the Swamp: Reshaping Education for Public Service." *Journal of Policy Analysis and Management* 14(2): 202-220.

Shulman, Lee. (1991). "Professing the Liberal Arts." Lecture given at the 1991 Institute on Integrating Service With Academic Study, Stanford University.

Shumer, Robert. (1994). "Community-Based Learning: Humanizing Education." *Journal of Adolescence* 17: 357-367.

Stanley, Mary. (1993). "Community Service and Citizenship: Social Control and Social Justice." In *Rethinking Tradition: Integrating Service With Academic Study on College Campuses,* edited by T. Kupiec, pp. 59-62. Denver, CO: Education Commission of the States and Campus Compact.

Stanton, Tim. (1990). "Liberal Arts, Experiential Learning, and Public Service: Necessary Ingredients for Socially Responsible Undergraduate Education." In *Combining Service and Learning: A Resource Book for Community and Public Service,* edited by Jane Kendall and Associates, pp. 175-189. Raleigh, NC: National Society for Experiential Education.

Whyte, William F., ed. (1991). *Participatory Action Research.* Newbury Park, CA: Sage.

Sociology and Service-Learning: A Critical Look

by Kerry J. Strand

An important current trend in higher education is what is commonly called "service-learning" — where community service and classroom learning are joined in the academic curriculum. Many educators from a wide variety of disciplines have detailed the benefits of service-learning, with particular focus on its usefulness as a means to expose students to diversity, engage them in the world outside the academy, and otherwise prepare them for responsible democratic citizenship (Morrill 1982; Rubin 1990). Advocates emphasize its pedagogical value as well, citing the centrality of experience to intellectual growth and the ability of service-learning — when it is done right — to achieve that elusive aim of truly engaging the student in the business of learning (e.g., see Kraft and Swadener 1994; Siegel and Rockwood 1993).

Sociologists are well represented among service-learning teachers and advocates, as firsthand experience in the community provides a promising means to explore firsthand the content of what we teach in courses dealing with topics such as social problems, social inequality, gender, ethnicity, social movements, political sociology, and social change. Community service furthers our aims by helping students develop an appreciation for social and cultural diversity, an understanding of the sociological imagination, and an ethic of responsibility for improving the communities and society in which they will live throughout their lives (Ender et al. 1996).

Despite the exciting and enormous potential of service-learning, however, I believe that there are pitfalls associated with using it to teach undergraduate sociology, as it can reinforce modes of thought and patterns of learning that are incompatible with our pedagogical aims. My first purpose is to draw attention to some of these pitfalls in the hope that recognizing them will make it easier to avoid or counteract them in our teaching. Second, I will offer some concrete suggestions as to how we might structure the service-learning experience to ensure that it enhances, rather than undermines, sociological understanding and the critical consciousness that is central to that understanding.

Sociological Thinking and Critical Consciousness

Sociology is essentially a "subversive" discipline — in the best sense of that word — whose perspective is inherently and inescapably critical. Although much of the research literature on critical thinking in higher education sees it as a cognitive skill having to do with the ability to formulate and evaluate arguments or lines of reasoning (Kurfiss 1988), the critical thinking that is central to sociological thought is of a slightly different kind. That is, it is not so much a skill as an attitude or predisposition — a "critical consciousness" — that compels us, in the words of Paulo Freire, to "problematize" the natural, cultural, and historical reality in which we are immersed. This kind of critical consciousness is what Peter Berger (1963) refers to when he talks about the "debunking motif" of sociology, what C. Wright Mills (1959) places at the center of the sociological imagination, and what those of us who teach sociology strive to inspire in our students as they come to understand ideas such as the sociology of knowledge, ideology, latent function, false consciousness, and the most basic sociological precept that human behavior is shaped by social forces — forces that are themselves not immutable but rather products of human action and interaction. As we encourage such thinking, we invite students to challenge conventional wisdom, seek information that counters prevailing assumptions, and consider divergent views and ideas, even (and perhaps especially) if they conflict with the beliefs and assumptions that students hold most dear. Richard Paul contends that to teach critical thinking this way (in what he calls the "strong sense") requires that we push students to "explicate, understand, and critique their own deepest prejudices, biases, and misconceptions . . . " (1982: 3). To teach sociology, for most of us, is to do our best to get students to engage in just this sort of thinking: to question, examine, challenge, and propose alternatives to the taken-for-granted social world as they have come to know it, both through their own experience and as they have been taught or told about it.

In a more concrete sense, this means that those of us who teach undergraduate sociology must provide solid evidence and persuasive arguments in support of alternatives to conventional thinking about things such as the causes of poverty, the consequences of immigration, the distribution of economic resources, trends in race, gender, and class inequality, and how the political system works. While a few students come to us predisposed to question conventional wisdom about society and social problems, most do not. Instead, most come to sociology with preestablished ideas about human behavior and society buttressed by emotional commitments to what they think *is*, as well as what *should be*, in their own and others' social lives. Because of this, we work hard in our classes to get students to consider new data, new ways of interpreting information, new lines of reasoning, and new assumptions about what humans are like, how the social world operates, and what makes a good and just society. Indeed, in some respects it is the very *separateness* of the classroom from the "real world" that makes it possible for teachers of undergraduate sociology to accomplish our goal of getting students to think critically and in new ways about the taken-for-granted world in which they are otherwise immersed. This same "separateness" may also make it easier for students to recognize aspects and levels of social reality — social structure, power, inequality, stereotyping, ideology — that are so easily obscured in everyday life.

Service-Learning and Sociology: How Good a Fit?

I believe that incorporating a community service requirement into under-graduate sociology courses does not invariably contribute to enhanced understanding of course material, or of the sociological perspective generally. Instead, service-learning can subvert our efforts by subtly promoting asociological and individualistic thinking about society and human behavior, encouraging reliance on personal experience rather than systematic analysis as a basis for knowing, and reinforcing rather than challenging stereotypical views of different social groups (including, especially for female students, gender-related expectations). Although these service-learning "pitfalls" are not inevitable, I believe that recognizing the forms they take is an important first step toward avoiding them.

One danger is that service work can reinforce individualistic thinking about social problems and human behavior. Most of us work hard to disabuse students of the common American tendency to "psychologize" about human behavior. As we gently steer them instead toward sociological insight, we try to help them see that the roots of social problems lie not in individuals but in social structure. Our aim, in the words of C. Wright Mills, is to "translate personal troubles into public issues" and to help students recognize that these troubles are "capable of solution [not] by any one individual but only by modifications of the structure of the groups in which [they] live] and sometimes the structure of the entire society" (1959: 187). But service-learning can actually be an obstacle to achieving that aim. Most students work in direct-service agencies, typically in one-on-one service-providing roles. While such agencies clearly need assistance and students derive personal benefits from, for example, tutoring low-income children or working in a soup kitchen, this kind of experience does not in itself help students acquire an understanding of the causes of illiteracy, poverty, racism, or hunger.

Nor does this type of service — like the traditional voluntarism that, according to Vernon Jordan, serves as little more than a "band-aid dispenser for a sick society" (1983: 403) — turn our students into agents of social change. On the contrary, such work supports rather than challenges the status quo, and as such it resonates with conservative political policies and rhetoric (reminiscent of George Bush's famous "one thousand points of light") that would absolve government of any responsibility for alleviating major social ills such as homelessness and poverty, and for adequately funding important social needs such as health-related research, quality day care, and programs for groups such as old people and people with various kinds of disabilities. Much of what we value as a society is indicated by the price tag, and the fact that we rely on individual assistance to provide needed services to significant segments of our population — children, the infirm, the elderly, the poor, and the sick — says important and not very good things about our national priorities. Encouraging or requiring our students to participate as "volunteers" implicitly reiterates the common view that social problems can be significantly alleviated or solved through individual efforts, and in so doing implicitly condones existing social arrangements, rather than challenging or changing them.

Along these same lines, the service experience that empowers a student may in fact further "depower" the people with or for whom the student works, as such "help" may impose silence and passivity on the recipients (Freire 1973). And even the most well-intentioned students often end up working for agencies and organizations that routinely dehumanize and control the people they were designed to serve. Some programs and policies have as their explicit aim the social control of certain client populations (e.g., see Abramovitz 1989). More typically, such control is rooted in norms and practices that emphasize efficiency, conformity to professional standards, "treatment," and remediation — practices that are unlikely to change as long as these organizations remain dependent on prevailing political and economic interests that they are therefore loathe to challenge. As a result, many of our students are participating in organizations that are of dubious value to the people the programs claim to serve, and that consequently may do more to perpetuate than to alleviate the social problems the organizations purport to address.

Another service-learning pitfall that sociologists need to be wary of is the subtle advocacy of personal experience over systematic analysis as a source of information about social problems and social life. Advocates of experiential learning typically maintain that experience itself is a valuable source of knowledge and understanding. While there is surely some truth to that assertion, it doesn't jibe well with social scientists' efforts to have students recognize that personal experience is only one source — and not a terribly valid or reliable one — for understanding the world. Beginning sociology students are notoriously skeptical about generalizations that are inconsistent with their own experience. Instead, they are far more likely than not to take as truth what seems true in their own lives. The inferences that our service-learning students are likely to draw from their contacts with social service agency clients are not, one suspects, the sort that encourage investigation of the systemic causes of those clients' social situations. On the contrary, such anecdotal evidence seems far more likely to reinforce the conventional "victim-blaming" explanations of social problems that sociologists most dislike. A student who works in a homeless shelter and sees that many of the men are unshaven and smell of alcohol and use the shelter only in very bad weather is very ready to conclude that their homelessness is *their own choice.* Here again, personal experience may do more to undermine than to promote sociological understanding, as it can bolster rather than challenge students' biases and misconceptions.[1]

This same kind of pitfall can undermine our efforts to help students appreciate social and cultural diversity. While we may value the opportunity for service-learning students to come to know people whose social status and characteristics are different from their own, it is also true that such contacts may work to perpetuate rather than contradict negative stereotypes. In part, this is because the people with whom students come into contact in service agencies or other settings where they frequently work — prisons, group homes, shelters, soup kitchens — are not representative of the social categories from which those people come, but rather are likely to be the most needy and downtrodden members of those groups (poor African Americans, single mothers, etc.). More generally, students' experience with diverse people not only is fleeting but may also be distorted by the power and prestige inequalities built into the helper-helpee roles. As a result, the exposure to social and cultural diversity that community service offers does not necessarily lead to the greater tolerance and understanding that we would hope for in our students.

A final pitfall has to do with the aim of instilling in students an "ethic of service." This idea assumes that students, by virtue of their service-learning experience, will develop a lifelong habit of participation in civic life and a lifelong commitment to working for the common good. This goal seems like a worthwhile one, but do all of our students need a service-learning experience to develop such a commitment? In fact, most women in our classes are likely already to have a commitment to service, at least as indicated by their career aims. More important, most of these students — service-learning or not — will do volunteer work of some sort throughout substantial portions of their lives: in their children's schools, in ladies auxiliaries at the church or the hospital, as Girl Scout leaders and Sunday School teachers, in raising money for the Cancer Society, the March of Dimes, or the PTA. The majority of volunteers in the United States are women — a fact that is seldom noted by service-learning advocates, most of whom fail to acknowledge the gender-relatedness of service. In fact, the commitment to service that is an oft-stated aim of service-learning is an integral part of *gender role* learning for American females: an extension of their traditional nurturing functions and caretaking role and analytically parallel to housework — both forms of "women's work" that are socially necessary, defined as part of our obligations as wives and mothers, and, of course, unpaid (see Berk 1988; Gold 1971; Ollenburger and Moore 1992). Feminist sociologists, in particular, are committed to a pedagogy that helps all students — but especially women — "problematize" societal gender proscriptions and examine in a critical way their own gender role learning. The goals of service-learning are not obviously compatible with such a pedagogy, particularly where female students are concerned.

Service-Learning: Social Action and Critical Reflection

I have suggested that service-learning, despite its enormous promise as a way to engage our students and accomplish our teaching goals, nonetheless carries with it some potential pitfalls as a pedagogical tool for teachers of undergraduate sociology. The final task here is to explore some ways to avoid these pitfalls and to make service-learning more effective as a means to help students acquire a sociological perspective and learn to apply that perspective to understand and act upon the social world. Of greatest importance, I believe, are how we design our service-learning requirements and how we work with students to help them connect their service experiences with course material.

One new and promising direction in our approach to service-learning has already taken hold among some faculty both within and outside of sociology: that is, a move away from service as servicing/charity work and toward service as social action for social transformation. Sometimes this means we deliberately broaden our definition of "service" to include organizations dedicated to social change (feminist groups, unions, environmental organizations, hunger groups, human rights organizations) and actively encourage students to seek such placements. Some faculty have made service a class project, so that the students join a collective community effort of some kind — seeking funding for local youth or day-care programs, opposing the building of a local incinerator, working to get the city government to enforce housing regulations, fighting to improve working conditions of local miners — to bring about some change or meet some need that the community itself has identified.

Those of us whose students will continue to choose more conventional, service-oriented sites — the majority, I presume — nonetheless can think more carefully about which kinds of service experiences and organizations best fit the aims of our teaching. These might include organizations whose work brings about some measure of real improvement in people's lives and that seem to be committed to community self-determination, human dignity, justice, and equality. We also might pay particular attention to issues such as gender typing and gender exploitation in certain kinds of agencies and in the ways in which those agencies use their paid and unpaid staff, with a particular eye toward giving our female students experiences that are empowering rather than exploitative of their gender training.

Finally, while most of us would agree that some amount of classroom discussion is integral to a quality service-learning experience, I believe that the way we structure the academic component of service-learning is especially crucial in sociology courses. The classroom is the place where we seem to have the best opportunity to see to it that students' service work — even when it is of the one-on-one, direct-service-work-in-an-established-agency variety — promotes our pedagogical aims. This would seem to require not only that we commit a significant amount of time to discussion and reflection but also that we conscientiously introduce topics, readings, and written assignments that help students think critically and analytically about their service work and its links with course concepts and perspectives.

The possibilities here are numerous. One is to make community service itself the focus of discussion and sociological analysis, perhaps by assigning readings and raising provocative points to get students to think critically about "doing good." For example, much of what is written and assumed to be true about America's philanthropic tradition says that we are an exceptionally generous, democratic, and egalitarian people and that these superior qualities are responsible for the long-standing tradition of American voluntarism (e.g., see O'Connell 1983). In our classes, we might help students juxtapose mainstream roots of the American philanthropic tradition (Tocqueville, Mather, Emerson, Rousseau, Addams) with its "underside" by exploring topics such as the ideological bases of historical and popular thinking about voluntarism, the history of women and philanthropy and its feminist critique, ways that voluntarism and "helping relationships" may be used to control, the negative impact of policies and programs on the people they are ostensibly designed to serve, and the less altruistic reasons some people volunteer, including the promise of salvation, feelings of pity and self-righteousness, boredom, an effort to enhance one's prestige, or the desire to appease the "have-nots" in order to maintain class inequalities — hence, one's own position of privilege — rather than to effect any real change in the lives or life chances of the poor and other disadvantaged groups.

In other ways, we need to be creative and persistent in our efforts to help students make connections between sociological thinking and every aspect of their service experience. In journals, written assignments, and class discussions, students should be forced to wrestle with questions such as:

• Who benefits from what this organization does? Is anyone harmed by its efforts? How and why?

- Why are people involved in this work?
- What are the causes and consequences of the problem that this agency/organization addresses? How could/should this problem be addressed differently?
- What structural changes would have to take place to help alleviate this problem? How might such changes be instigated and implemented? What are the barriers to making changes?
- Can one envision a society in which this agency is unnecessary? What would such a society look like? Is it achievable?
- Who has power in the city, in this organization, and in relationships within the organization? How is that power exercised?
- What are the sources and consequences of the inequality of power? How do other forms of social inequality — race, class, gender, age, sexual orientation — bear on the work of this organization and on one's own work within it?
- What is the impact of "service" on the "clients" and on others within the community?

When service-learning is effectively linked with sociological inquiry, the benefits for teaching and learning can be far-reaching. Students are equipped to analyze and reflect on their experiences by virtue of the guiding framework of the sociological understanding and critical consciousness that they bring with them from their academic coursework. They begin to recognize the pervasiveness — and the flaws — of individualistic thinking about the causes and consequences of social and community problems, and gradually are equipped to consider the viability of alternative strategies for addressing these problems and to debate the effectiveness of individual versus collective responses. They begin to understand, sometimes in a profound and compelling way, how sociological concepts — social power, social class, poverty, inequality, labeling, ideology, social control, rationalization, bureaucracy, discrimination, community, and countless others — play out in the real world and help us to make sense of it. Students who come out of our classes and institutions with this capacity for critical analysis — along with the passion and compassion that so frequently come from service experiences — are students who have been served well by service-learning. They are equipped to think analytically about their society and are inspired to assume roles as community leaders and agents of social change. We can't do much better than that.

Note

1. Hondagneu-Sotelo and Raskoff (1994) make a similar point.

References

Abramovitz, Mimi. (1989). *Regulating the Lives of Women: Social Welfare Policy From Colonial Times to the Present*. Boston, MA: South End Press.

Berger, Peter L. (1963). *Invitation to Sociology*. Garden City, NY: Doubleday.

Berk, S.F. (1988). "Women's Unpaid Labor." In *Women Working*, edited by A.H. Stromberg and S. Harkess, pp. 287-302. Mountain View, CA: Mayfield Press.

Ender, Morten G., Brenda M. Kowalewski, David A. Cotter, Lee Martin, and JoAnn DeFiore, eds. (1996). *Service-Learning and Undergraduate Sociology: Syllabi and Instructional Materials*. Washington, DC: American Sociological Association.

Freire, Paulo. (1973). *Education for Critical Consciousness*. New York, NY: Seabury Press.

Gold, Doris. (1971). "Women and Voluntarism." In *Women in Sexist Society*, edited by V. Gornick and B.K. Moran, pp. 533-554. New York, NY: Mentor Books.

Hondagneu-Sotelo, Pierette, and Sally Raskoff. (1994). "Community Service-Learning: Promises and Problems." *Teaching Sociology* 22: 248-254.

Jordan, Vernon. (1983). "We Cannot Live for Ourselves Alone." In *America's Voluntary Spirit*, edited by Brian O'Connell, pp. 401-405. New York, NY: The Foundation Center.

Kraft R.J., and M. Swadener, eds. (1994). *Building Community: Service-Learning in the Academic Disciplines*. Denver, CO: Colorado Campus Compact.

Kurfiss, Joanne G. (1988). *Critical Thinking: Theory, Research, Practice, and Possibilities*. ASHE-ERIC Higher Education Report, No. 2. Washington, DC: Association for the Study of Higher Education.

Mills, C. Wright. (1959). *The Sociological Imagination*. New York, NY: Oxford University Press.

Morrill, Richard L. (1982). "Educating for Democratic Values." *Liberal Education* 68(4): 365-376.

O'Connell, Brian, ed. (1983). *America's Voluntary Spirit*. New York, NY: The Foundation Center.

Ollenburger, Jane C., and Helen A. Moore. (1992). *A Sociology of Women*. Englewood Cliffs, NJ: Prentice-Hall.

Paul, Richard. (1982). "Teaching Critical Thinking in the 'Strong' Sense: A Focus on Self-Deception, World Views, and a Dialectical Mode of Analysis." *Informal Logic* 4: 3-7.

Rubin, Sharon G. (1990). "Service-Learning: Education for Democracy." *Liberal Education* 76: 12-17.

Siegel, S., and V. Rockwood. (1993). "Democratic Education, Student Empowerment, and Community Service: Theory and Practice." *Equity and Excellence in Education* 26: 654-670.

Building Campus-Community Connections:
Using Service-Learning in Sociology Courses

by J. Richard Kendrick, Jr.

Service-learning is an approach to education that is rapidly gaining ground as a learning technique (Cohen and Kinsey 1994; Parker-Gwin 1995), and it has been well described by other contributors to this volume. While service-learning is coming into its own as an accepted teaching technique (Cohen and Kinsey 1994: Markus, Howard, and King 1993) and there are excellent resources available to those who are interested in designing service-learning components (Lieberman and Connolly 1992), the questions I set out to answer are to what extent is service-learning being used in courses in sociology, in what kinds of courses is it being used, and how?[1]

This article will discuss its use in sociology courses and present a set of dimensions for classifying service-learning techniques. The dimensions are inductively derived from a nonrandom sample of 39 course syllabi and case studies, published and unpublished.[2]

I discovered that sociology courses in colleges and universities across the country incorporate service-learning at all levels — from Introduction to Sociology and Social Problems to upper-division courses such as Gender Studies and Collective Behavior. In some courses, service-learning is used to supplement or enhance the classroom experience. In others it is the other way around: classroom work is used to analyze the service experience, and it is the service experience that drives the learning. For this second category of courses, the service experience is central, and students meet in seminars periodically to discuss and analyze their service experiences. In many cases, these courses take the form of a service-learning internship or a field research experience. A third category of courses integrates service and learning to such an extent that it is difficult to assess where one leaves off and the other begins. Often, the work students do is defined not in terms of hours to be committed but in terms of tasks to be accomplished so that the end product is of value to the agency being served. The learning takes place in the field as much as (or instead of) in a classroom setting.

These findings fit nicely into Sigmon's (1994) typology of service-learning experience. At the two poles of a continuum we could place his concept of "service-LEARNING," in which classroom learning is primary and the service experience provides a context for applications of concepts learned using traditional classroom techniques (lecture, reading, discussion), and "SERVICE-learning," in which service is the primary experience and the classroom work provides a vehicle for student reflection about what they are gaining from their community involvement. In the middle of the continuum sits what Sigmon considers to be the ideal, "SERVICE-LEARNING," in which the service and the learning are given equal weight — one being intricately interwoven with the other. When service and learning are properly integrated, the service contributes to learning in the classroom and the classroom experience enhances what students gain from service. Each augments the contribution of the other, producing an experience for teachers, students, and agency participants that is greater than anything that could be achieved by a single component standing alone.

Whether the courses are service-LEARNING, SERVICE-LEARNING, or SERVICE-learning ones, my analysis of the 39 syllabi and case studies revealed that the course designs vary along nine dimensions: obligation, location, scope, intensity, structure, integration, social service/social change orientation, skills development/concept application, and evaluation. These dimensions provide descriptive insight into how service experiences are implemented, and they provide a set of guidelines for instructors to consider as they design their service-learning courses.[3] While I made these dimensions as discrete as possible, there are areas of overlap and interaction among some of them that I will point out as I discuss each one.

Obligation

Obligation refers to the extent to which the service component is a required element of the course. In many courses, students who enroll in the course must complete a service-learning requirement, but in others it is one of several options. In nearly two-thirds of the courses I examined, the service experience is mandatory, and several instructors make the requirement clear in the titles of the courses (Community Involvement; Life on the Fringe of Society: A Service-Learning Course). Students who are uncomfortable with the requirement are advised to find another course more compatible with their interests and schedules. In 11 of the courses, the service-learning requirement is one option among several that students may choose. Courses in which service-learning is optional typically allow students to substitute some other experiential learning (for example, students may apply course learning to their work environments) or research paper project. The extent to which service-learning is required seems to vary with the degree to which service is central to the course experience. Courses that are built around service (SERVICE-LEARNING) seem more likely to make service a requirement.

In an extended discussion of this issue on a service-learning listserv between October 1995 and January 1996, some participants argued that students must have the option of serving or not; otherwise, the voluntary nature of the service is defeated. Others claimed that students choose service when they sign up for a course (or a curriculum), and the service component is no more involuntary than any other course component — library research, field research, homework assignments, or mandatory reading. In either case, instructors usually indicate they are flexible in meeting the needs of students who may be unable to meet the course's service requirements, such as full-time jobholders or the disabled. Consequently, in analyzing course syllabi on the obligation dimension, one might assume that service is optional in cases where faculty are simply building in alternatives for students who cannot complete a service experience. The option to waive the service requirement is employed rarely, if ever.

Location

Where the service is to take place (on campus or off campus) is an important aspect of designing service-learning courses, but it is one feature difficult to assess from reading course syllabi. In fact, I couldn't tell in nearly half the courses (44%) where students are expected to serve. For those courses with information about location, it appeared that most instructors (77%) had established service sites off campus. In some courses (23% of those for which the syllabus contained location information), instructors allow students to choose on-campus alternatives, such as recycling programs or campus social services or advocacy programs.

One factor that guides decisions about where students serve is whether or not it is a goal of the service-learning course to get students off campus and into the community. Alternative models of service include bringing service opportunities to campus. Some projects, such as survey preparation, administration, and data analysis, can be brought from agencies to the classroom. In addition, agencies may be interested in exposing people in the community to the campus through programs such as tutoring teenagers at risk of dropping out of high school, English as a second language, or adult literacy. It was not possible to evaluate the extent to which instructors followed this model.

Scope

Scope refers to the types of agencies in which students participate and the variety of experiences a student gains in the performance of service. Making decisions about which agencies students will serve depends on learning objectives — where students are most likely to see course concepts in action or develop the skills being modeled in the course. A large majority of courses (72%) allow students to select between agencies or programs within agencies. Once students make a selection, they typically perform all of their service with a single agency (85% of the courses). In some courses, such as Bryn Mawr's course on the sociology of HIV/AIDS and Bentley's Introduction to Gender Studies, instructors limit participation to agencies that provide services directly related to the subject matter of the courses, such as HIV/AIDS services or gender issues, respectively. In other courses, such as Appalachian Communities at Virginia Tech, students rotate among a variety of community events, from attending square dances to participating in food distributions and other projects, to give students insight into the various types of community services and functions in a neighborhood, town, or region.

Intensity

The intensity of the service-learning experience consists of two elements: the number of hours students serve and the level of responsibility of their service. One may place these two aspects of the intensity dimension on a grid, with hours on the horizontal axis and responsibility on the vertical axis. Some service experiences may involve a large time commitment and a high degree of responsibility; others may involve smaller commitments of time and fewer responsibilities.[4]

The number of hours served by students is related to the use of service-learning in the course. When it is added to traditional, introductory sociology courses such as Social Problems and Introduction to Sociology, anywhere from 15 to 20 hours of service are required over a semester, while courses that are field centered require more. Of the courses I examined, only one asks for as few as 10 hours of service for a semester, seven courses (18%) require 12 to 15 hours, 15 courses (38%) require 20 to 25 hours, and four courses (10%) require 40 hours. Among the rest, course requirements range from 56 hours up to 117 hours over a semester. In some of the SERVICE-LEARNING courses, the number of hours to be devoted to a service project is not specified on the syllabus. Rather, the task to be accomplished is described, and it is assumed the hours devoted will be commensurate with the goals to be accomplished, whether these involve an educational program to advance recycling in a neighborhood or an assessment of the child-care and transportation needs of working-class families in a community.

In exchange for the time spent performing service and processing the experience, some instructors (13%) reduce the number of classroom hours to give students time to do the work of integrating their service and course learning. In some cases, classes are canceled for a portion of the semester, while in others there are fewer class meetings per week or the length of each class meeting is reduced.

The responsibility aspect of the intensity dimension was impossible to evaluate with any precision from course syllabi. One would need to know more about the specific tasks of service assignments to determine the extent of the responsibility students have in the agencies for which they work. Nevertheless, a rule of thumb that seems to apply is that the fewer the hours served, the less responsibility one takes on. Courses with the largest time commitment to service-learning seem to be associated with the greatest levels of responsibility for the participants. These courses come closest to Sigmon's ideal type of SERVICE-LEARNING. They are often driven by community needs as well as academic objectives, since they provide students with opportunities to practice skills such as action research, participant observation, interviewing, needs assessment, program development, and evaluation. Student projects result in products of value to the agencies served (presentations to community groups or public officials, pamphlets, newsletters, fundraising programs, reports, educational videos). Learning occurs as much from the evaluation of the usefulness of the students' work by agency representatives as it does from evaluation by faculty. Examples of courses that appear to achieve this level of integration include The Social Psychology of Recycling, Community Involvement Seminar, and Preparation for Fieldwork: Perspectives in Human Ecology (see Ender et al. 1996).

Anecdotal evidence and research indicate that those experiences from which students learn the most involve fairly responsible tasks that contribute something meaningful to the agencies students serve (Hedin 1989; Mintz and Hesser 1996). Students cannot take on very much responsibility without a significant investment of time, because it takes time for agencies to train their volunteers in the tasks of the agency. In addition, this dimension is related to scope (the range of experience a student gets), because it is possible to build in more scope the more hours a student is required to serve. Hours committed, scope, and level of responsibility work together. The more time invested, the more likely the service will be meaningful to all involved in setting it up.

Intensity of experience is not sufficient to guarantee learning, however. Instructors must include ways for students to process what they are learning by attending to structure (extent to which course requirements and learning outcomes are specified) and integration (extent to which the service experience is tied to classroom learning objectives and vice versa).

Structure

Structure directs student learning in a course and helps students to see how the service experience is related to course content. In some courses (33%), the learning experience is highly structured: The tasks students are to perform are clearly defined, and the learning outcomes are determined in advance. Instructors prepare handouts or handbooks with detailed lists of questions students are to answer in journals or papers. For example, in Introduction to Human Society and Human Community and Modern Metropolis at Augsburg College, students are given field study journals in which to record descriptions of their visits to their service agency and to write interpretations using a specified set of course concepts. A social movements course at Catholic University comes with a set of questions students are to answer about the social movement organization in which they participate. The questions guide students in the application of course concepts as they are introduced in class.

Other courses (59%) are much less structured: Students have wider latitude to decide how to approach their experiences, and the learning outcomes are open-ended. Twenty of the courses use a set of general questions, which are included on the syllabus, to guide students' learning. Three of the courses use much more open-ended approaches. My analysis of these syllabi indicated that many faculty seem to be following the advice of Hondagneu-Sotelo and Raskoff (1994), combining open-ended journal writing with a set of questions to guide students in their analysis of their service experiences. In my Introduction to Sociology course, for example, I ask students to keep a journal and record a description of their experience followed by an analysis relating at least one relevant course concept to their experience. Students seem less likely to flounder around trying to figure out how to relate the service-learning to their courses when instructors give them some ideas about how to tie the two together. It is through structuring students' learning from service that instructors begin the process of integration.

Integration

Integration links the classroom and service experiences, bringing the service into the classroom and the classroom learning into the service experience. To promote students' learning from their service experiences, faculty and agency supervisors must provide opportunities for students to analyze their experiences and receive feedback as the course and the service progress. Integration of service with academic objectives can occur in the field as faculty, students, and supervisors meet whenever possible to discuss progress, and it can occur in the classroom when students discuss their experiences with faculty and their classmates, or agency representatives participate as guest presenters and discussion leaders. In some courses, the integrative component is minimal, while other courses combine service with formal classroom work.

The most popular technique by far is some form of written response to the service experience in the form of a paper (87% of the courses). The paper requirements vary a great deal, ranging from short analysis or reflection papers to term paper–length assignments. Many faculty are very creative with the writing assignments they make in their service-learning courses. Students may be asked to write a letter to the editor on behalf of an issue or agency, write a letter to a politician, create materials (pamphlets, fundraising appeals, newsletters) for use by the agencies they are serving, or write reports to be delivered to agency staff or government officials.

Other integrative assignments include journal writing (used in 56% of the courses), classroom discussion (56% of the courses),[5] and oral reports in class (46% of the courses). In at least three of the courses, representatives of the agencies with which students participate come to the classroom. Only two course syllabi spelled out that exams will be used as a way of processing service-learning, although it is undoubtedly the case that in many other courses faculty ask students to apply course learning to their service experiences on their examinations.

Another way of looking at integration is to examine the density of integrative techniques: How many courses use one or more of the methods of integrating service and learning? Research shows that integration is key to extracting learning from service (Conrad and Hedin 1982; Hamilton and Zeldin 1987; Hedin 1989), so the better job one does of integrating service with the curriculum, the more learning that takes place. Limited as I am to describing those techniques listed in course syllabi, I found that seven courses (18%) use four or five different methods, more than two-thirds (69%) of courses use two or three methods, and five courses (13%) use only one of the techniques.

Social Service/Social Change Orientation

What I am denoting as a *social service* experience are those Coles (1993) describes as "community service" (such as tutoring, helping in youth programs, visiting the elderly and the sick); an experience with a *social change* orientation is characterized by involvement in social and political struggle (service involving activism and advocacy). In his syllabus for Introduction to Sociology, Sam Marullo makes a similar distinction between experiences that have as their goal amelioration of social problems, those I would classify as social service oriented, and experiences that are aimed at advocating for structural change, those I would classify as social change oriented. Whether a course's service-learning is oriented toward social service or social change depends a great deal on what the instructor wants students to learn from their service experiences.

It is important to recognize that it is not always possible to clearly separate service experiences into one category or another. Whether a particular service experience is social service or social change oriented depends to some extent on the mission and values of the specific agency with which students work, as well as on the student's role with the agency. Agencies themselves may be placed on a continuum of social service versus social change, and the student's role may be similarly classified. As a result, a student may work with an agency that emphasizes social service, and he or she may have a social service role. On the other hand, a student may be placed with a social service agency but be given a social change role to play. Similarly, students placed with social change agencies may have a social change or social service role to play, depending on the specific assignment. Consequently, to evaluate a particular student's experience, one would have to know exactly what the student did for a particular agency — social service work, social change work, or some combination.

Nevertheless, it is useful in planning and categorizing service-learning courses to consider where students' tasks might be placed within a matrix of social service versus social change. Do the objectives of the course emphasize student experience with social service or with social change, and are there reasons for emphasizing one over the other? Of those courses I could classify based on information provided in the syllabus or supplemental materials (49% of the courses), many (68%) emphasize social service over social change. Several (16% of those I could classify) emphasize a combination of social service and social change, and several more (16%) seem to focus on social change exclusively. As might be expected, instructors of Collective Behavior and Social Movements seem to be the most likely to fall into the last category, using participation in social and political movements to demonstrate the dynamics of advocacy.

This is not to say, however, that it is only in these courses that the connection between social service and social change can be examined. Parker-Gwin's analysis of her service-learning courses at the University of California-Los Angeles and Virginia Tech points out how social service opportunities can be used to discuss groups oriented toward social change:

> We analyzed the relationship between the community agencies through which the students were volunteering and the larger social movements of which they were a part. . . . They understood how working within conventional organizations could contribute to social change. . . . We discussed the tension between treating the "symptoms" of a social issue and addressing the underlying causes of the problem. (1995: 4)

Furthermore, research on the effects of service-learning on student attitudes indicates that social service work can affect students' attitudes toward social change — its importance and their own sense of efficacy in pursuing it (Giles and Eyler 1994; Kendrick 1996; Markus, Howard, and King 1993). The discrepancy between what students can be encouraged to learn from social service as compared with social change settings may not be as large as one might think. Some courses make this link explicit by having students develop action-research skills in a social service context. However, in placing these experiences on the social service versus social change matrix, the goal of the action research must be considered — to improve service or to foster activism and advocacy.[6] Within my limited set of syllabi, I found no courses in which the explicit goal of an action-research agenda is to evoke advocacy or identify avenues of social change.[7]

Skills Development/Concept Application

Like the social service/social change dimension, whether an instructor emphasizes skills development (the ability to apply relevant course skills and learn new ones) or concept application (the ability to use relevant course concepts to analyze one's service experience) depends on what an instructor wants students to gain from their classroom learning and service experiences. In some courses (5%), service experiences are designed to reinforce skills developed in the classroom or to build new skills that are not or cannot be taught in the classroom. For example, students may practice their action-research skills by participating in a needs assessment for a social service agency, or they may work on teaching skills through a tutoring program. In other courses (46%), service opportunities provide students with contexts in which to see sociological principles and concepts in action. The goal of the experience is to use new concepts to analyze the world and give students the opportunity to practice thinking sociologically. Typical of this approach are questions from Sandra Enos's Workshop in Sociology at Rhode Island College:

> *Where do social problems come from? What are the reasons for poverty, homelessness, violence, etc.? When you consider these problems, do you usually examine the individuals involved and try to figure out how specific behaviors and attitudes have contributed to the problem, or do you usually examine larger factors? What are the pros and cons of each approach?*

Some courses (28%) encourage students to apply the skills they have developed as sociologists as well as their knowledge of the discipline in the agency, so the goal of the service-learning includes both concept application and skills development. For instance, Bryn Mawr's course in the sociology of HIV/AIDS gives students experience in data analysis — quantitative and qualitative — and the papers students write at the end of the course integrate course concepts with their experiences, often proving helpful to the agencies with which students serve (Porter and Schwartz 1993). In addition, there are several courses with field research orientations in which the goal is to give students practice with skills and concept application while at the same time meeting the research needs of social service agencies.

Evaluation

Evaluation of the service experience can consist of a number of different assessments by the individuals involved: evaluations by faculty of student learning and the service experience; evaluations by students of the course and the service experience (including its integration with coursework and the agency's interactions with the student); evaluations by the agency of student performance, the usefulness of students for the agency, and satisfaction with faculty (or other staff) supervision of student participants (Driscoll et al. 1996; Giles, Honnet, and Migliore 1991; Hesser 1995).

My analysis of the syllabi revealed a wide range of evaluation techniques used by faculty for assessing student performance, from awarding points for completion of a service assignment to more extensive evaluations that include journal assessments and papers. In 90 percent of the courses, student learning is evaluated based on papers they write about their experiences in which they apply course concepts to their service opportunities. More than half the courses (54%) use participation in class discussions to assess service experiences, nearly half (44%) evaluate student journals, and in-class presentations are assessed in 41 percent of the courses. Very few instructors (5%) explicitly describe using exams to evaluate students' learning from service, but the use of exams may be significantly understated, as I mentioned earlier. Some instructors base a portion of a student's grade on completion of the service experience as evidenced by submission of a service log (31%).

Evaluation of the service experience by agency representatives is not mentioned on most syllabi, although there are a number of courses (36% of those examined) in which agency supervisors evaluate student performance, and in at least one course there are meetings between the students involved, faculty, and agency supervisors to discuss the service experience.

It was more difficult to tell how students evaluate the course. Six of the course syllabi (15%) make it clear that students will be expected to evaluate their experiences. In my own course, Introduction to Sociology, I evaluate student learning outcomes using journals and papers, while students evaluate the service-learning component of the course using an open-ended questionnaire administered separately from the college's regular course evaluation. In other courses, the service-learning and the course evaluation are included on the same instrument using Likert scale–type questions or open-ended questions.

None of the syllabi mentioned any evaluation of the experience by community agencies, other than their evaluations of individual student performance. However, agency evaluation of the contributions of students — and whether any benefit is worth the agency's involvement — is an important element of maintaining a good relationship between the campus and the community. Agencies are, after all, providing the learning opportunities for our students.

Conclusion

My analysis of 39 sociology course syllabi revealed that there are a variety of courses, from introductory courses to advanced ones, in all kinds of institutions of higher education, from community colleges to research universities, using service-learning as a teaching strategy. The service-learning approach clearly consists of a continuum of techniques. On one end are service-LEARNING courses, which allow students some freedom to define their own experiences and learning outcomes, involve a limited commitment by students, and offer opportunities for processing the experience in the context of a more traditionally based course. In the middle are SERVICE-LEARNING courses, experiences that have clearly defined student roles and learning outcomes, require students to spend a great deal of time in service, and are highly integrated into the structure of a course so that a reciprocal and synergistic relationship exists between the service experience and the classroom experience. At the other end are SERVICE-learning courses, in which students spend a great deal of time in service, somewhat less in integrating their experience with their academic training. Courses throughout the continuum can offer experiences with a social service or social change orientation, that emphasize skills development or concept applications, and that can be narrow or broad in scope.

The ends of the continuum should not be viewed as positive and negative poles. Service-learning has different applications in different course contexts. Sociologists interested in using service-learning in their courses could benefit from the continually evolving knowledge of what constitutes "good practice" (Mintz and Hesser 1996; Sigmon 1994) in the field of service-learning. There are many helpful resources for constructing service-learning courses, such as the Campus Outreach Opportunity League's (COOL's) manual *Education and Action: A Guide to Integrating Classrooms and Communities* (Lieberman and Connolly 1992) and the National Society for Experiential Education's two-volume set *Combining Service and Learning* (Kendall and Associates 1990). Campus Compact produces a variety of materials to assist faculty with the development of service-learning courses, as does the American Sociological Association. Daily discussions of good practice in service-learning take place on the service-learning discussion list sponsored by the University of Colorado-Boulder. Last, but certainly not least, the essays and syllabi in this volume are an excellent resource.

Adherence to the principles of good practice ensures that the service being provided is useful to the agencies served, that students performing the service are learning from the experience, and that the academic integrity of the learning is preserved. Much has been written about how to construct effective service-learning courses, and new research is emerging documenting the positive outcomes of service-learning experiences. The syllabi and case studies I analyzed for this article — some of which appear in this volume's appendix — demonstrate the growth of the field of service-learning in sociology. Practitioners of the technique within the discipline are making important contributions to the field of service-learning by presenting papers at conferences, offering workshops to teach others their methods, and publishing relevant research. As service-learning continues to evolve from our knowledge of and experiences with the experiential education and faculty-development movements of the last two decades, we will learn even more. However, it is already clear that service-learning, properly implemented, offers many advantages for students, their communities, and the faculty who use this approach. By drawing upon the models of service-learning that others have provided, assessing those models in the light of good practice, and using the research that tells us what is working and what is not, we can continually refine our methods and move toward even more effective ways to integrate service with learning in our courses.

Notes

1. When I started my research, I discovered examples of experiential learning (but not service-learning) in all kinds of sociology courses — an introduction to sociology course (Hamlin and Janssen 1987); urban political economy (Chaichian 1989); criminology, juvenile delinquency, and social deviance (Greenberg 1989); and research methods (Takata and Leiting 1987). In addition, there were examples of integrating experiential learning with applied courses (Seem 1989) and suggestions for integrating aspects of applied sociology into introduction to sociology courses (Ruggiero and Weston 1991). I came across few articles and only one example of a syllabus that integrates service-learning with a sociology course (Bradfield 1992). Now, however, more attention is being given to service-learning in sociology, including sessions at regional sociology conferences and the American Sociological Society's (ASA's) national conference, as well as a service-learning syllabi set compiled by the ASA (Ender et al. 1996).

2. A general call for contributions (syllabi from courses with service-learning components) was issued in a newsletter of the Eastern Sociological Society. A request for contributions was sent to schools listing service-learning courses in *Education and Action: A*

Guide to Integrating Classrooms and Communities published in 1992 by the Campus Outreach Opportunity League. I issued a call for contributions to the service-learning listserv originating at the University of Colorado-Boulder and searched UC-Boulder's service-learning database. Two syllabi were collected at the 1996 meeting of the Eastern Sociological Society. I obtained syllabi for a number of other courses through personal contacts, and Garry Hesser sent me the syllabi included in this volume.

3. There have been helpful discussions of many of these dimensions on UC-Boulder's service-learning listserv. Archives of these discussions can be found at *http://csf.colorado.edu/sl.*

4. In order for courses to be service-learning courses, there must, by definition, be some degree of student participation in service. Therefore, I have excluded from the scope of this project experiences that are exclusively observational, such as field research courses in which students are observing but for which there is no evidence of service. An interesting discussion of short service experiences took place on UC-Boulder's service-learning listserv in December 1995.

5. It could probably be assumed that discussion is used in nearly all service-learning courses as an integrative technique. However, this analysis is based on those techniques that are explicitly described in course syllabi.

6. While there are several examples of courses in which students do field research, such as The Social Psychology of Recycling and Preparation for Fieldwork: Perspectives in Human Ecology (see Ender et al. 1996), the goal of the research in each case seemed to be to improve service delivery.

7. See Divinski et al. (1994) for a discussion of the obstacles to doing social change work in academic settings. Markus, Howard, and King (1993) discuss the role of social change in service-learning courses on pp. 417-418 of their article on service-learning outcomes.

References

Bradfield, C.D. (1992). "Introductory Sociology." In *Education and Action: A Guide to Integrating Classrooms and Communities*, edited by T.M. Lieberman and K. Connolly, pp. 198-203. St. Paul, MN: Campus Outreach Opportunity League.

Chaichian, M.A. (1989). "Urban Political Economy: Designing the Course 'Sociology of Dubuque.'" *Teaching Sociology* 17: 56-63.

Cohen, J., and D. Kinsey. (1994). "'Doing Good' and Scholarship: A Service-Learning Study." *Journalism Educator* 48(4): 4-14.

Coles, R. (1993). *The Call of Service: A Witness to Idealism.* New York, NY: Houghton Mifflin.

Conrad, D., and D. Hedin. (1982). "The Impact of Experiential Education on Adolescent Development." *Child and Youth Services* 4: 57-76.

Divinski, R., A. Hubbard, J.R. Kendrick, and J. Noll. (1994). "Social Change as Applied Social Science: Obstacles to Integrating the Roles of Activist and Academic." *Peace and Change* 19: 3-24.

Driscoll, A., B. Holland, S. Gelmon, and S. Kerrigan. (1996). "An Assessment Model for Service-Learning: Comprehensive Case Studies of Impact on Faculty, Students, Community, and Institution." *Michigan Journal of Community Service-Learning* 3: 66-71.

Ender, M., B.M. Kowalewski, D.A. Cotter, L. Martin, and J. DeFiore, eds. (1996). *Service-Learning and Undergraduate Sociology: Syllabi and Instructional Materials*. Washington, DC: American Sociological Association.

Giles, D.E., and J. Eyler. (1994). "The Impact of a College Community Service Laboratory on Students' Personal, Social, and Cognitive Outcomes." *Journal of Adolescence* 17: 327-339.

Giles, D.E., E.P. Honnet, and S. Migliore. (1991). *Research Agenda for Combining Service and Learning in the 1990s*. Raleigh, NC: National Society for Experiential Education.

Greenberg, N. (1989). "An Experiential Learning Approach to the Teaching of Criminology, Juvenile Delinquency, and Social Deviance." *Teaching Sociology* 17: 330-336.

Hamilton, S.F., and R.S. Zeldin. (1987). "Learning Civics in the Community." *Curriculum Inquiry* 17: 407-420.

Hamlin, J., and S.J. Janssen. (1987). "Active Learning in Large Introductory Courses." *Teaching Sociology* 15: 45-54.

Hedin, D. (1989). "The Power of Service." *Proceedings of the Academy of Political Science* 37: 201-213.

Hesser, G. (Fall 1995). "Faculty Assessment of Student Learning: Outcomes Attributed to Service-Learning and Evidence of Changes in Faculty Attitudes About Experiential Education." *Michigan Journal of Community Service-Learning* 2: 33-42.

Hondagneu-Sotelo, P., and S. Raskoff. (1994). "Community Service-Learning: Promises and Problems. *Teaching Sociology* 22: 248-254.

Kendall, J.C., and Associates, eds. (1990). *Combining Service and Learning: A Resource Book for Community and Public Service*. 2 vols. Raleigh, NC: National Society for Experiential Education.

Kendrick, J.R., Jr. (Fall 1996). "Outcomes of Service-Learning in an Introduction to Sociology Course." *Michigan Journal of Community Service-Learning* 3: 72-81.

Lieberman, T.M., and K. Connolly. (1992). *Education and Action: A Guide to Integrating Classrooms and Communities*. St. Paul, MN: Campus Outreach Opportunity League.

Markus, G.B., J.P.F. Howard, and D.C. King. (1993). "Integrating Community Service and Classroom Instruction Enhances Learning: Results From an Experiment." *Educational Evaluation and Policy Analysis* 15: 410-419.

Mintz, S.D., and G.W. Hesser. (1996). "Principles of Good Practice in Service-Learning." In *Service-Learning in Higher Education*, edited by Barbara Jacoby, pp. 26-52. San Francisco, CA: Jossey-Bass.

Parker-Gwin, R. (1995). "Connecting Service and Learning: How Students and Communities Matter." Unpublished paper. Virginia Tech.

Porter, J.R., and L.B. Schwartz. (1993). "Experiential Service-Based Learning: An Integrated HIV/AIDS Education Model for College Campuses." *Teaching Sociology* 21: 409-415.

Ruggiero, J.A., and L.C. Weston. (1991). "Teaching Introductory Sociology Students About the Practice of Sociology: The Practitioner's Perspective." *Teaching Sociology* 19: 211-222.

Seem, J.E. (1989). "Designing Applied Courses." *Teaching Sociology* 17: 471- 475.

Sigmon, R.L. (1994). "Linking Service With Learning in Liberal Arts Education." Washington, DC: Council of Independent Colleges.

Takata, S.R., and W. Leiting. (1987). "Learning by Doing: The Teaching of Sociological Research Methods." *Teaching Sociology* 15: 144-150.

Unpublished Syllabi

Austin, M., University of Louisville: Voluntarism

Boyd, T., Berea College: Field Experience in Social Policy Studies

Chin, J., LeMoyne College: Internship in Sociology, 1995

Edwards, B., Catholic University: Social Movements, 1994

Enos, S., Rhode Island College: Workshop in Sociology

Fine, E., Virginia Tech: Appalachian Communities

Golemba, B., St. Leo College: Social Problems

Hesser, G., Augsburg College: Introduction to Human Society,1995

Kendrick, R., SUNY College at Cortland: Introduction to Sociology, 1994

Marullo, S., Georgetown University: The Contemporary City, 1995

———, Georgetown University: Introduction to Sociology, 1995

———, Georgetown University: Race and Ethnic Relations, 1996

Ogburn, L., Middlesex Community College: Life on the Fringe of Society, 1995

Ostrow, J., and J. Cronin, Bentley College: Community Involvement, 1996

Parker, R. Virginia Tech: Introductory Sociology, 1994

Porpora, D., Drexel University: Participatory Sociological Theory

Tuominen, M., Denison University: Social Movements: Women, Organizing, and Change

Vann, B., Loyola College of Maryland: Self and Society, 1996

———, Loyola College of Maryland: Social Inequality, 1996

A Multicultural and Critical Perspective on Teaching Through Community:
A Dialogue With Jose Calderon of Pitzer College

by Sandra Enos

Jose Zapata Calderon is an associate professor in sociology and Chicano studies at Pitzer College, in Claremont, California. After graduating from the University of Colorado, he returned to northern Colorado as a community organizer for 14 years. At Aims Community College and the University of Northern Colorado, he taught courses that connected students with research in the Mexican-American barrios in Weld County. As an advocate ethnographer, Calderon has published numerous articles and studies based on his community experiences and observations. The type of research and teaching methods described below have served as a catalyst for other endeavors.

In 1991, after being hired as an assistant professor at Pitzer College, Calderon led the development of a multiethnic coalition, the Multi-Cultural Community Association, to find solutions to ethnic tensions between Latino and Asian students in the Alhambra School District. As a parent in the district, he was also elected as the chair of the Alhambra School District Human Relations Advisory Committee. A grant that he wrote to Campus Compact in 1994 resulted in a course, Community and Social Responsibility, cotaught with sociology professor Betty Farrell. This class allowed Pitzer students to carry out participant observation and multicultural study plans in the Alhambra School District high schools. The project resulted in the development of multicultural and conflict resolution classes in the school district, the initiation of a conflict resolution program at Pitzer College, and continued funding by the Edison Company and other foundations.

For the last three years, Calderon has taken a class of (on average) 30 students to study and work with the United Farm Workers union in La Paz, California. In return for the union's hospitality and shared knowledge, the students contribute their skills and abilities to various segments of the farmworker community. On the last day of their stay, students present skits depicting what they have learned from the experience. This class was honored as the Curriculum-Based Alternative Spring Break of 1995 by the

BreakAway Foundation. In the spring of 1996, together with film/video professor Alex Juhasz, Calderon taught a class, Film and Diversity, in which students created videos focused on issues of diversity, as part of a Ford Foundation–funded "ism" project. Most recently, Calderon has taught a class called Restructuring Community that focuses on the practical consequences of urban growth, the emergence of "growth machines," and alternatives to uneven development and inequality. The class provides students with service-learning experiences through local city governments as well as community organizations.

ENOS: Can you tell me about how you came to integrate service-learning into your classes?

CALDERON: It came out of resolving a problem that I really had trying to connect the world of community activism with academia. I went to graduate school with the idea that academia would provide more flexibility to survive, on the one hand, but also to continue this tradition that I had, which was to use knowledge to create social change, or to develop policies based on building a better quality of life. After I graduated from the University of Colorado in the early 1970s, I was involved in community organizing for about 14 years before coming back and working on a Ph.D. I think the only reason I survived in the sociology Ph.D. program at the University of California-Los Angeles (UCLA) was because I found a means to apply what I was learning in the classroom to my concrete lived experience. Otherwise, I would have never stayed there. I was able to apply it to community service and activism, particularly in the city I was living in when I was working on the Ph.D., and to involve my entire family in particular sites we had been organizing in.

When I graduated from UCLA and was hired as a professor at Pitzer, I sought to continue this practice in all my classes. As a result, one of the most successful classes and a catalyst for more service-learning here at Pitzer was when I applied for funds from Campus Compact.[1]

Betty Farrell and I developed and cotaught a class where we placed students in the Alhambra School District to do participant observations, on one hand, and give service, on the other hand. They worked with teachers and carried out mentoring and tutoring. In some cases, our students even helped to teach classes.

In the second semester, students helped teachers to develop multicultural lesson plans. Out of this, we were able to hook up with a coalition of parents, the Multi-Cultural Community Association, that I was part of. We were able to work together in advancing some structural changes in the schools. Through our efforts, a multicultural education curriculum was more institutionalized, a conflict resolution class was established, and alternatives to a traditional tracking system were implemented. These experiences helped solve my dilemma of how to connect the classroom with social change, and it gave me motivation to go even deeper into service-learning. Discovering Campus Compact and the connections to other people who were carrying out service-learning in other parts of the country motivated me and other professors on the Pitzer campus to integrate community service into our classes.

My lived experience as a farmworker also became an asset to this process. I grew up working in the fields alongside my grandparents, who were farmworkers all their lives. When I began teaching at Pitzer College, I wanted to develop a class that could let students feel what I felt when I went out to work with Cesar Chavez and the United Farm Workers (UFW) after I graduated. That experience had changed my life in terms of wanting to come back and organize in my own community back in Colorado. So in order to bring a flavor of that experience to my students, I developed a class called Rural and Urban Ethnic Movements, where students go work and live with the farmworkers. In preparation for their going, I utilize a number of books and a lot of literature that has been written about the farmworkers. The ties that I developed in the early 1970s have provided me with the contacts to allow for the kinds of relations that have developed between students at Pitzer and the United Farm Workers. In return for the union's hospitality and shared knowledge, the students work in various departments of the union. When they return to Pitzer, they organize a memorial celebration and support the union's boycott efforts throughout the year.

That pretty much relates to how I came to integrate community service. It came out of a passion, of trying to figure out how I could connect this passion for community activism and social change with the classroom and do it in such a way that I could survive in academia.

There seems to be a common profile of faculty who are drawn to the practice of service-learning.
A lot of the faculty whom I have met who are involved in service-learning have had some type of community organizing and service background. Because of their past experiences, they struggle to make education a non-alienating, relevant experience. Usually, these individuals care immensely about the state of the world and its inhabitants, and they are using their energies to make it a better place to live. I put myself in this group. Although we have stumbled over many hurdles, we tend to be optimists. We are constantly looking for new angles to teach, learn, and organize. There are never enough hours in the day to do all of this — but somehow service-learning creates the balance and the link.

I have students work with autobiographies in my class, and I clearly see this distinction. Many minority students do come from lower socioeconomic backgrounds, from immigrant families. Their fathers and mothers may be janitors now, may no longer be just farmworkers, but they have that background. Consequently, they have particular issues that emerge on the campus that sometimes, unless there are other individuals on campus like myself who are sensitive to them, they hold in, and it can result in their dropping out. Those issues involve the lack of funds and feeling alienated, particularly if there isn't a whole lot of material about the history and identity of their particular community. Those histories need to be represented, and I think that is what diversity and multiculturalism are all about. It's not just something that minority students or women or gay and lesbian students need to know about, but something that the majority population needs to know about so that they can all be aware and work together on common issues. That's where the real issues emerge — the issue of affirmative action, the issue of making sure that history books are representative of the contributions of all groups.

My view is that in order to understand our commonalities, it is important to recognize our historical differences and why those differences exist. Then I think real unities develop, not just unities developed on superficial, feel-good levels, but unity based on an understanding of each other and where we do have commonalities.

Do you think that community service provides a platform where students can experience the sort of things that you are talking about? Students are in the world but may not be seeing the world. Do your students need the link to the community and to the academy to see what it is you are trying to teach?

A lot of students come right out of high school and are full of theories and ideas that they were taught in high school or by their parents. I find many students who come out of communities where they were not exposed to people of color or to issues having to do with race, gender, class, or gay and lesbian issues. In the Rural and Urban Ethnic Movements class, we get students from all different stratification levels. The students who are the most affected are not necessarily the minority students, because I think they know something about the social situation. The students who have been somewhat isolated and have not been exposed to the conditions of farmworkers and how farmworkers have emerged to organize themselves are the ones who begin to question why there has been this massive movement, there have been all these books written about it, and they have not been taught about it. The direct experience with the UFW affects them on a long-term basis, because it doesn't just follow how they have been taught in the past out of a book or a teacher feeding them abstract information.

The impact is long term; that is why it is hard to evaluate the effect of service-learning after one semester. Usually, students say that they had a positive experience and that they learned a lot. But the long-term impact is what we don't get right away. For example, I had this very conservative student who used to question the legitimacy of unions. He went on the service-learning alternative break. I recently got a letter from him in which he wrote that the class and experience had changed his entire life. He wrote that he decided to go into social welfare and empower people. Before, his outlook was to go into corporate America and make lots of money. His is not an isolated incident. If we started asking people involved in service-learning all across the country, I think we would find that this transformation occurs among many students. They end up working with the homeless, in unions, in non-profits, in agencies, and in the community. Their values are now to use their lives, their knowledge, and their values to build a better community. That is what I have found. Again, some of the students who are most affected are not just students from minority backgrounds but those other students.

Have you made any changes in your courses since you began with service-learning?
Many times over. I definitely learn new lessons every time I teach, and I use these lessons to continuously restructure my courses. One of the things that I have learned is to integrate more student-centered learning. Over and over, I have read Ira Shor's *Empowering Education* alongside *Pedagogy of the Oppressed* by Paolo Freire. These books have helped to take me away from traditional methods of lecturing and to understand the meaning of student-centered learning and that learning is a two-way process between students and teachers in the classroom. This method allows me to use problem-solving and critical-thinking techniques to draw out students. It allows for a continual process of reenergizing students, and I get energized as well. It certainly energizes me a lot more that students are energized when they return from their community site and are able to reflect upon it in relationship to class concepts. In my Social Stratification class, for example, I ensure that the students learn about some of the classical theories that emerged from Marx, Durkheim, and Weber. However, these theories become more concrete when we are able to talk about them in their relation to local communities or to the students' service experience. This really makes for more dynamic learning.

Service-learning has also led me to change the requirements for my classes. I primarily give essay examinations, and ask students to write reflection papers and research papers based on ethnographic methodologies. I especially promote that students learn about what participatory action research and advocate research are all about. I bring in books such as William Foote Whyte's *Participatory Action Research*, Michael Burawoy's

Ethnography Unbound, Jim Thomas's *Critical Ethnography,* and Orlando Fals-Borda's *Breaking the Monopoly With Participatory Action Research.* These books all demonstrate that it is good for students to be involved, to do research, to put themselves into the place of others, and to represent the voice and views of the oppressed. In terms of the books and articles I use for the class, I try to pick out materials that directly relate to lived experience and the type of community service that students carry out. I particularly like biographies and autobiographies. I now make it a practice at the beginning of each semester to allow students to review the syllabus — this has come out of my experience with Invisible College [an association of service-learning educators] and Campus Compact — to propose changes, and address any holes in the content. This practice allows us to make a contract with each other. I also periodically throughout the semester discuss with the students how the class is going and consider any changes that they might have. Many of these changes and modifications in my classes have come as a result of my deep involvement with service-learning and with individuals throughout the country who have shared their lessons with me.

Do you think Pitzer is an unusual school in terms of its location, its student body, its ability to accommodate the sort of work you do? Your president supports your work, I know. I can imagine that other institutions are more conservative in their orientation to service. While students on many campuses might be encouraged to serve soup in a soup kitchen, there may be fewer schools that have students out in the community doing critical analysis of the public schools and proposing reform and policy change.
Right. We have an administration and a faculty that are very supportive of service-learning. One of the foundations of our college, since its founding in 1963, is to integrate interdisciplinary intercultural perspectives as part of the liberal arts curriculum. Way back then, Pitzer had already begun to adopt three educational objectives. These were the interdisciplinary perspective, the intercultural perspective, and what was called a concern with the ethical implications or social consequences of the relationship between knowledge and action.

Pitzer is also unique in placing responsibility for educational quality with its faculty and its students. Rather than, for example, having academic departments, we have field groups. Academic departments, the faculty felt, lead to academic entrenchment and cut out the interdisciplinary character; they also create turf wars. Instead, Pitzer faculty organize themselves into what are called field groups that have no budgets and really have no department chairs. Field groups access curriculum with a concentration, and they make tenure recommendations. Faculty have membership in multiple field groups, not just one, so the system itself allows for continual development of interdisciplinary courses and [initiatives] where faculty from many disciplines can find common ground. So there are a lot of faculty here from different disciplines that I coteach service-learning courses with who are strong colleagues. For example, last year I cotaught a course with professor Alex Juhasz called Film and Diversity. This course combined our strengths in video, and race and ethnic relations.

Another thing that has allowed Pitzer to advance is the Ford Foundation Diversity Initiative. Six years ago, the college began the process of introducing diversity into the curriculum. Over a two-year period, eight seminars were held involving two-thirds of the faculty. The purpose was for faculty to figure out how they would redesign their courses to be more inclusive of the role historically underrepresented groups played in the development of the United States.

Within this context, a broad array of courses with increased outreach to the community have flourished. So today, although there are some individuals who believe that service-learning lowers academic standards in higher education, on the whole here we have full support. Through our development of service-learning models, we are able to provide evidence that it is helping to enrich higher education. With those who are skeptical, we have shared studies that have come out of Campus Compact and other sources. We have shared articles written about how service-learning has advanced collaboration with local communities. We have been a catalyst for creating examples of how service-learning is academically rigorous. Our class with the Alhambra School District, for example, was a class that was academically rigorous for the students by making concrete connections between books, theories, and lived experience. The faculty support here has led to the institutionalization of a "social responsibility" objective that requires the students to take at least one class during their term here involving community service, community-based fieldwork, or an internship. This has been made a prerequisite for graduation. The Faculty Council also recently decided to give lab credit for courses that have a service-learning component. These initiatives have advanced the development of a career and community services center, which is able to help faculty with some of the logistics in developing classes that have a service-learning component. Our work in the Alhambra School District also led to the development of a conflict resolution center, which was initially funded by a grant. The campus is now looking into long-term funding, because the project is serving so many schools in the region.

Overall, Pitzer's history of innovative education together with recent service-learning initiatives have led to strong support by the faculty and administration.

Have you found that your own research and path of investigation have changed any by virtue of what the students have been involved in?
I think that it has been sort of a dual learning experience. For example, as the students began to work in the Alhambra School District, their observations resulted in a number of concrete findings that served as a foundation for a lot of changes in the school. As they shared those experiences, it influenced me to further expand the research that I was carrying out. We began to collaborate on the research. Some students used their data to write their thesis papers. The class that Betty Farrell and I cotaught culminated in an article that appeared in *Teaching Sociology*. It also helped to fulfill our needs for doing research — which is necessary for promotion. I think a lot of young faculty are hesitant to go into service-learning because they are told that it will not help them in obtaining tenure. My own tenure recommendation included a substantial segment on the contributions I had made through service-learning. I would say that it is now being seriously considered in the evaluation of other faculty, as well. This didn't come overnight; it involved the creation of service-learning models and other faculty members' seeing the significance and importance of its being part of the tenure process. During my term at Pitzer, I've learned how to balance my teaching and service-learning with my research.

As service-learning becomes popular and faddish, and faculty talk about placements for students and work in the community, they worry that students aren't prepared and that maybe they don't belong in the community. On the other hand, do you think the potential benefits of students' being in the community supersede the need for a perfectly created placement in the community by a faculty member?
I lean toward the viewpoint that there are no guarantees in service-learning. It is positive in itself that some professors are attempting to try it out. I think that is where those of us who are involved in service-learning play a role. Those of use who have had a lot of experience in service-learning need to be catalysts on our campuses and share our experiences with others who are just beginning to get excited about it.

At Pitzer, we have institutionalized yearly meetings where we talk about our plans for how we are going to advance the service-learning curriculum on campus, what needs still are unmet. Every Friday, we have also institutionalized the meeting of a learning circle that brings faculty and students together to discuss service-learning projects and take up concrete issues on campus.

What are some of the lessons we share? One of the things we've learned is that service-learning means making a commitment to a particular site for a long period of time. The difference between students and faculty is that students usually take a course for one semester or carry out service-learning until they graduate and then they are gone. But that's not true with faculty. We're around for a longer period of time. I think too many communities have been burned by service-learning practitioners who parachute in to involve students over one semester or to gather research for a particular project, and then very little is given back to the community. What we have learned is that when those individuals go back to the community, they are not very well respected or accepted. Sometimes, they burn the field for other, sincere faculty who want to work there.

So, to me, it is better from the very beginning if service-learning is treated as a collaborative effort between the campus and the community and the institutions involved. That's why service-learning, if it is done well, takes so much time. I think faculty have to know that. The key to a successful service-learning class or a research project lies in the initial planning. For sure, it has to be carried out with the voice of the participants at the selected site. Throughout the term of the project, there has to be communication among all those involved. And when the term ends, it is important that faculty and the students summarize the results together. You can't guarantee that students aren't going to say or do things that might be insensitive or unconscious, but those are the risks we have to take. In the case of the Rural and Urban Ethnic Movements class, for example, not only do we have the class time to prepare students through readings, videos, and discussions, but we are also bringing speakers from the farmworkers themselves to talk about the issues. We also hold evening meetings where members of the UFW come and talk to the students about what they can expect when they go there. At the same time, we help the site by letting them know who the individuals are who are coming and what skills, abilities, and questions they are bringing with them. If we as faculty have developed a strong relationship with the site, and they know that we are going to be there for the long term, they will respect us. If mistakes are made, they will let us know, because it is that kind of relationship.

You have taught sociology for a while. Do you think service-learning is a particularly good tool to teach sociology as you understand the field?
I have always thought of sociology in terms of praxis and in terms of how the Brazilian educator Paolo Freire defined our capacity as human beings to create culture. I was an activist before I became a sociologist. How can we live in society, study social relations, teach about social problems, without actively promoting practical solutions? This involves seeing the world as a local community being connected to much larger worlds.

I have long grappled with the question of how to relate my academic world to a better society. Wherever I go to speak, I raise the question as to the role of higher education in helping to advance human development. What should be the role of higher education in promoting participation in the issues that are really facing us right now: a clean environment, quality of life, adequate child care, a quality education? My view is that higher education should meet these challenges head on. We have resources that can be utilized, not to "help" communities but to collaboratively utilize the energies and resources — research, teaching — to work with and alongside communities because we are part of those communities. The role of higher education should be to help develop campus-community partnerships that can present alternatives to some social, political, economic, and environmental inequalities.

We should be asking ourselves some questions: How can I use the position that I have in teaching, learning, and research without losing my humanity? How do I ensure the values of caring for others, values that may have come from experiences in activism, in the community, and in trying to build a better world? This is to me what sociology should be all about. We do have the capacity to be active participants in the process of social change. We can connect the tools of knowledge to finding solutions to the economic and social realities of our communities. Of course, we have to focus because we can only do so much. But to me, that's what sociology should be all about, not just carrying out research that gathers dust in some library.

It also occurs to me that we can look at higher education as an institution in the larger society that has basically been a somewhat neutral actor in some settings. High on the hill — doing the job of educating students — it is able to maintain a detached outlook on matters that are of important interest to the communities that surround it. How do you, as an active member of the community and as an engaged researcher, function in an institution that may have a smaller purpose than the one you think the organization or institution should be about?

It can be very frustrating sometimes unless there's some perspective to it. There are conservative professors who definitely teach their class with a bias. They say it is not biased. However, the theories that they use in the classroom have a bias to them. We also have a bias, and I don't hold back from relating to students my positions. The one thing that we can provide in this place that pretends to be neutral is that we can give students something that they may not have gotten elsewhere. To develop critical thinking in my classes I present literature so we can examine both sides of an issue. That allows for a lot of dialogue. Then if service-learning is tied to it, it becomes an even larger dialogue and more concrete.

At the same time, I think we can have a perspective and utilize that perspective to understand that faculty teach in a lot of different ways and that a thousand ideas can flow. This type of teaching can give room to be able to create critical thinking to help students to question and think to create change. This type of teaching gets away from the banking method of instruction, where the flow of knowledge is channeled primarily from the teacher to the student. I find my place within the institution by, on the one hand, being clear about the positions I hold on certain issues, while at the same time allowing students to critically think about their positions and where these positions fit into the larger picture.

I know that you've done a bit of traveling to campuses that are doing service-learning. What is your analysis of the variety of practices that are assumed under the service-learning rubric?

There are sharp differences in how various practitioners and institutions implement service-learning. There are those who primarily focus on the "service" aspect. Although the service-learning experience may have course materials and class discussions, its main goal is to place students in a particular institution or organization to provide a service. Still, this type of service-learning does benefit the community, and it affects students and faculty, as well. In some cases, this may be the first introduction to getting involved and giving service.

Another type of service-learning, which I am interested in, is based on a mutual process of empowerment, in which students, together with the community, are involved in a collaborative effort to find solutions to particular issues or problems. This type of service-learning requires the faculty and students to immerse themselves alongside community participants to do reflection and to collectively develop theories and strategies related to the problems that they are facing.

As service-learning is becoming more popular, there are new questions that are emerging in its application in institutions of higher education. In some institutions, the issues of liability, management, and governance have come to the fore. In others, the issues of control and power relations are becoming a reality. In one college I know, a professor got students involved in researching and protesting land development policies in an African-American community. It turned out that some of the developers were also on the college's board of trustees. This created tremendous conflict between the interests of the college, the land interests, and those interested in protecting the quality of life in their community.

For me, these are positive developments. As we begin to explore new types of service-learning, it makes for very exciting research and for finding new ways to deal with these issues. It is natural that once service-learning is embraced by faculty and students, it will move to other levels that can include policy making and social change. When it moves to this level, there are no guarantees as to the involvement and support of the institution. There are no guarantees as to whom the students will confront, including those in powerful positions related to the institution. I don't see this as a negative, but it certainly moves beyond the "safe" models that many institutions are comfortable with — the internship, service, and volunteer models. I personally support all these different models, because they serve different purposes and constituencies at different times and under different circumstances. At the same time, they can build upon each other.

It has been interesting speaking both with you and with Frank Furstenberg from the University of Pennsylvania, because you have both been involved as sociologists in work with public schools. You have significantly different entry points to the school setting and significantly different ways of determining the problem to be addressed.

As I have mentioned before, my entry point comes from my activist background. Coming from this background, I really laud students who get involved with community leaders and other participants in finding solutions to practical problems in their communities. I try to show through example that there is a need to get involved. There are many students coming out of high school these days who have a history of community involvement. The higher education experience can put a damper on that quality. Some of these students have a tendency to turn away from the academy and drop out.

I think service-learning can make a real difference for these students. I know that it makes a difference for faculty who have come out of an activist history and are trying to find a means to exist in academia without being co-opted and without losing the values that give social meaning to their research or teaching.

My research and activism correspond with aspects of the participatory action research approach, particularly in the explicit connections made between social research and action. However, in my situation, in the city of Monterey Park, I became an activist before I became a social researcher. Consequently, I had to resolve the issue that my data were collected in the dual roles of researcher and advocate. I began to call this type of research "advocate research": a type of research where one could be involved in the process while simultaneously seeking to describe the world of the participants through their eyes. Of course, as ethnographers we have to seek to represent all sides. However, our involvement can give us an "in" that allows us to more fully understand the participants and to summarize the lessons learned.

What kind of impact do you think all this activity on the part of higher education is having on communities?

Certainly, the communities that I have been working with have been empowered to see campuses as having tremendous resources that the community can take advantage of. The labor unions, for example, are actively seeking to develop stronger ties among labor, campuses, and community activists. I am heartened by the efforts being made by labor organizers as well as faculty to become part of the communities that they live in — collaborating with neighborhood groups to advance local organizing efforts and political campaigns.

As the research efforts on our campuses are being used to create and change policies, the divide between campus and community is being diminished. Our communities don't see the campus as an island, and, more important, we don't see ourselves as an island. We see ourselves as an appendage of a larger community.

As students and faculty get involved in local political issues, they also begin to see that they can be a political force in the community. They no longer see themselves as travelers passing by, but as individuals with a stake in the decisions being made. Service-learning certainly helps to bring all these aspects together. Pitzer College, as an example, is developing a reputation locally and regionally as a place where there is a culture of service-learning. We get calls all the time from schools that want to utilize our resources in conflict resolution, early outreach, and curriculum transformation. As we get known for that sort of work, the strengths and advantages of service-learning get known.

This sounds like a wonderful example and somewhat unique in its bilateral and multilevel organizational involvement.
Yes, students and faculty are involved at all levels. It is based on where professors find their passion. Many service-learning practitioners come out of a background of activism. They realize that they have lost their idealism along the way. They find that they are so caught up in academia that they have lost ties with the community. The reason why some professors shy away from service-learning is that they don't have ties to the communities around them.

We are being innovative at all levels. Some professors have involved students in local unions. They have learned to use email and the Internet to communicate with union organizers and community members in other cities and in other nations. Some students are part of a partnership between the nearby city of Ontario and Pitzer that includes students' living with families in the targeted area, intensive writing courses with a focus on urban issues, and seminars led by a variety of scholars, agency directors, and community workers. These various curriculum initiatives have been complemented with institutional grants from the Irvine and Mellon Foundations. With these funds, faculty-development grants are providing opportunities for professors to develop classes in their fields that integrate experiential learning or to participate in internships themselves.

Do you find there are unique kinds of teaching and learning opportunities that are afforded by service-learning that cannot be achieved in any other way?
Yes. Through service-learning, students were "doing" diversity and multiculturalism without realizing it. In various classes that I have been involved with, students were drawn from different backgrounds in terms of race, class, gender, and sexual orientation. What I found is that the students, in the process of working together in service-learning projects, have developed a sense of collectivity. In the case of the UFW experience, students work together in teams doing data entry, public action mailings, archival research, etc. In return for the union's hospitality and shared knowledge, the students present a reflection of what they have learned through the medium of theater. The beauty of this project is that it brings together students from diverse backgrounds to work together and to think critically and creatively. When they come back to campus, these ties are not lost but enriched. These are results that we cannot replicate in the classroom. These are results that reenergize me as a professor and remind me about the concrete meaning of collaborative learning.

Are you able to weave in sociological knowledge? What concepts and theories are students pointed to?
This is one thing that we are very careful of doing. In my Social Stratification class, I ensure that students learn about classical and contemporary stratification theories. However, I take it one step further and have students figure out how to apply these theories to multicultural novels and class presentations. In this class, for example, a group of students from varied ethnic backgrounds read the book I Know Why the Caged Bird Sings, by Maya Angelou, and applied its content to various stratification theories. In the process, they found connections to their own lived experience and shared their collective interpretation through the creation of a wall-size mural. As they worked on the project, I observed how students from varying ethnic, class, and gender backgrounds could come together to produce a masterpiece.

In a couple of classes that I cotaught with sociology professor Betty Farrell, Social Responsibility and Community, and Roots of Social Conflict in Schools and Communities, students participated in a weekly seminar organized around varied readings about the region, including educational stratification, demographic changes, and the nature of the Latino and Asian Pacific people's experiences.

In the Rural and Urban Ethnic Movements course, students learn about social movement theories and the difference between use values and exchange values as applied to the concepts of place, growth, gentrification, and community development. By virtue of their experience in the community, they are able to critically evaluate these theories.

In the courses that focused on local school districts [Alhambra and Garvey], most of the students wrote in their evaluations of the class that it was most difficult because of the requirements: extensive reading, fieldwork, traveling to the site, working independently with the students, taking field notes, coding, and writing up the final results. As mentioned before, we ensured that the books that they were reading were concretely related to the site that they were involved in. This was also ensured through the Rural and Urban Ethnic Movements class. There are now a lot of books on the history, origins, and strategies of the farmworker movement. In the class, we spend a lot of time looking at all the different sociological theories that relate to this particular social movement. When we go out into the field, students see the theories in practice and how different strategies are being applied. As a result, their reflection papers are not based just on emotion or personal reflection but are about how the theories can be applied to what they have learned and observed.

For faculty, helping students to link experience to theories is a real challenge. I know that I am always trying to move students beyond their own experience so that they become awakened to the importance of reading and critically examining texts and meaning. In some cases, in a course such as The Family, for instance, the students want to base all their learning on lived experience, and often challenge our research because they are aware of a personal exception to the rule. Helping students to see the world in new ways via experience and theory is designed not to rid them of old ways of thinking but simply to help them understand where their own perspectives come from.

One of the lessons that I have learned about student-centered education is that if it is applied well, it leads to a more interactive classroom, where the roles of the faculty member are made more equal to those of the student. This is a good thing. However, I have also found (particularly in introductory courses) that many students have not been exposed to particular theories or different ways of looking at issues. Some students in this situation often become comfortable with sharing their experience but slight the importance of doing the readings. As professors, we can shirk our responsibilities if the class becomes primarily focused on lived experience. The students need to learn to be dialectical and critical of the various sides and implications of classical and contemporary issues and theories in the literature. They need to ask challenging questions: Why do people have different positions on issues? Why are individuals and groups stratified at different levels? How did I, as an individual, get stratified in the position that I am in today? Students should be able to explain the historical, economic, political, and social foundations of how individuals and groups have become stratified at different levels and how inequality in positioning is explained in different ways by contending theories and theoreticians.

Overall, I think that this type of learning by "doing" sociology will stay much longer with them than if it were knowledge being taught merely out of a book. I am learning, more and more, how to develop combinations of lived experience, theory, and praxis in the classroom.

Do you find that students who come from backgrounds that are similar to the communities and people being served are having experiences that are different from students from more-privileged backgrounds?

Both are affected in deep ways. From reading reflection papers, I find that the more-privileged students respond in awe at having experiences with communities such as the farmworkers' communities in La Paz and Delay. They are struck time and time again by the realities that these communities have to face on a daily basis and how they are able to survive through resistance and organization. The service-learning experience often influences these students to change their career goals. Now, they begin to think about how they can use their lives after graduation.

However, I have found that the students who come from those communities are not surprised, but instead spend most of their time searching for answers. They are more affected by the strategies and efforts that the community advocacy organizations are carrying out to change things. These students become more interested in returning to their communities and using their education to join the efforts of others. Many minority or underrepresented students (including women and gay and lesbian students) fall in this category. They are sensitive to the issues on campus, issues that have a lot to do with their survival. These issues involve the lack of funds, role models, financial aid, and a relevant learning environment. Often, if the institution lacks a multicultural curriculum and faculty who can understand where the students are coming from, such students will drop out. All students and faculty need to realize that the inclusion of the underrepresented in the curriculum is something that serves not only the underrepresented but everyone, regardless of background. This country was built on the backs of diverse people. Unfortunately, some benefited and some didn't. That story needs to be told so that students from all backgrounds can sincerely and genuinely work together on common issues. The service-learning experience impacts both types of students, but the impacts are quite different.

As I look at the field of service-learning, it occurs to me that we have not established a useful framework that helps people to really understand what we mean by "community work." There are a variety of competing meanings here, and I think we assume understanding and agreement where none exists.

I think that we need a deep dialogue on this issue. The community, as a whole, is made up of many competing interests. Those who are corporate growers, developers, polluters — interests that may place profits over quality of life — are all part of what we call "community." When we talk about community, we are talking about a geographical, political, or spiritual place that is very diverse. This place has different levels of stratification, power relations, backgrounds, and ideologies. When you and I talk about community, we have a common sense that we are talking about communities of people who are facing inequality or who are trying to improve their living environment.

Ultimately, what communities we serve can have institutional implications, and this can result in conflict with the traditional power and decision-making interests. We need to debate some hard questions. What are the ethics of service-learning? Do we treat all communities the same? What communities are we talking about when we say that service-learning is all about "collaborating with the community"? This is an important question — because service-learning can be used to oppress and domesticate communities, to do all the things that we say that we are not about.

As we teach and develop critical thinking, some may take it to mean that it is only about "criticizing" and being oppositional. People today are asking for positive solutions, not just to hear what you are against. In this context, it is important to present and learn about all sides of issues that are affecting our communities. Our students need to learn the intricacies of research methodology and its strength in producing various options, answers, and outcomes. This sort of openness and exchange should be a hallmark of our service-learning classrooms. We have to teach our classes in such a way as to allow divergent perspectives to flow from the literature and from the students themselves.

It is my perspective that in the larger society students are not provided with many different ways to look at the world. The dominant understanding of inequality has a tendency to blame the "individual" for his or her "inadequacies." There are other theories and explanations that focus on the historical and systemic foundations of inequality. Students should learn to weigh the strength of the evidence for these explanations. What is liberating — as both Ira Shor and Paolo Freire would agree — is that first attempt at dialogue and critical analysis. From this can emerge consciousness that moves to the level of practice — empowering practice. If we as educators, who have direct contact with the students, are not the catalysts for this type of learning and community work, the students will most likely not get it from anywhere else.

Note

1. Campus Compact, a national organization with offices in more than 20 states, works with member campuses and higher education in general to advance the practice of service-learning and community service on college campuses.

Service-Research Projects in the Urban School: A Dialogue With Frank Furstenberg, Jr., of the University of Pennsylvania

by Sandra Enos

Frank Furstenberg, Jr., is the Zellerbach Family professor of sociology and research associate in the Population Studies Center at the University of Pennsylvania. His recent books include *Recycling the Family* with Graham Spanier (1984), *Adolescent Mothers in Later Life* with J. Brooks-Gunn and S. Philip Morgan (1987), and *Divided Families* with Andrew Cherlin (1991). He has published numerous articles on sexuality, pregnancy, and childbearing by teenagers, as well as on divorce, remarriage, and stepparenting. His current research projects, supported in part by the Zellerbach Family Fund, focus on the family in the context of disadvantaged urban neighborhoods, adolescent sexual behavior, cross-national research on children's well-being, and urban education.

Furstenberg's work in the inner city is propelled by his personal interest in inner-city youth and their environment along with his research interests in low-income families and their children. Public schools offer opportunities for interventions that provide services and connect families to schools. Furstenberg is intrigued as well by the potential involvement of the community, the university, and the public schools in improving the state of the larger community. In terms of university-based research, Furstenberg argues there has been little work on communities that either has met community needs or has involved community members in its design or execution.

As involved citizens, Furstenberg and his wife started a program in local schools independent of any scholarly interests he had in the local community. Called College Works, this program aimed to ease the transition from high school to college for youth from inner-city schools and required close collaboration with the local school system and the Philadelphia School Collaborative. Furstenberg grew even more aware that children in these schools face enormous challenges in their attempt to get a good education and find their way to postsecondary education. Public school children lack information and counseling about opportunities. Furstenberg and his colleagues started thinking about the need to involve the family and the neighborhood in schools and to assist families in managing risk and opportunity.

In 1994, Ira Harkavy, director of Penn's Center for Community Partnerships, asked Furstenberg to teach a course that would connect his research interests with his teaching.[1] Given his orientation to research in the inner city and his growing interest in school-based intervention, Furstenberg readily agreed.

Furstenberg started teaching service-learning courses in 1994. Students in this first class were both enthusiastic about working in local schools and worried about what this might entail. This senior experience involved a two-semester research project. He characterized the class as "an adventure" and proposed that the students take leadership of the course and of their learning. Some students who were accustomed to dealing with traditional instructors and their assumed authority initially experienced difficulty. In the first classes of the semester, the students read about urban schools, and early in the semester they visited the schools to work out the details of their assignments and structure their own experiences. For many, this was a disorienting experience. The challenges in finding "things to do" simulated "real-world" challenges where actors have to figure systems out, negotiate with teachers, and get their bearings in an unfamiliar world. As the semester progressed, students gained their footing. Penn students worked with high school students to design a survey to guide the development of the service-learning program. These reports by students were eventually submitted to school administrators.

The course was repeated the following year with a more collaborative relationship with the schools and a more deliberate focus on a specific problem, i.e., what to do about preventing pregnancies in the schools. This question was focused in two ways: to identify programs that could most effectively reduce pregnancies in the schools and to design an optimal strategy for working with the schools on this intervention. This more focused approach to the myriad problems faced by inner-city children provided students with a more coherent framework for their work in the schools. The students structured the academic experience, producing videotaped interviews with teen parents, arranging for speakers to attend class sessions, meeting with school teachers, and producing papers for review.

ENOS: **In placing students in the community, we aim to teach them a great deal. Sociologists observe that actors can be "in the world" but not observ-**

ing the world and what is going on. What are the connections between sending Penn students out to the community and what you expect they will learn by virtue of that assignment?

FURSTENBERG: I think that students come to Penn with a certain interest in the urban environment. Otherwise, they would not come to this sort of school. At the same time, a sizable minority, and perhaps a majority, come here with a deep apprehension about the urban environment. Relatively few of them are familiar with or have lived in the inner city of large cities. This environment is intimidating to the students. For many, it is alien and downright frightening. To bridge that distance between the world of the advantaged and the world of the disadvantaged is a formidable problem. Although presumably a lot of social science courses take up these issues, what students read and what students experience are quite different.

They also come to and enter neighborhoods and environments few of them have dared to go into. Their parents may not have been pleased to learn that these students were in these so-called dangerous schools and dangerous environments. In fact, these settings do have real risks. Students were encouraged to be careful and prudent in the way that they related to and entered these environments, but they also learned to be comfortable in a world that many of them wouldn't have been prior to this experience. That was another dividend of the course.

In teaching the course, I found almost immediately that having students read about urban education and situating them in an urban school were different as day and night. It was for the students an entrance into a world that they for the most part had no idea existed, at least in the form in which they perceive it. Most of my students know what it means to be bored in high school; most know there are good teachers and there are bad teachers; most students know that students vary in their aptitudes and tastes for schooling. However, few realize how stripped away the urban schools are of any of the amenities that Penn students have received — amenities such as an organization that worked, an organization that was relatively responsive to parents' concerns. Of course, parts of urban schools do work in one way or another, but generally the schools aren't up to the task of engaging their students in ways that are going to really give them a sense of preparation for the future, a sense of what the future requires of them and considers how the future might draw on their talents and capacities. Moreover, many school teachers simply are not invested in their students; they don't really believe their students will have a place in later life. This really is sharply different from the experience that most Penn students had in high school.

It seems that the connections between your students and the students in the schools are especially meaningful for the Penn students and for the

sort of learning that goes on.

The Penn students were close enough in age to these young adolescents to identify with them and far enough away to be of some help to them. The process of really engaging them in the classrooms, in the hallways, after school, over on the Penn campus, was eye-opening in a truly monumental way. It allowed students to experience "there but for the grace of God go I"; to see that these kids were not very different from where the Penn students and their classmates had been. The Penn students also sensed something of the despair that the high school students feel and the disparity between what they would like to have and what they're getting. These lessons, I think, would be impossible for me either as a teacher or as a researcher to convey in a convincing manner, in a manner that really gets inside their heads and enters their bloodstreams, that really enters their mentality.

I found that because the Penn students were working collaboratively and talking to each other about their experience outside the classroom, it wasn't a kind of lone experience the way traditional classroom learning tends to be. Their collective consciousness was so raised by this and so affected by it that more than a few of them really altered their career plans and decided to go into urban education. They also became galvanized in their commitments to doing community service on a more permanent basis.

Of course, we selected students who were receptive to this, and I wouldn't say for a minute that this transformative experience would automatically happen to every student at Penn were he or she placed in similar circumstances. However, both the class experience and the off-site experience worked to create a powerful amalgam that I think really was a creative educational experience. The students had a kind of epiphany that made them aware of the sociology of disadvantage and disadvantaged communities and institutions, and also aware of their own circumstances and responsibilities in addressing those kinds of issues.

One general lesson that I took from this experience is that it may not be possible to convey this sort of knowledge except by directly engaging students in an environment they are trying to understand and ameliorate. They learned a lot about urban schools. They learned a lot about urban communities and urban families. They learned a lot about the way society is structured. A by-product of this experience was that students recognized how privileged they are. This made them also feel less "entitled" and more "analytical," [more inclined] to give something in return.

The good side of this is that if they were strictly doing research or studying communities, they would have been cheated a little bit, as would the communities. In the research-only instance, they are taking but not fully giving in a reciprocal relationship. Another benefit was that this source provided access they could not easily obtain except by fully entering into the situation and the institution. Were they to talk to the teachers or students in a casual way, they would have seen these communities quite differently from what they did by starting out by teaching in the classroom or running small projects with the students. They learned a good deal about the students through those [interactions]. They learned to differentiate among the students and teachers — the ones who cared and the ones who didn't. What it did was to break down the tremendous stereotypes that exist — either the conservative stereotypes that poor students don't care or the left-wing stereotypes that if you did only a little of this and a little of that, then the situation could be changed. They became aware of how complex the situation is and how much change is needed and how radical the changes have to be. It did not necessarily create a sense of hopefulness, but neither did it make them disengage, because they experienced the difference that they made by being in the situation.

Those who teach service-learning invest a lot of time and energy in this sort of pedagogy. We are asking faculty and students to do some new things, to experiment with learning and teaching. What do you think the costs and benefits are here?
From my point of view, I found that the students took a great deal of responsibility once the class began. They assumed much more responsibility for organizing this learning experience and sharing responsibility for it, and that was a really important asset of this kind of course. Students became active agents in their own learning rather than passive receivers. As active agents, they become much more creative in how they devised ideas and projects, and bolder and more ambitious than they might otherwise have been. The course took an enormous amount of time, their time and my time — mine as a kind of supervisor and hand-holder and facilitator, and theirs as people who were assuming more adult-like responsibilities and becoming less dependent on me.

That creates a gratifying relationship between the students and me. I find that if some of the student alumni from the two courses see me, they throw their arms around me and give me a big hug. That isn't the normal relationship between students and the faculty. Even if they call me "Dr. Furstenberg" (and I've invited them to call me by my first name as graduate students do), the normal distance between students and faculty had diminished as a result of the kind of collaboration that we had in fashioning the course together. This change in relationship is a feature that I especially appreciated. The service-learning experience did change their relationship with me as a teacher. This was a wonderful bridge experience between the way they might function in the world of work and the usual way they function in school. As smart and as motivated as they are, students usually take assignments and do what they are supposed to do, as opposed to creating the assignments and doing as much as they can. That was a very appealing dividend of the course for them.

When students talk about their community service experiences in class, they reveal an enormous amount of information that is a rich source for discussion and further investigation and research. Have you found that your own research has been modified or enriched by virtue of the work your students are doing?
Indeed it has. The experience got me much more deeply involved in work in urban education. It was an area in which I have no academic experience. By virtue of this course, I became much more deeply involved in what schools are about. As a result, I've gone on to develop a research agenda related to urban education that I think would not have happened were it not for this course. In some ways, I too was immersed in the urban schools and found the experience sufficiently provocative to think about projects and interventions, both of which I am doing. I am now doing a longitudinal study about the Philadelphia school system and thinking about a possible intervention involving collaboration with the local high school I worked in. Both of these endeavors are connected to the two years I taught the class. In that sense, it was a great learning experience for me, as well.

It also, in many ways, gave me a kind of legitimacy as someone who was not just extracting a pint of blood from my research site but was giving a pint of blood just as the students were. I taught a course for some of the staff of the school simply because I was asked to by the principal. I and my teaching assistants helped supervise some of the students at Penn. In some ways, we were tested to see how interested we really were. People wanted to know who was benefiting from this work and how.

One thing has impressed me in speaking to faculty about this kind of teaching. Faculty do believe in their hearts that students can really come to adopt a sociological perspective in these classes that they can't grasp in any other way — understanding the structure and form of how to be and think like a sociologist.
I think that is very true. I think these students enter a world that is unfamiliar and they have to be instructed into the ways of that world. [This results in] the anthropological benefit of being an outsider who learns to be more comfortable in an unfamiliar culture. One needs to rely on knowledgeable informants. As a result of this exposure, students look back at the world that is familiar in a way that changes it and that makes it all different again. Students realize that the taken-for-granted qualities of their own social world can't be taken for granted in the same way. The role that

resources play, that access and information play, can't be overappreciated.

Take a concrete example. Students consider how high school students from inner-city schools think about entering the middle-class world and how far away it is for them — how much these poor kids need to know. These encounters made the Penn students much more aware of power and privilege. Of social structure as it really exists; the way it structures access to resources and opportunities; the way it structures cognition, knowledge, and beliefs; the way it structures understandings, behaviors, and norms. I don't think students can get that kind of knowledge without going outside of the campus world. The community experience *renders* the academic work. There's a kind of "Aha! This is what I was reading about. This is what sociology is really about."

Many of our majors who take five or six or seven courses in sociology never really learn or acquire the sociological perspective, the "sociological imagination," as C. Wright Mills referred to it. Students need to understand the way in which individuals' private concerns are expressed in public issues and the ways in which individual biographies get built up in social structure that fashions opportunities and life courses. Those kinds of things have a certain verbal familiarity to the students. They are acquainted with all of that kind of understanding, but it isn't alive for them. When it becomes alive, suddenly their black-and-white world is now technicolor and has a three-dimensional quality instead of a flat aspect. Students must reconcile different accounts in these situations and come to understand the complexity of the social world and of solving problems and reconciling perspectives.

[To be sure,] this type of academic learning has a quality of simulation. It is somewhat contrived. But the community work is real. As they go into this reality, they come to apply the understandings from their textbook learning that are latent. These understandings become activated, and students use these sociological concepts and perspectives in a different way. Once they start using them, it is like learning how to ride a bicycle. They know how to do it now. You can't teach someone how to ride a bicycle by telling them how to ride the bike, or how to swim by telling them how it is to swim. Learning sociology by service-learning is like learning to ride a bike or learning to swim.

Similarly, once you really know how to do sociology, you can never not do it. We have far too much of telling students how we do it or how it should be done and not enough letting them do it. This is the doing of sociology that I think occurs in these service-learning courses. One challenge here is how to help students think about action and about how to make a difference in the situations they are encountering.

There is great support among a small number of faculty who want to do this sort of work but find themselves without sympathetic and enthusias-

tic colleagues in their discipline or on their campus. What do you think are some ways to advance the practice among our colleagues?

Faculty who are interested in incorporating community service into their teaching need a supportive academic system and a core interest in learning about ways to become a better teacher. Supports might include learning about models of teaching and research from respected peers, recognition that this is valued and valuable work.

To spread the word and bring on additional faculty, it is important to have students' testimonies about the learning that goes on in these courses. Students sell the course to other students, and that pushes faculty to get involved.

As we've touched upon earlier, Penn, a highly respected institution of higher learning, is situated in the middle of a distressed urban community. Can you set the context here and discuss the role of your work within that institutional setting and the role of Penn as a player in the community?

Penn is situated in and is virtually surrounded on at least three sides by inner-city communities of low-income and working-class blacks as well as a sprinkling of professional blacks and whites. It is essential that Penn work in its community. While it doesn't entirely quell the hostility that exists between the university and the community, between the privilege of the campus life and the underprivilege of the community life, it certainly helps. It commits the university in the right direction. Penn is becoming more related to its community in a way that it hasn't always been, and the students feel a part of that community. However, there are all sorts of problems going on in the community and between the university and community. I don't want to suggest in any way that service-learning can make a dramatic difference in what happens in the community.

Even if the university were fully committed to a partnership with the community, it could not be more than a very helpful institution. It cannot solve all the problems of the community. Our work in the community certainly changes the kind of inward stance of the university and the completely blocked position of the community for the better. This work signifies a small measure of balance and exchange.

Penn is doing a lot of that kind of work, and I hope it will do even more in the future. I think there is a lot of room for growth. If students are going to come to an urban school in an urban environment, we would be completely remiss if we did not try to develop this kind of relationship and advance it in the future. It is imperative that we set an example for our students, faculty, and staff. We simply cannot disengage from the community without great costs to ourselves and society.

Note

1. At Penn, service-learning is incorporated into a larger framework called "academically based community service." At the Center for Community Partnerships, Ira Harkavy leads an effort that involves more than 40 faculty in community service work in local public schools. Disciplines include sociology, history, nutritional anthropology, classics, and journalism. In addition to the representation from many disciplines, an institutional commitment of funding and administrative support characterizes the Penn program. Tying this effort to the core institutional mission and a recognition that the futures of the community and the university are intertwined are important hallmarks of Penn's work in West Philadelphia (Benson and Harkavy 1994).

Reference

Benson, L., and I. Harkavy. (Fall/Winter 1994). "1994 as Turning Point: The University-Assisted Community School Idea Becomes a Movement." *Universities and Community Schools* 4(1-2): 5-8.

Service-Learning as Symbolic Interaction

by Barbara H. Vann

As the body of literature on service-learning continues to grow, writers in a number of disciplines have begun describing how service-learning ties into their discipline. Sociology is perhaps one of the easiest disciplines to link with service-learning, and sociology instructors have long agreed about the potential value of experiential community service-learning as a pedagogical tool for integrating concepts students learn in the lecture hall with focused perceptions of society (Corwin 1996).

Marullo (1996) has described service-learning as a pedagogy that offers "a crucible for learning that enables students to test theories with life experiences, and forces upon them an evaluation of their knowledge and understanding grounded in their service experience" (7). In fact, Myers-Lipton (1996) has found that service-learning promotes development of a sociological imagination, which, as C. Wright Mills explained,

> . . . enables its possessor to understand the larger historical scene in terms of its meaning for the inner life and the external career of a variety of individuals. It enables him [sic] to take into account how individuals, in the welter of their daily experience, often become falsely conscious of their social positions. (1959: 5)

Service-learning provides students with the opportunity to discover the larger structural issues that are behind the seemingly individual problems and needs encountered in their service experiences.

And yet, although the linkage between sociology and service-learning is well established, little has been written about a theoretical grounding of service-learning specifically in sociology. This essay is a beginning attempt to explore the relationship between service-learning and symbolic interaction. One of the claims service-learning makes is that theories and concepts about social interactions, human relationships, and institutional operations are understood better when they are observed firsthand (Chesler 1993; Miller 1994). For sociologists, the laboratory for applying, testing, and evaluating claims about human nature and social relations is the larger society. Service-learning assignments enable students to take what they learn in the classroom and test this knowledge against the reality they observe at their service site. As Marullo (1996) states:

> This experience not only enables them to understand better the material they are learning but also helps them to place their own life experience in a broader context by providing a comparative base of a different reality.

Especially for the typically more affluent students at a private liberal arts college, but also for university students in general, exposure to the living conditions of the poor is a very educational experience. (123)

The remainder of this essay will focus on the ways students' understanding of symbolic interactionist concepts aids their process of discovery in the rich milieu provided by the service-learning site.

Service-Learning and Symbolic Interaction

Symbolic interaction is the interpretive work of human encounters, or the process through which we attach meaning to one another's conduct (Blumer 1962). These meanings are the product of social interaction, and are modified and handled through an interpretative process. That is:

Humans create and use symbols. They communicate with symbols. They interact through role-taking, which involves the reading of symbols emitted by others. What makes them unique as a species — the existence of mind and self — arises out of interaction, while conversely, the emergence of these capacities allows for the interactions that form the basis of society. (Turner 1978: 329-330)

"Role taking" refers to the process we employ when we use a person's behaviors as the basis for our inferences about his or her identities (McCall and Simmons 1978). The central idea of role taking is that the individual can imagine a situation from a perspective other than that afforded by his or her role in the situation. A role provides an individual with a vantage point from which to view the situation and from which to construct his or her own action. By "taking the role of the other" an individual is able to understand the meaning of a given situation and act accordingly.

We learn to take the role of the other via socialization, or, rather, this is how socialization occurs and how the self develops, according to George Herbert Mead (1934). In theoretical terms, role taking requires identification *with* and identification *of* others (Stone 1962). Identification with others occurs as one tries to imagine how others are seeing and conceiving a given situation. Before identification with others can occur, however, an individual must be placed, generally based on social attributes such as gender, age, race or ethnicity, and social class and on physical attributes such as appearance, demeanor, and language.

Once an individual has been placed, we are able to predict his or her conduct because we have identified him or her as a type of person who is likely to behave in ways similar to others of that type. The process of role taking depends on this ability to typify (Hewitt 1994). The largest part of our everyday conduct occurs within routine situations with relatively congruent definitions. We can easily know what roles are to be played, and generally know what to expect. We rely on the usual cues to identify those with whom we are interacting, and generally identification with them is not difficult. The construct of role taking presents a good starting point to illustrate the linkage between service-learning and symbolic interaction. As in any other type of interaction, individuals are presented with opportunities for role taking while interacting in community service settings. A service-learning experience, however, is rarely a routine situation for the majority of students. Students engaging in such an activity, especially for the first time, are uncertain about the roles they or other interactants will play, and they frequently do not know what to expect in terms of behavior. This uncertainty may well lead to difficulty in role taking on the part of students. One way students can process the meaning of this difficulty is by applying symbolic interactionist concepts to their service experience, thereby achieving greater understanding of the perspectives of those they meet, it is hoped. In some cases, this understanding actually aids students' ability to interact within the service setting.

In the pages that follow, I will use the concept of role taking in a service-learning context to begin to identify a theoretical linkage between symbolic interaction and service-learning. The specific aspects of role taking described here are typification and role taking, role taking with those perceived as cultural strangers, and the relationship of role taking to power. All these constructs I cover in my introductory sociology course called Self and Society, a course framed within the symbolic interactionist perspective and drawing heavily on Erving Goffman's dramaturgy. Early in the semester, we study urban interaction, and students are introduced to concepts such as cultural strangers, avoidance behaviors, and the norm of anonymity. About halfway through the semester, we spend several weeks focusing on the politics of interaction, in which we explore the effects of gender, race/ethnicity, and social class on interaction. We pay special attention to the phenomena of deference and power. It is at this point that students are encouraged, but not required, to participate in a service experience. Their assignment is as follows:

Assignment 3: Gender, Class, and Racial/Ethnic Inequality: The Effect of Position in the Stratification Structure on Interaction

For this assignment, choose a setting in which to observe interaction among individuals of different backgrounds based on gender, race/ethnicity, or social class. A likely setting would be a meal program such as Beans & Bread or Our Daily Bread, or some setting in which people who are "cultural strangers" meet. Observe long enough to determine what patterns of behavior, norms, etc., are in operation. After gathering your data, write up

*your analysis in terms of how position in the stratification structure affect-
ed interaction. Pay particular attention to such things as demeanor, appearance, setting, props, gestures, and language. Be sure to address the role
power plays.*

The following section examines what might be described as the problematic role taking that may occur in service-learning experiences. I use student responses to the above assignment to illustrate how their understanding of symbolic interactionist concepts aids their process of discovering the
social world — in this case, the social world of impoverished individuals.

Typification and Role Taking

According to Gregory Stone (1962), all interaction involves two levels:
our observation and response to discourse, and our observation and
response to appearance. These serve as bases for typification — our expectations and assumptions about a particular role, situation, person, or object.
Typifications serve as a means of organizing and cataloguing knowledge,
and subsequently affect the course of interaction (Hewitt 1994).

Very little about people is actually visible to observers. Physical appearance (expressed in dress, posture, and facial expression) and a few overt
words and deeds constitute all that is directly accessible to others. We rely on
these cues, however, to understand not only who an individual is but how
interaction with that individual should (or shouldn't) proceed. These cues
allow us to predict the conduct of others because they identify them as types
of people who are likely to behave in ways similar to others of their type. The
very process of role taking depends on this ability to typify (Hewitt 1994).

When individuals are poor, they are not able to manage the impressions
given to others to the same extent as can individuals who have more in the
way of material resources. The cues used by others to typify them are not
necessarily under their control. Poor individuals may appear unkempt, dirty;
they may smell bad. They may be missing teeth. They may carry all of their
belongings in bags or shopping carts. Their demeanor may, in fact, be that of
someone who feels he or she is at the bottom of the stratification structure.

When students first come into contact with such individuals, they make
preliminary judgments based on these cues. Certainly these judgments may
be negative. The following is from a student paper: "The first subject I
observed was a white, working-class male, in his mid 40s, dressed in dirty
clothes and rather unkempt. He wore a cheap, stained baseball cap and
filthy generic tennis shoes." *Dirty, unkempt, cheap, stained, filthy, generic* — this
student has no difficulty attaching undesirable social characteristics to this
individual based on appearance. Analogously, another student makes
assessments based on the demeanor of those encountered: "Some guests are
very outgoing, wanting to talk to anyone and everyone, while there are also

those that seemed ashamed to be there and come in, sit down, eat, and leave without a word." Based on her experience with meal guests at a soup kitchen, this student uses their demeanor to classify them, attribute social characteristics to them, and interpret their behavior.

A framework of analysis such as Goffman's presentation of self (1959) provides students with a means of understanding how factors such as appearance, props, and demeanor affect interaction. With this understanding, students may develop more empathy, and engage in less judgment and negative stereotyping. The student who wrote the following seems to have used such a framework to understand the lack of interaction in a particular setting:

> Some people took their sandwiches and left, thereby engaging in no interaction whatsoever. Some would use props such as cards and alcoholic beverages to deter any interaction with those who were serving them, while others would just minimize eye contact. Other avoidance behaviors included bitter facial expressions in which the homeless either expressed discomfort or tried to make us feel uncomfortable, all in part to minimize interaction.

Finally, some students not only become aware of the way appearance and demeanor work to affect their perceptions of those they encounter but are also able to understand how they themselves manage others' impressions. The following student, a white male who is in fact very well spoken, came to such an understanding:

> When a group of African-American men were talking while eating their sandwiches, I approached them and asked how they were doing. At first, they were fairly reticent in talking to me, but as the conversation continued, I found that they had tried to bring me in. I found that I was talking in a streetwise fashion rather than a more refined and educated manner that I usually did.

In an attempt to present himself as more similar to the men than perhaps he really is, this student is aware of his manipulation of the cues that those with whom he was interacting used to make assessments of him.

Role Taking and Cultural Strangers

The preexisting stereotypes of poor and homeless individuals held by students (as well as by the general population) often serve to cast these individuals as "cultural strangers," defined as those who occupy symbolic worlds different from our own (Karp and Yoels 1993). Identification with those perceived as cultural strangers is more difficult than identification with those with whom we believe we share similar backgrounds. Often, in service-learning situations, students and those being served assume that they do not share similar backgrounds, particularly in terms of social class. This may well lead to difficulty in role taking. Students may not readily identify with those they are serving due to fear, negative stereotyping, or just because they have never been in such a situation before. For example, one student, upon learning that what she had thought was a shelter for homeless women was actually an organization serving mentally ill and drug- and/or alcohol-addicted homeless women, "went ballistic": "How dare they put me in a service spot where there were mentally ill women without warning me! All of my stigmas about people foaming from the mouth and women thrashing about while I had to hold them down came to my head."

Employing sociological concepts such as "cultural strangers" may provide students with analytical tools that they can use to frame their experiences in a less threatening manner. For example, viewing poor or homeless individuals as cultural strangers may assuage some of the guilt and fear felt by students coming into contact with such persons for the first time. Because interactants do not appear to share the same symbolic backgrounds, there is no automatic expectation that they will understand each other or feel comfortable together. And by attempting to view themselves as those they are serving view them — for example, as white, upper-middle-class, privileged college students — students may attain a level of understanding that enables them to take the role of the other. The following example is from a student paper:

> I have determined that people who have some social characteristic in common have a greater ability to interact than those with no social traits in common. I conversed briefly with a white male. I am a white male. I was dressed in torn jeans, a dirty t-shirt, and sneakers with holes. We appeared to be on similar economic levels.

Another student focuses on difference:

> Many of the homeless, realizing that they were of different racial or ethic backgrounds than most of those who were performing service, made remarks suggesting that we didn't understand the "hardships of the black man." It was true that most of the homeless individuals were African American, but [these statements from the homeless] exemplified how social situations such as these made communication difficult, particularly between groups of different racial backgrounds.

And of course, on many occasions students learn very quickly that they and those with whom they are interacting are not cultural strangers, but share much in common.

> My first day at the facility was extremely uncomfortable! When we walked

in, C. told us to sit in the living room until dinner was over. Then she asked one of the women, M., to sit and talk to us. She was telling us how she can play the harmonica and about all of her different physical ailments. Nothing different from what my grandma would talk about.

As students begin to grasp the social and cultural similarities and differences between themselves and others, role taking often proceeds more easily.

Power and Role Taking

When people interact, they may cooperate in the pursuit of common goals, but they may also compete for scarce resources or engage in conflict over which actions to take. The exercise of power depends in part on one party's control of resources that are valuable to and desired by others. Ascribed status characteristics such as social class, race or ethnicity, gender, and age bear directly upon this process.

Students engaged in service-learning (at least many of the students enrolled at the kind of liberal arts institution where I teach) are very likely to occupy higher status positions than those they are serving. This is particularly the case with students working with poor and/or homeless individuals. Not only is there an extreme difference in social class, but often there are racial or ethnic differences, as well. I think that it is this asymmetry between students and those they are serving that causes some of the problems encountered in service-learning. Because of many students' position in the stratification structure, a position privileged by virtue of social class and often by virtue of race or ethnicity, they are somewhat "crippled" in their ability to role-take when interacting with individuals who occupy less-privileged positions. Over and over, in student papers, I am struck by their expectation of gratitude on the part of those they are serving and their sense of outrage when this is not forthcoming. They often do not seem capable of "taking the role of the other" to an extent that would allow them to understand that their expectation is based on their privileged position.

However, this is certainly not always the case. A number of students have been able to see themselves as they imagine others see them, and they comment on the nature of this asymmetry. For example, a student who worked with our Care-A-Van project handing out sandwiches to homeless individuals analyzed the interactional difficulty in these terms: "These actions appeared to be examples of asymmetrical deference, which exists between unequals. The homeless apparently thought that we were social superiors to them and responded by not interacting with us." By analyzing his experience in terms of Goffman's (1967) notion of asymmetrical deference, this student recognizes his own position vis-à-vis the homeless individuals with whom he is interacting. Throughout the paper, this is something the student struggles with, sometimes acknowledging it, as above, and other times lapsing into what may feel most natural to him, as when he describes himself as "talking in a streetwise fashion rather than a more refined and educated manner that I usually did." He is such a savvy student, however, that he goes on to analyze his actions further: "This appeared to be, although I was unaware of it at that time, an example of creating an appearance of unity when it may not in fact exist. In this case, the homeless, although of a lower socioeconomic position and a different race, had a sense of power over me."

One of the less obvious ways power is exercised is through control of the physical setting in which interaction occurs. Particular contexts often define powerful and powerless roles. Power holders have the ability not only to control the physical elements of a situation but also to control how people in that situation will act. One student provides an insightful description of a soup kitchen:

> It was evident that the volunteers and security guards were in power in this structure. But some guests tried to reverse the power structure by their use of language and bearing a demeanor that put them in charge. But in the end, the security guards would have the last word, having ultimate power in being able to tell people to leave.

This student is able to capture not only the power inherent in roles in this particular context but also interactional struggles for power that play out through language and demeanor.

Conclusion

As a result of a community service project and a series of assignments in which students analyze their experiences sociologically, I think a case can be made that service-learning entails a deeper level of understanding than that achieved by more-traditional pedagogical means. Students can apply symbolic interactionist concepts to all of their everyday circumstances. Their applications are deepened through service-learning. Rather than merely observing everyday interaction, these students participate in settings within which they are forced to figure out their own and others' roles. They must then closely examine what this process entails. That is, by viewing service-learning as symbolic interaction, students are able to get at the meaning behind their own and others' actions within the interactional setting of the community service site.

The above discussion is intended as a beginning effort to lay out a theoretical linkage between symbolic interaction and service-learning. A fuller examination would focus on various features of impression management, including self-management techniques involved in maintaining and saving face, e.g., the use of verbal and nonverbal accounts and disclaimers.

Finally, what is the impact on the self for students engaged in service-learning? I would like to think that they are better citizens for their experience. Is it because they have learned to take the role of the other in the company of individuals with whom they might not ordinarily interact? Students appear to deal with and process the meaning of role taking differently by applying symbolic interactionist concepts to their service experience, with the result that they achieve greater understanding through this application.

References

Blumer, Herbert. (1962). "Society as Symbolic Interaction." In *Human Behavior and Social Processes*, edited by Arnold M. Rose, pp. 179-192. Boston, MA: Houghton Mifflin.

Chesler, Mark. (1993). "Community Service-Learning as Innovation in the University." In *Praxis I: A Faculty Casebook on Community Service-Learning*, edited by J. Howard, pp. 27-40. Ann Arbor, MI: OCSL Press, University of Michigan.

Corwin, Patricia. (July 1996). "Using the Community as a Classroom for Large Introductory Sociology Classes." *Teaching Sociology* 24: 310-315.

Goffman, Erving. (1959). *The Presentation of Self in Everyday Life*. Garden City, NY: Anchor Books.

———. (1967). *Interaction Ritual*. Garden City, NY: Anchor Books.

Hewitt, John P. (1994). *Self and Society: A Symbolic Interactionist Social Psychology*. 6th ed. Boston, MA: Allyn & Bacon.

Karp, David A., and William C. Yoels. (1993). *Sociology in Everyday Life*. 2nd ed. Itasca, IL: F.E. Peacock.

Marullo, Sam. (1996). "Sociology's Contribution to the Service-Learning Movement." In *Service-Learning and Undergraduate Sociology: Syllabi and Instructional Materials*, edited by Morten G. Ender, Brenda M. Kowalewski, David A. Cotter, Lee Martin, and JoAnn DeFiore, pp. 1-13. Washington, DC: American Sociological Association.

McCall, George J., and J.L. Simmons. (1978). *Identities and Interactions*. Rev. ed. New York, NY: Free Press.

Mead, George H. (1934). *Mind, Self, and Society*, edited by Charles Morris. Chicago, IL: University of Chicago Press.

Miller, Jerry. (Fall 1994). "Linking Traditional and Service-Learning Courses: Outcome Evaluations Utilizing Two Pedagogically Distinct Models." *Michigan Journal of Community Service-Learning* 1: 29-36.

Mills, C. Wright. (1959). *The Sociological Imagination*. New York, NY: Oxford University Press.

Myers-Lipton, Scott. (1996). "Service-Learning: Theory, Student Development, and Strategy." In *Service-Learning and Undergraduate Sociology: Syllabi and Instructional Materials*, edited by Morten G. Ender, Brenda M. Kowalewski, David A. Cotter, Lee Martin, and JoAnn DeFiore, pp. 21-31. Washington, DC: American Sociological Association.

Stone, Gregory. (1962). "Appearance and the Self." In *Human Behavior and Social Processes*, edited by Arnold Rose, pp. 87-116. Boston, MA: Houghton Mifflin.

Turner, Jonathan. (1978). *The Structure of Sociological Theory*. Rev. ed. Homewood, IL: Dorsey.

The Joys of Your Troubles:
Using Service and Reflection to Enhance Learning in the Community College Sociology Classroom

by Martha Bergin and Susan McAleavey

Perhaps the primary reason for many faculty members' use of service-learning lies in the power of reflection to integrate the lessons of one's life into course content. However, a brief story about Martha Bergin's first service-learning student illustrates clearly why structured reflection is also important for discipline-related learning to occur. Utilizing a performance theory (Geertz 1973; Goffman 1959; Schechner 1985; Turner 1982, 1988) approach to reflection as it applies in an academic setting allows us to achieve deeper insight about its processes. Through examples of assignments taken from Sue McAleavey's sociology classes, we can explore concrete applications of *preflection*, *intermediate reflection*, and *summary reflection*. Finally, because the teaching experiences described here all took place in a community college, the final section comments on the community college as a context for implementing service-learning in sociology.

Struggling Toward Service-Learning: Ali's Story

His name was Ali,[1] an international student from Pakistan. Large of body, slow of movement, with quick, warm, brown eyes, he was the first of my[2] students ever to take me up on the notion of doing service-learning. To me, it really was a "notion," in that I had not previously participated in service-learning, and I was not an instructor for whom the idea occurred "naturally" or spontaneously. As much as anything else, I had finally offered service-learning so that I could say I had offered it. Now, of course, I had to journey down that road I had indicated it was my intention to travel.

"Is it all right if I use the hours I'm volunteering for Dr. Counts's psychology class for this class, too?" Ali asked, seeming to take mental measure of my capacity for cooperation or resistance. Quickly I did some mental calculations. We would have to allow some "double dipping," I reasoned. Otherwise, as service-learning became more popular, students would have to do 20 service hours for this class and 10 for that and another 20 for this, and the situation could quickly become more stressful than beneficial.

I heard myself saying,

Well, yes, you could, but obviously you'll be writing a different paper for me than you will for Dr. Counts. You will need to identify and analyze psychological issues for Dr. Counts, and to identify and analyze sociological issues for me. Of course, they will be interrelated, so I wouldn't expect the papers to be about completely different things. But I will expect you to be very mindful about "where you are" intellectually — and to be able to understand and write about the difference between a sociological issue and a psychological issue. Do you think you can do that?

"Sure," answered Ali. "That won't be a problem. I could do that!" Ali's pleasure radiated from his wide grin and relaxed posture. I think he found the situation quite amusing and felt that he had gained an advantage by negotiating to avoid some work. And as I looked into his dancing eyes, I did wonder whether I had spoken too soon. But when it came time for Ali to turn in his written paper, I began in earnest my own learning curve around service-learning.

The first thing I realized was that I should have asked him to show me drafts of his work earlier in the semester. Ali's final paper failed dismally to differentiate between psychological and sociological issues. Written about his experiences working at the campus child-care center, Ali's comments were in large part limited to developmental observations about individual children and to descriptions of how individual parents interacted with their children when dropping them off and picking them up. While some of his work referenced issues of socialization, few such references were clearly drawn. I decided that, although it was very late in the semester, I would have to do some of the coaching I now knew I should have been doing all along.

"What do you think," I asked Ali, "is the role of factors such as social class, educational level, and culture in explaining the behaviors of these individual parents and their children?" Questions like that got Ali thinking. He began to develop an appreciation of the difference between ideas whose domain is psychology and those whose domain is sociology, and of the possible interrelationships between these two perspectives. He decided to rewrite his paper and began to improve his analytical abilities. We ended the project, at Ali's request, when he had revised his paper so that he had earned enough points to obtain a B in the class, as that was his personal goal.

Ali was now satisfied with his service-learning experience, but emotionally and intellectually I was left reeling. In my five years of teaching, both as a graduate associate at a university and as a community college instructor, I had neither encountered nor attempted to use a pedagogy with as much potential for both instructor and student. Although the interactions between me and Ali had been hurried and limited in focus to "fixing" his paper, I realized that no student in my classes had ever had an opportunity to do such grounded intellectual work or to attempt such a challenging analysis. I doubted whether many of my former students could do better than Ali's first try at identifying sociological issues as those issues emerge in real-life situations.

From that first experience on, I was hooked. I wanted all of my students to have the quality of intellectual opportunity that Ali had experienced, and I wanted to do the kind of teaching and learning with every student that I had been doing with Ali. I began in earnest to think about how I could motivate more of my students to choose service-learning and about how I could best structure my time to help them utilize their service experiences to learn sociology in that very personal, experiential way service-learning made possible.

Implementing Service-Learning in the Community College

If anything clearly defines community college students, it is their diversity. Students at Mesa Community College (MCC) range in age from 17 to 84. Some have been members of a national all-academic team, while others have recently completed basic skills classes. Among those students for whom English is not a first language, some are first-time college students, while others hold degrees in law, philosophy, or medicine obtained in other countries. Often, MCC students have bachelor's degrees or master's degrees obtained in this country and are in the process of changing careers or broadening their skills.

Community colleges serve the community not only by providing educational programs appropriate to educational years 13 and 14 but also by serving as a base for lifelong learning. Here one finds students who work full time, part time, two or three jobs, as well as students who are parents, students who take care of their parents, and any combination of the above. Many MCC students co-enroll at Arizona State University (ASU). Fifty-one percent of ASU's transfer students come from the Maricopa Community College system, with the lion's share of these students transferring from MCC, the largest college in the system, with an enrollment of 23,000 students.

Since community college students often have been raised in and have children they are raising in the community in which they are asked to serve, such an institution can be an excellent context for service-learning. Many returning students are already deeply engaged in community and civic activities, and future leaders of the Mesa community are likely to attend MCC. Indeed, alumni of MCC include city councilpersons, state and U.S. representatives and senators, as well as key business leaders.

If, then, the community college is fertile ground for service-learning, what are some of the ways in which its instructors can help its students to capitalize on what they are experiencing? An MCC student, Dan Lepianka, illustrates the important divide between voluntarism and service-learning: "I'd been volunteering at my site — the AIDS Project — for three years before

I started with the service-learning program, and I've gotten so much more out of it since I did this under a faculty, with all the requirements for learning from the experience."

Certainly the above-described story about Martha and her student Ali illustrates a need for thoughtful planning and course-related reflection. We know that reflection helps students to examine and own their experiences, and to develop conceptual frameworks for understanding the significance of their service experiences (Bringle and Hatcher 1997). But how exactly does reflection work, and what are some of the theoretical underpinnings for reflection as a learning tool?

Understanding Reflection: A Performance Perspective

Performance theory (Sartre 1956; Schechner 1985; Turner 1982, 1988) and other dramatistic approaches to social analysis (Burke 1969; Geertz 1973; Goffman 1959) address the processes that make reflection an effective pedagogical strategy.

Reflection is a process that can be understood as an aspect of the broader category of the *reflexive* dimension of human experience (Turner 1988: 96-97). Reflexivity, in turn, is an aspect of Turner's "social drama" (1982, 1988) and can be explored in depth through the conceptual framework of performance theory. Grounded in an epistemology of "knowing through bending back," or reflecting, on experience, self-reflexive experience — such as reflecting on one's actions, thoughts, and feelings at a service-learning site — is that category of experience where one comes to know oneself by encountering oneself as reflected by something.

Scrutinizing one's face in a mirror is the primary example of and metaphor for such activity, but reflexive experience can occur anywhere. For example, if someone is having a bad day and thinks, "Everyone is so disagreeable today," it is quite possible that the person perceives others as disagreeable because he or she is in a "bad mood." Thus, the quality of this person's interactions is showing him or her the quality of his or her own emotional and mental processes at that time. This is also an example of a type of reflexive experience by which one can draw erroneous conclusions about events. Certainly in the traditional sociology classroom, where we strive to teach students to question assumptions and clarify values, we encourage them to engage in self-reflexive practice in the context of their lives. Such practice, however, is limited by a lack of specific emotional involvement. In the service-learning classroom, where emotion and intellect coincide, mindful and deliberate reflection can be a powerful tool for greater awareness of the reflexivity of specific experiences.

Using Reflection in the Sociology Classroom

Since community college sociology instructors typically have 40 students in their classes, have no teaching assistants, teach a minimum of five courses, and participate in other college activities (committee work, etc.), reflection activities have to be manageable within these constraints. What, then, are some procedures that, without being overly burdensome to faculty, can help sociology students to engage in reflexive practice?

Sue McAleavey's (1996) sociology classes employ three sequential processes — namely, *preflection*, or speculation about an activity; *intermediate reflection*, documenting their beginning journey; and *summary reflection*, thinking back about an activity — in order to build blocks of reflexive thinking. These processes are woven into class assignments by requiring students to write a learning plan prior to beginning their experience, submit regular journaling of their experiences for instructor feedback, participate in classroom-based small-group reflection activities, write an analytical summary, and give a final class presentation.

Preflection and the Learning Plan

The foundation for the service-learning experience is created through a learning plan (see the figure on page 98), which has two parts. The first, Part A, explores students' personal motivations and expectations about their chosen service site. The second, Part B, requires students to specify learning goals to be pursued that connect course content to their service activities. Supplemental readings help the students to broaden their understanding of sociological concepts and theories beyond the class text, and are divided into site-relevant categories. Therefore, in addition to targeting discipline-related goals, preflection encourages students to become aware of preconceptions and expectations they might have about the upcoming service experience. Since sociology inevitably offers students the opportunity to examine diversity and multicultural issues, speculations about the service situation can prove invaluable later on, particularly if the student's expectations are not met. Violation of expectations is an event that lies at the core of the intercultural experience (Ting-Toomey 1994: 360).

Requiring students to respond to structured questions creates an opportunity for "handles" that the instructor can "grasp" later as he or she facilitates classroom reflection, helping to pinpoint in any substantive area issues that the students may be working through, such as the intercultural experience, social roles, or value judgments. An example of a preflection that contains handles for such discussion is provided in the following speculations from a student's learning plan:

Learning Plan

It is important that you play a big part in shaping *your learning* from your service experience according to your particular interests and service site.

The learning plan will be an ongoing process: i.e. as you learn more about your site and the work there, and as you learn more about sociology, your journaling should reflect an integration of experience and sociological theories and concepts.

I want you to submit the following (parts A and B) before you start your service placement:

A.   **i) the reason for your choice of placement**
      ii) what you hope to accomplish there by volunteering
      iii) what you would like to learn while there

       EXAMPLE:
       i) I chose Jr. Achievement because I'm a business major and I think this sounds upbeat, I couldn't handle anything sad...
       ii) I want to tell the children how important it is for them to stay in school, and will use myself as an example. "Look at me, thirty years old and going back to school for the first time in years to get my degree, *you* do it differently."
       iii) I want to learn something about business since that's my major and how to communicate information. I also want to learn why the dropout rate is so high, and what I can do to prevent my own son from doing that.

PLEASE NOTE: I also want you to refer to the sheet "Service Site-Related Readings" for assistance with sociological references, relevant concepts and theories. Initially, choose one reading (your text would be easiest to start with) and use that information for this second part of your initial learning plan.

B.   **Two sociological concepts / theories that sound interesting for me to examine while at my service site ...[name of site]... are ...[topic #1] ... and ...[topic #2]...**

       EXAMPLE:
       I am going to be at Children's Action Alliance, and would like to look at the concepts of *groupthink* and *group conformity* as they may or may not apply in the legislative committees that I will have a chance to observe. I will also be looking to see if I can observe these and any other group dynamics at my office site.

PLEASE SUBMIT THIS LEARNING PLAN TO ME BY THE FOURTH WEEK OF THE SEMESTER AT THE LATEST. I EXPECT YOU TO ADD TO PART "B" AS THE CLASS PROGRESSES BY INCORPORATING MORE SOCIOLOGICAL TERMS ETC. INTO YOUR JOURNALING.

While I'm working at Middle Ground Inc., there are many things that I would like to learn. I'm not exactly sure what I'll be doing, except that the work will involve helping prisoners and their families, informing them of their rights and responsibilities. One of the things that I would really like to know is why these prisoners did the things they did.

This writing sets forth a very common expectation, a "taking-for-granted" that the student's presence will be helpful, and perhaps a deeper and unstated assumption that the student expects his or her presence to be positively received. If the student finds that he or she encounters quite a different reception, or finds that he or she spends much more time listening, perhaps, than "informing," then these surprises can be explored and used to spark a search for further learning.

An example of Part B of the learning plan is provided by Kurt, who demonstrates the specificity of his orientation toward sociology and the service-learning situation:

I expect that becoming involved in the Mesa community as a coach and volunteer will teach me quite a bit about sociology, such as giving me a chance to look at status hierarchy. This entails the different socioeconomic groups present in the community. Erving Goffman in explaining "Impression Management" states, "Individuals enter the presence of others and commonly seek to acquire information about them. . . . They will be interested in his/her socioeconomic status, conceptions about his/her self, his/her attitude toward them, competence, trustworthiness, etc." It will be interesting for me to evaluate each different child's attitudes while they do the same to me.

By articulating the concepts he wishes to explore, Kurt creates a clear starting point, which may lead him to better understand some broader interactions among social groups in his community. Another example is provided by Part B of a different student's learning plan. Amy has chosen to serve in a tutoring program for junior high students in a low-income area. She frames complex questions about testing, where others might accept test scores at face value:

Can test results really give a clear and concise picture of a child's aptitude, intelligence, or interest? Does this grouping or separation produce an effect of alienation or resignation? For example, does a student who is not fed into a college prep program resign himself as unworthy of attending college? Are such classifications merely an attempt to fill the needs of society through social placement? Are there junior high school–level students aware of this going on in their own experiences? If so, how does it affect their attitude and mindset? Does social placement sacrifice the individual?

Amy's readings have enabled her to learn about various theories that she can then use her service experiences to substantiate or reject.

Similarly, another student, who chose to do her service at the Salt River Maricopa Pima Indian Community (SRMPIC), wrote:

> *Social integration is the degree to which people feel part of or identify with social groups.*
>
> *It is very important to feel a sense of belonging to a group, but I think that being in a situation where I will be a minority and facing different norms will be an excellent way for me to learn . . . about myself, groups, subcultures, Native Americans' social integration . . . and how their culture affects teaching styles.*

These types of exploration of academic concepts can develop through the semester into a more seasoned, or intermediate, type of reflection, one defined by Keith Morton (1995) as "thick reflection."

Midsemester Intermediate Reflection

Intermediate reflection is addressed through journaling and classroom activities. Using faculty feedback on their journals and working in supervised discussion groups, students have an opportunity to move toward "thicker" reflection. Chris Koliba (1996) and Keith Morton (1995) talk of such reflection as a "genre of questioning" designed to bring students to understand how the same event might have different meanings for different people. In this way, "focus is not only on the strategies involved but [also] on the assumptions that underlie the action" (Reason 1994: 330). The role of faculty is to help students to "make sense" of a social situation through a multifaceted understanding of the terms and social forms through which it can be constructed. In a sociology classroom, this has particular significance in terms of understanding concepts such as stereotypes, the Thomas Theorem, ethno-methodology, labeling theory, and the social construction of reality.

However, students have varying degrees of skill in writing, as well as varying capacities for abstract thought processes, and reflexive practice is not an automatic skill for many of them, any more than it is for faculty. Students must, therefore, not only be guided as to faculty expectations for grading purposes but also should be provided with specific questions to assist in the journaling process itself. In addition, giving weekly assignments so that students can focus on examples of whatever sociological concepts are being covered that week and can include such concepts in their journaling represents still another important way to help them to make course connections.

However, dialogue must be extended beyond journal exchanges, and class time must be given to allow reflection to take place long enough to allow deeper processes of discovery and examination to take place. In preparing for classroom reflection, it is advisable to design a series of low-risk activities, building to higher-risk self-disclosure activities that develop trust among participants. A small-group "graffiti" exercise where students artistically depict their response to the question "How can you best represent your service experience at this point in time?" is an example of an enjoyable, nonthreatening, trust-building exercise that can yield informative insights. Further into the semester, one can ask for students to share what they are learning about themselves and about the current appropriateness of their learning plans, both Parts A and B. Students may be asked to share with the class ways in which their service experiences have illuminated class material for them or, perhaps, have raised issues concerning concepts in the curriculum.

The task here is for faculty to be prepared to address issues that, in a perfect world, would arise only some three weeks later, to be able to grasp "teachable moments" in grounding students' experiences in content knowledge. Faculty should, for example, be able to refer to the course text(s) in order to illustrate such connections, whenever the relevant information is needed. For faculty who have themselves been taught in a more traditional, orderly, and sequential fashion, such an approach may not always be easy. For example, Hillary, whose learning plan excerpt appeared earlier, remarked later in her journal:

> I am amazed at how close this community is. . . . The lady I worked with most explained to me that this closeness has good and bad aspects to it. She said it is good to have people you can count on, but it is sometimes "too close," and there is lots of gossiping and not much personal space.

Hillary's reflections stimulated conversations on different ways of enforcing norms, positive and negative sanctions, conformity versus deviance, individualism versus collectivism — concepts not usually taught together.

An example of reflections that encouraged "thicker" classroom reflection around the idea of equality of opportunity appeared in Amy's journal toward the end of the semester:

> As a privileged child with well-educated parents, I never considered the possibility that all children didn't have the same stimulation, encouragement, and life chances that I enjoyed. . . . It is so clear to me that involving oneself in the community is, perhaps, the only way to truly appreciate the social, political, and educational reality that exists in our society. When living a comfortable life, it is easy to convince oneself that all people are capable of succeeding if they just "work hard enough."

Leslie, who spent time with the Adult Probation Department, wrote:

*One of the objectives I had with this service-learning was regarding stereo-
typing individuals. . . . I personally thought of people that were on probation as "bad seeds" or "troublemakers." . . . However, I have found that people often make mistakes. . . . Maybe the love of money is indeed the root of
all evil.*

This entry provoked deeper discussion in class about values in a capitalistic
society, the purpose of imprisonment, and students' beliefs in rehabilitation.
Moreover, both of these entries illustrate how preflection and intermediate
reflection can work together to engage students in active and purposeful
learning experiences. Although reflection often occurs spontaneously in the
classroom, particularly during those rewarding times when the class has a
"really good discussion," deliberately designed reflection is a necessary tool
to help students unpack, examine, and reintegrate their service-learning
experiences.

Summary Reflection

Summary reflection in the context of service-learning can bring an individual not only to analyze the sum of his or her experiences as they relate to
learning plan and course content but also to address issues of personal development — finding something to live for that is greater than the self, and
exploring social justice and the meaning of citizenship. The latter can be a tall
order for faculty who may not wish to get involved in such issues. It is, furthermore, unrealistic to suppose that most students can grow to fully appreciate all facets of service-learning involvement within one semester (hence,
the implications of this approach for learning communities and sequentially
linked courses). However, despite these constraints, the written directions
given to students for both their journaling and their summaries can assist in
eliciting further "thick reflection," or insights on the bigger picture.

Anita's analytical summary provides a good example of how values and
perspectives on life can begin to change:

> *Working in the community setting such as this one is a bit awkward. I have
> much more than these people do, and I hope they aren't judging me or feel
> that I'm judging them. I don't judge any of them. I've learned to appreciate
> what I have, and I am thankful that I don't have to accept hand-me-downs
> or charity. I now hold back more on what I spend on my own daughter. I've
> learned that her happiness is more important than the label on the clothes
> she's wearing or the amount of toys she possesses.*

"When we quit thinking primarily about ourselves and our own self-
preservation, we undergo a truly heroic transformation of consciousness. . . .
A hero is someone who has given his or her life to something bigger than
oneself" (Campbell 1988: 126). Thus, reflection in service-learning brings a

student to that particular type of threshold experience wherein he or she can develop a sense of being the growing, changing, risk-taking, and efficacious hero of his or her own life. In her analytical summary on her time spent with an advocacy group assisting Central American refugees, Sandy reflected on issues that attended her accomplishment of such a passage:

> I was angry when my instructor said to focus more on my experience and personal growth. . . . I found that it was easier to deal with the apparent injustice of American actions in Central America if I suppressed my feelings. . . . I have changed for the better because of my internship [sic] experience. Before I began the internship, I believed that I cared about other people simply because I would never have personally acted with the intent to hurt another. However, I have learned that when nice people fail to act, that inaction can be injurious or even fatal for others. During my internship, I came to the realization that it is not someone else's responsibility, but mine and every other American's.

Another student, Eric, stated in his summary:

> Volunteering at the Emergency Shelter Hotline was eye-opening for me. I realized we have a terrible time housing and providing shelter for the homeless. . . . I also learned that this is political, such as sending people to other states with bus tickets and weeding out unwanted people in our community. The public should become more involved in making sure there is enough room for everybody, and by keeping an eye on who they put in office.

After serving in a "Success for All" reading program at an inner-city school, Sylvia reported:

> During my experience, I was able to make connections between the issues that related to the effects of poverty and the life chances of children from impoverished homes. More importantly, this service-learning experience has made me more aware that major social problems do have solutions . . . but a school like this cannot continue to survive on its own. Local politicians need to recognize that funding for additional community programs [is] desperately needed to improve the social environment for these children. . . . I understand now that I personally have to take an active part through volunteer service as well as supporting policies that can improve the lives of the growing families in these situations.

To again invoke Campbell's terms, these students have all made a hero's journey.

Some Concluding Reflections on Reflection

Exploring and developing reflection is an indispensable facet of developing a service-learning classroom. Reflection is a key process through which humans develop and retain awareness of themselves and their environments, grow and change, review and expand, create analogies, and consider new contexts for experience. Preflection, intermediate reflection, and summary reflection are powerful tools available to the sociology instructor who aims to maximize the effectiveness of service-learning.

Looking back down the road as these skills have developed in our own lives and in the lives of our students, we can easily see what we could have done better. Developing student guidelines and techniques for classroom reflection is a constant work in progress, an acknowledgment of the gifts and insights we have learned through our work and the work of our students. Truly these rewards are the joys of our troubles.

Notes

1. We have changed the names of all students, except those who specifically requested their names remain associated with their work.

2. Use of first person in this section refers to Martha Bergin.

References

Bringle, Robert G., and Julie A. Hatcher. (Fall 1997). "Reflection: Bridging the Gap Between Service and Learning." *College Teaching* 45(4): 153-158.

Burke, Kenneth. (1969). *A Grammar of Motives*. 1945. Berkeley, CA: University of California Press.

Campbell, Joseph. (1988). *The Power of Myth*, with Bill Moyers, edited by Betty Sue Flowers. New York, NY: Doubleday.

Geertz, Clifford. (1973). *The Interpretation of Cultures*. New York, NY: Basic Books.

Goffman, Erving. (1959). *The Presentation of Self in Everyday Life*. Garden City, NY: Anchor Books.

Koliba, Chris. (1996). "Thick Reflection." Paper presented to the National Society for Experiential Education, Snowbird, UT.

McAleavey, Sue. (1996). "Historical Overview and Current Models of Service-Learning at Mesa Community College." In *From the Margin to the Mainstream: The Faculty Role in Advancing Service-Learning*, edited by Terry Pickeral and Karen Peters, pp. 29-37. Providence, RI: Campus Compact, National Center for Community Colleges.

Morton, Keith. (Fall 1995). "The Irony of Service." *Michigan Journal of Community Service-Learning* 2: 19-32.

Reason, Peter. (1994). "Three Approaches to Participative Inquiry." In *Handbook of Qualitative Research,* edited by Norman K. Denzin and Yvonna S. Lincoln, pp. 324-339. Thousand Oaks, CA: Sage Publications.

Sartre, Jean-Paul. (1956). *Being and Nothingness,* translated by Hazel E. Barnes. New York, NY: Citadel Press.

Schechner, Richard. (1985). *Between Theater and Anthropology.* Philadelphia, PA: University of Philadelphia Press.

Ting-Toomey, Stella. (1994). "Managing Intercultural Conflicts Effectively." In *Intercultural Communication: A Reader,* edited by Larry A. Samovar and Richard E. Porter. 7th ed. Belmont, CA: Wadsworth.

Turner, Victor. (1982). *From Ritual to Theater: The Human Seriousness of Play.* New York, NY: PAJ Publications.

————. (1988). *The Anthropology of Performance.* New York, NY: PAJ Publications.

Service-Learning Through Meta-Reflection: Problems and Prospects of Praxis in Organizational Sociology

by Hugh F. Lena

> *If you tell me something, I hear you; if you show me something, I see it; but if you let me experience something, I know it.*
>
> — Chinese proverb

This essay describes an ongoing experiment with service-learning in a course on organizational sociology in which students are expected to learn the organizational theory literature and to practice what they have learned about organizations by organizing the class through community service. As with any sociology course in organizational theory, students learn about organizational structures and processes, power, conflict, leadership, decision making, organizational environments, and change, but, in addition, the course requires students to put their knowledge to use by organizing themselves. As is typical of service-learning courses, students in this course are required to perform a minimum number of hours of service each week, but rather than performing service in an organization or community beyond the walls of the college, students are initially required to engage in service to their own classroom community. Once they have done service for the class and have learned from their successes and failures organizing themselves, they are able to put to use what they have learned about organizations. Thus, the objectives of the course are for students not only to take responsibility for their own learning but also to know more about organizing and organizations by *experiencing* them. This paper explores some of the problems and prospects of this approach to service-learning in sociology.

The Foundations of Organizational Service course is designed to enhance students' learning about organizations and to increase their appreciation for putting their knowledge to use in a practical and meaningful way.

Some of the ideas in this paper are adapted from presentations at the annual meetings of the American Sociological Association in August 1995, and the Invisible College of Campus Compact in June 1996. The author wishes to thank Thomas R. King, Christopher Caruso, Margaret Clifford, Christopher Drury, Nicholas Longo, and Dylan Randall for the many hours of contentious conversation from which this paper sprang.

In addition, the course seeks to transform students' learning by addressing some of the problems that confront higher education today. After briefly describing some issues in pedagogy and higher education, I discuss some of the ways this course approaches these issues within the framework of service-learning and the creation of democratic learning communities, and I explore some of the problems and prospects related to service-learning in courses in organizational sociology.

The Call to Service

Higher education has come under fire, both from within and outside the academy, for its failure to meet the needs of students and society. Among the criticisms that have been leveled, perhaps most damning is the failure of American higher education to instill in students a desire to become critically engaged in ideas, in an awareness of the profound social problems of our times and recognize the importance of civic education and responsibility in a democratic society (see, for instance, Bloom 1987; D'Souza 1991; Kimball 1990; Loeb 1994). For a growing number of academics, service-learning is a pathway to educational and pedagogical reform that promotes civic responsibility in a democratic society and contributes to educational excellence.

According to many critics, traditional pedagogical methods often encourage passivity among students and discourage them from taking responsibility for their own learning. Many faculty fall into the teaching pattern, reinforced by their own educational socialization, that Freire calls the "banking system of education" (1968: 58). Instead of communicating, the teacher issues communiqués and makes deposits that the students patiently receive, memorize, and repeat. Often the last-minute cramming for examinations and spewing back information amounts to little more than "academic bulimia" (Schilling and Schilling 1994). Service-learning offers the promise of an alternative pedagogy.

To date, much of the research and writing about service-learning has concentrated on definitions of service-learning (Honnet and Poulsen 1989; Kupiec 1993; Stanton 1987), student learning outcomes (Hedin 1989; Miller 1994), civic education (Barber 1994; Boyte 1993), developing meaningful partnerships with communities (Harkavy 1993; Kendall 1990), course development (Miller 1994), pedagogy (Fox 1994; Palmer 1993), and stimulating faculty interest in service-learning (Hammond 1994; Jacoby 1996; Stanton 1994). Principles and practices of service-learning have also been discussed within individual disciplines, including sociology (Chesler 1993; Daly 1993; Kendrick 1995; Lena 1995; Parker-Gwin 1995). A review of this literature suggests several lingering problems with service-learning.

Service-Learning Issues

One of the most pressing issues facing those who wish to integrate service-learning into academic courses is its lack of a well-articulated conceptual framework. As a relatively new social and cultural phenomenon, service-learning remains ambiguous in its definition, scope, and purposes. Is service-learning merely another name for experiential education? Is it a field or a social movement? Is it a discipline? Does it represent a paradigm change in higher education? What, if any, are the distinctive epistemological foundations of service-learning?

In a recent paper, Goodwin Liu (1995) asks a number of probing questions about whether service-learning represents a paradigm change in higher education. Using Kuhnian terminology (Kuhn 1970), Liu contrasts the traditional paradigm in higher education, which consists of generating and codifying knowledge dispassionately then imparting that knowledge from teacher to student, with the paradigm of service-learning, which values subjective experiences, knowledge put into action, and reciprocal learning between teachers and students. The traditional knowledge paradigm is foundationalist — knowledge grows in a linear, cumulative manner — and dualistic. Service-learning challenges this approach on epistemological, academic, and pedagogical grounds. It is antifoundationalist. It centers service in the academic enterprise, thus elevating that service to the level of scholarship. It reconceptualizes students as active learners, not empty vessels to be filled with knowledge by teachers, and sees the campus not as an ivory tower but as an engaged, institutional citizen. In this way, community service becomes not merely charity, but a reciprocal process with benefits for students, the academic institution, and community partners. For Liu, service-learning challenges the linear, normative, and putatively empirical bases of the traditional knowledge paradigm by valuing pragmatic discourses in which context-dependent knowledge drives epistemological questions. While Liu's argument can be criticized (cf. Richman 1996), his model of the epistemological foundations of service-learning has much to commend it.

Overreliance on the banking system of education has contributed to our educational malaise, but there are a number of structural elements in higher education that also reinforce passivity and discourage active learning. Distributional requirements in many curricula force students into large survey courses with perfunctory coverage of subject matter that holds little interest for them. Departments, faced with administrative cuts or threats of cuts, increase enrollments and engage in survival strategies designed to market their disciplines, tailoring course offerings to external pressures. These organizational forces often function counterproductively when it comes to learning outcomes.

A second structural determinant, one that establishes the conditions for the first, concerns the organization of undergraduate education itself. Education operates like a marketplace, where many students shop around each semester for a schedule that fits with their own preferred use of time rather than one that embodies well-considered educational choices (Gimenez 1989). Relatedly, the current organizational arrangement of classes leaves students little time to reflect, to conduct research, or to engage in self-directed styles of learning. Last, but not least, is the organization and ecology of most college classrooms. Indeed, even the layout of the typical college classroom, the positioning of teachers and students in the room, and the authoritarian manner in which decisions about course organization and evaluation are made reinforce counterproductive, nondemocratic methods of teaching and learning.

Democratic Learning

As noted above, there has been renewed interest of late in overcoming the structural barriers to active participation of students in their learning (Freire 1998; Shor and Freire 1987). Included among new teaching initiatives is a call to "empowering education" (Shor 1992), critical pedagogy (Giroux 1992, 1997), and the creation of democratic learning communities (Beyer 1996; Lempert 1996). For Shor and others, empowering education is conceived of as a force for individual and social change. By empowerment, Shor does not mean that students can do whatever they like in the classroom. Neither can the teacher do whatever she or he wants. The learning process is negotiated, requiring mutual student-teacher respect and authority, and commitment to the public welfare. Education can then take place in a more democratic, collaborative atmosphere, allowing for the formation of a true learning community.

Increasing numbers of educators affirm the value of linking students' lives and experiences to their academic study (Palmer 1998). They acknowledge the importance of student "voices" in classroom learning. Using reflection to integrate students' experiences, especially experiences derived from service to others, with their academic study is one good way of "bridging distances" between concepts and lived experiences. However, successfully utilizing reflection presents a challenge, because doing so places us in the middle of the learning/teaching experience (Morton 1993: 90). Students are both attracted to and wary of this process, since it promises them an opportunity to better understand what they experience and value but also requires them to rethink experience in terms of abstract, sometimes contentious, concepts. When such experience is derived from our own learning community in the classroom, reflection is particularly difficult.

To say that the classroom can be a democratic learning community does not require equality in every dimension, but it does assume that all members of the academic community take part in community activities. Suggesting that students accept a measure of responsibility for their own learning seems odd — after all, it is their learning that is the focus of a course. However, most classrooms are not run democratically. To the extent that service-learning values the experiential dimension of learning and encourages the creation of democratic learning communities in the classroom, it runs contrary to many of the norms and conventions of contemporary higher education (Beyer 1996; Giroux 1997). Thus, in addition to epistemological challenges and issues related to community involvement, service-learning presents pedagogical challenges that will be difficult to address within traditional academic curricula (Varlotta 1996).

The course described in this essay represents an attempt to explore some of these issues as well as the creation of democratic learning communities. It offers lessons on the promise of using the classroom as a community in service-learning courses. It also describes some of the pitfalls in creating democratic learning communities in the classroom.

The Course and Its Context

Foundations of Organizational Service is designed as an introduction to theoretical and methodological principles of organizations, organizational behavior, and group processes that are essential to understanding how service is provided in, through, and with organizations and associations. Through both content and instruction, the course addresses issues critical to the sociology of organizations. In addition to examining theoretical and methodological approaches to organization, bureaucracy, and management, the course covers critical dimensions of organizational and group phenomena such as leadership, motivation, decision making, power, and conflict.[1]

Furthermore, the course is distinctive in a number of important respects, three of which respond to the issues raised earlier concerning pedagogical strategies, service-learning issues, and possibilities of democratic learning environments. First, the course is embedded within a full-blown academic program in Public and Community Service Studies, which is itself innovative and thrusts students into a bewildering array of responsibilities and obligations within and between their courses. This permits faculty to experiment with collaborative activities and communication vehicles beyond the constraints of traditional class time. Second, the course has a unique service component attached to it through which students can explore some limits of community in service-learning. Third, the course is structured to maximize opportunities for reforming the classroom to make it more of a democratic learning community.

Foundations of Organizational Service is a required course for both the major and minor in Public and Community Service Studies at Providence College. Housed within the Feinstein Institute, the program was piloted in the 1994-95 academic year, and its first students were selected through a competitive process (Hudson and Trudeau 1995). Beginning with the 1995-96 academic year, an academic major and minor were formally approved, and registration for the course was open to all students. However, most of the students who elect the course are majors or minors in the program and are also taking a year-long practicum that requires them to receive training as "teaching assistants" in other service-learning courses. In this capacity, they work with service-learning faculty and community partners to coordinate service placements in those courses, lead reflection sessions for those students, and assist faculty in class discussions and on projects. In addition, they also have their own service responsibilities. Thus, students in the course are enmeshed in a complex array of overlapping activities and responsibilities that holds the potential for community-building opportunities and encourages collaborative work. They know each other well and have common class and social activities. This context makes it easier to explore the limits of community building within the class. Vehicles for communication in the class are illustrative.

Since the campus is wired for electronic communications, we have integrated multiple forms of communication into the course. Students make extensive use of email and newsgroups to share ideas, make queries, and schedule out-of-class activities. These multiple forms of communication extend the boundaries of collaborative work beyond the confines of class time, and encourage participation by members of the class who are reluctant to participate orally in class discussions. Moreover, all the written work in the course is submitted to the professors electronically, and comments and evaluations are returned electronically, either via files attached to email messages or through an Internet-based, collaborative writing program.[2] We have "paperless papers"! In one semester, several of these assignments are submitted by two-person teams of students, who share their responses to a question, edit each other's work, and receive the same grade. This collaborative writing works so well that students have made their papers required reading for future class meetings, and lingering issues or concerns have became future paper topics.

Another innovative feature of electronic communication is the course's "virtual syllabus," which is complete only on the last day of class. At the beginning of the semester, a draft outline for the course with a few "hyperlinks" to organizational sites and email links to members of the class is provided as a webpage. Since the students are expected to flesh out the syllabus according to their wishes and interests as the course progresses, teams of students take responsibility for learning how to write and manage the web-page; and as other teams of students plan the direction of the course in consultation with the class, the web teams incorporate their suggestions in the developing syllabus. If students (or for that matter others on campus) want to check on upcoming assignments, email members of the class, post events and social activities, or search the Internet for information, they merely access the virtual syllabus. In addition, all electronic communications distributed via the class listserv are archived and may be searched by subject, author, or date of posting. While some of the students have grumbled about learning to use computers and have experienced the usual difficulties with electronic communications, the overwhelming result has been positive.

The Service Component

The course is also distinctive in its service component. Service to the class serves as a vehicle for understanding the classroom as one of the communities we can serve, since we conceive of service and community in broad enough terms to include communities on as well as beyond the campus.

From the beginning of the program, we have continually challenged the stereotypical notion of service as time spent with others who need our services based on some deficiency on their part (McKnight 1995). For example, Robert Coles describes service as "a challenge. Service means offering oneself to others as an example, as a teacher. Service is putting ourselves in another's shoes" (Coles 1993). This understanding of service suggests that it involves empathy, commitment, integrity, and authenticity as much as the kinds of activities one engages in while performing service.

Most students in the class have had extensive service-learning experiences within "other" communities beyond the campus, but when required to provide service to the class they find this an extraordinarily difficult thing to grasp. What we did not originally anticipate, however, is just how valuable it is to learn more about organizational service by sustained reflection on the rich texture of contributions to be made to a formative, and experimental, academic learning community. As students make service to each other more explicit, our reflection on that service allows them to appreciate the value of this kind of introspection for their understanding of the nature of service, community, and organization outside the walls of the classroom. If a traditional service-learning course means providing service alongside community partners and reflecting on those experiences in light of the academic content of the course, then we engage in *meta-reflection* — reflection on the service each student provides to the class with the explicit purpose of learning from it and changing subsequent service. As students practice what they learn about organizations, they learn from their practice organizing. Our goal is to improve class organization and its functioning by trying things out and then learning, through reflection, from our mistakes. This *service-as-praxis* requires more of each member of the class than merely linking service to substantive material; it necessitates that we use the link between service and content to change our service. Engaging in this kind of meta-reflection forces us to be much more introspective, with a higher capacity for what Parker Palmer (1987) calls "communal conflict" than would be necessary if the context of our service were "out there" with community partners. Effective service-learning in its traditional form is often very personal and transformative; but to the extent that we reflect on issues and problems of "others" in the community, we can find ourselves detaching ourselves from "them" in the learning process. However, if the objective of our service is reforming our own academic community of learning, reflection can become very close — and very uncomfortable. We believe it is discomfort like this that holds the potential for our students to take charge of their own learning and exhibit leadership amid confusion.

Our students have experienced remarkable successes and some frustrating setbacks as they have experimented with organizational practices in the class. For example, one semester they recognized the need for a set of goals and learning objectives for the class. Thus, several of the students asked each member of the class to write down his or her individual goals for the class. They then assembled those goals to create a collective statement of class mission and a vision that was later unanimously approved.[3] This was the smoothest example of organizational goal setting I personally have ever seen. However, on other occasions, the students have been less successful and even failed to articulate a guiding vision or goal statement despite recognizing that this was necessary. Early in the semester, the class often decides to create a number of committees (e.g., programming, evaluation, social support, communication) to coordinate service to the class. Sometimes these committees never get off the ground, while at other times they function quite well. When the students try to account for the differing success of such groups, they become more aware of governing structures and try to change them. Interestingly, they sometimes become concerned that students in successful committees have focused more on subsystem activities in their own functional areas than on the needs of the class as whole; i.e., these students "were becoming their position." One solution to this problem has been a system that allows individuals to rotate through different committees.

While reflection on service to communities beyond the classroom can be paradoxical for students — as well as faculty — it can become even more problematic if the experiences that are the object of reflection are those of the class community itself. Hence, we ask students to analyze the group and organizational features of their class "learning community" using the theoretical and conceptual material of the class. We ask them to engage in what I have already referred to as "meta-reflection." While we would not want service of this kind to replace the kind of service more typical of service-learning courses, we have found service-as-praxis particularly useful in a course about the sociology of organizations.

Democratic Learning Community

Finally, the course is experimental in the sense that its instructors strive to create opportunities for democratizing learning in the classroom. It is clear that in doing so we have the potential for helping students take more responsibility for their own learning, for developing greater mutual respect and learning among faculty and students, and for increasing flexibility in course design. We want to affirm the value of linking students' lives and experiences in their academic study and giving credence to student "voices" in classroom learning. We seek a negotiated learning process, one requiring mutual student-teacher respect and authority, as well as commitment to the collective. In short, we try to create a democratic learning community.

We do this by largely leaving the development of the syllabus and the organization of the class to the students. The faculty provide guidance on topics and readings, facilitate class discussions, and push the idea of required service in the class. Beyond that, students direct their own learning. They design various organizational and decision-making structures, course requirements, out-of-class activities, and even the "agendas" for class meetings. As they reflect on and evaluate the consequences of their service to the class, they redesign their organizational practices and procedures in an effort to improve on them. In this way, they learn about goal setting and organizational effectiveness by trying to formulate a mission and objectives for the course. They learn about the division of labor and resource allocation by assessing skills of class members and targeting needs in the class. They struggle to learn about power, reward systems, and motivation when they try to create an evaluation system. In other words, they experience organizing while learning about organizations.

While the students' struggle to create a democratic learning community in the classroom is often only a qualified success, they regularly do learn about working together to connect their knowledge and experience, recognize the paradoxes of structure, and question many features of their educational socialization. And while they raise many more questions about organizations than find answers, when they take responsibility for their own learning some remarkable things happen. Students rarely miss class and they schedule as many as 12 hours of meetings out of class each week. They are acutely aware of the importance of including everyone in class discussions and scheduled activities. To ensure that the class has heard diverse opinions and points of view, they invite visitors to class to play the role of devil's advocate during discussions. And while they are ever skeptical of their organizational knowledge, most of them come out of the course with a better understanding of the material than would have been possible in a traditional course, because they have experienced organizing even as they learned about organizations. By putting organizational theory to the test by practicing it, they become well prepared for community service and their organizational lives beyond the classroom.

Conclusions

In this paper I have described an ongoing experiment with a course on the sociology of organizations. The course is innovative in that it is designed to explore the possibilities for collaboration and learning beyond the classroom, in the use of the classroom as another community with which we can work in a service-learning course, and in our endeavors to enhance sociological understandings. As might be expected, this experiment has not been a complete success. Students' frustration with the course is often very high, and it sometimes takes a crisis before participants break through to a solution. Students and instructors devote an enormous amount of time to the course, and the pressures on students less committed to the course or its philosophy are intense. But perhaps the most troubling aspect of the course is students' perception that the more they learn about organizations, the less they really know. The structure of organizations became paradoxical and problematic for them. Since they have to learn about organizational structure even as they experience it, structure becomes something they seek but also fear. For many in the course, structure becomes the organizational crutch upon which they hang their dislike for bureaucracy, domination, and rules — a constraining demon but one for which, at the same time, they quixotically search. For those with substantial organizational experience, it is perhaps this lesson of the course that rings most true.

Notes

1. This description and analysis is based on the first four iterations of the course, which were team taught. The course has since been taught by other faculty, with somewhat different results.

2. Connect.net© is an interactive, collaborative word-processing program that allows faculty and students to read and write together by exchanging files over the Internet. It allows both synchronous and asynchronous writing and messaging, and permits instructors to grade papers online and create hotlinks to an online writing handbook.

3. The class "vision" statement — a combination of a mission and a vision statement — reads: "We, the members of the Foundations of Organizational Service, are dedicated to learn theoretical and practical issues concerning organizations in a democratic learning environment. We will achieve this through equal responsibility to discussion, service, and research. We will learn from our experiences, and those of others, by finding practical applications for our knowledge. Ultimately, we will have the ability to efficiently work through, in, and with organizations and to be able to effectively organize diverse peoples around a common goal. As a class, we will become a learning organization."

References

Barber, B.A. (1994). "A Proposal for Mandatory Citizen Education and Community Service." *Michigan Journal of Community Service-Learning* 1: 86-93.

Beyer, L.A., ed. (1996). *Creating Democratic Classrooms: The Struggle to Integrate Theory & Practice.* New York, NY: Teachers College Press.

Bloom, A. (1987). *The Closing of the American Mind.* New York, NY: Simon & Schuster.

Boyte, H.C. (1993). "What Is Citizenship Education?" In *Rethinking Tradition: Integrating Service With Academic Study on College Campuses,* edited by T. Kupiec, pp. 63-66. Denver, CO: Education Commission of the States and Campus Compact.

Chesler, M. (1993). "Community Service-Learning as Innovation in the University." In *Praxis I: A Faculty Casebook on Community Service-Learning,* edited by J. Howard, pp. 27-34. Ann Arbor, MI: OCSL Press, University of Michigan.

Coles, R. (1993). *The Call of Service: A Witness to Idealism.* Boston, MA: Houghton Mifflin.

Daly, K. (1993). "Field Research: A Complement for Service-Learning." In *Praxis I: A Faculty Casebook on Community Service-Learning,* edited by J. Howard, pp. 85-91. Ann Arbor, MI: OCSL Press, University of Michigan.

D'Souza, D. (1991). *Illiberal Education.* New York, NY: Free Press.

Fox, H. (1994). "Teaching Empowerment." *Michigan Journal of Community Service-Learning* 1: 55-61.

Freire, P. (1968). *Pedagogy of the Oppressed.* New York, NY: Seabury Press.

——— . (1998). *Teachers as Cultural Workers: Letters to Those Who Dare to Teach.* Boulder, CO: Westview Press.

Gimenez, M. (1989). "Silence in the Classroom: Some Thoughts About Teaching in the 1980s." *Teaching Sociology* 17: 184-191.

Giroux, H.A. (1992). *Border Crossings: Cultural Workers and the Politics of Education.* New York, NY: Routledge, Chapman & Hall.

———. (1997). *Pedagogy and the Politics of Hope.* Boulder, CO: Westview Press.

Hammond, C. (1994). "Integrating Service and Academic Study: Faculty Motivation and Satisfaction in Michigan Higher Education." *Michigan Journal of Community Service-Learning* 1: 21-28.

Harkavy, I. (1993). "University-Community Partnerships: The University of Pennsylvania and West Philadelphia as a Case Study." In *Rethinking Tradition: Integrating Service With Academic Study on College Campuses,* edited by T. Kupiec, pp. 121-128. Denver, CO: Education Commission of the States and Campus Compact.

Hedin, D. (1989). "The Power of Community Service." *Proceedings of the Academy of Political Science* 37: 201-213.

Honnet, E.P., and S. Poulsen. (1989). *Principles of Good Practice for Combining Service and Learning.* Wingspread Special Report. Racine, WI: Johnson Foundation.

Hudson, W., and R. Trudeau. (Fall 1995). "An Essay on the Institutionalization of Service-Learning: The Genesis of the Feinstein Institute for Public Service." *Michigan Journal of Community Service-Learning* 2: 150-158.

Jacoby, B. (1996). *Service-Learning in Higher Education.* San Francisco, CA: Jossey-Bass.

Kendall, J. (1990). "Combining Service and Learning: An Introduction." In *Combining Service and Learning: A Resource Book for Community and Public Service, Vol. 1,* edited by J. Kendall and Associates, pp. 1-33. Raleigh, NC: National Society for Experiential Education.

Kendrick, J.R. (March 1995). "Building Campus-Community Connections: Using Service-Learning in Sociology Courses." Paper read at the Eastern Sociological Society meeting, Philadelphia, PA.

Kimball, R. (1990). *Tenured Radicals: How Politics Has Corrupted Higher Education.* New York, NY: Harper & Row.

Kuhn, T.S. (1970). *The Structure of Scientific Revolutions.* Chicago, IL: University of Chicago Press.

Kupiec, T.Y., ed. (1993). *Rethinking Tradition: Integrating Service With Academic Study on College Campuses.* Denver, CO: Education Commission of the States and Campus Compact.

Lempert, D. (1996). *Escape From the Ivory Tower: Student Adventures in Democratic Experiential Education.* San Francisco, CA: Jossey-Bass.

Lena, H. (Winter 1995). "How Can Sociology Contribute to Integrating Service-Learning Into Academic Curricula?" *The American Sociologist* 26: 107-117.

Liu, G. (1995). "Knowledge, Foundations, and Discourse: Philosophical Support for

Service-Learning." *Michigan Journal of Community Service-Learning* 2: 5-18.

Loeb, P.R. (1994). *Generation at the Crossroads: Apathy and Action on the American Campus.* New Brunswick, NJ: Rutgers University Press.

McKnight, J. (1995). *The Careless Society: Community and Its Counterfeits.* New York, NY: Basic Books.

Miller, J. (Fall 1994). "Linking Traditional and Service-Learning Courses: Outcome Evaluations Utilizing Two Pedagogically Distinct Models." *Michigan Journal of Community Service-Learning* 1: 29-36.

Morton, K. (1993). "Reflection in the Classroom." In *Rethinking Tradition: Integrating Service With Academic Study on College Campuses,* edited by T. Kupiec, pp. 89-97. Denver, CO: Education Commission of the States and Campus Compact.

Palmer, P. (September/October 1987). "Community, Conflict, and Ways of Knowing: Ways to Deepen Our Educational Agenda." *Change* 19: 20-25.

————. (1993). "Is Service-Learning for Everyone? On the Identity and Integrity of the Teacher." In *Rethinking Tradition: Integrating Service With Academic Study on College Campuses,* edited by T. Kupiec, pp. 17-21. Denver, CO: Education Commission of the States and Campus Compact.

————. (1998). *The Courage to Teach: Exploring the Inner Landscape of a Teacher's Life.* San Francisco, CA: Jossey-Bass.

Parker-Gwin, R. (March 1995). "Connecting Service and Learning: How Students, Communities, and Institutions Matter." Paper presented at the Eastern Sociological Society meeting, Philadelphia, PA.

Richman, K. (Fall 1996). "Epistemology, Communities, and Experts: A Response to Goodwin Liu." *Michigan Journal of Community Service-Learning* 3: 5-12.

Schilling, K.L., and K.M. Schilling. (February 2, 1994). "Academic Bulimia: Binge-and-Purge Learning." *Chronicle of Higher Education:* A52.

Shor, I. (1992). *Empowering Education: Critical Teaching for Social Change.* Chicago, IL: University of Chicago Press.

————, and P. Freire. (1987). *A Pedagogy for Liberation: Dialogues on Transforming Education.* New York, NY: Bergin & Garvey Publishers.

Stanton, T.K. (1987). "Service-Learning: Groping Toward a Definition." *Experiential Educator* 12: 2-4.

————. (1994). "The Experience of Faculty Participants in an Instructional Development Seminar on Service-Learning." *Michigan Journal of Community Service-Learning* 1: 7-20.

Varlotta, L. (Fall 1996). "Service-Learning: A Catalyst for Constructing Democratic Progressive Communities." *Michigan Journal of Community Service-Learning* 3: 22-30.

Action Research:
The Highest Stage of Service-Learning?

by Douglas V. Porpora

Action research might arguably be considered the highest stage of service-learning. Service-learning is an attempt to unite two of the three usually separate functions that academic faculty are supposed to pursue: service and teaching. Yet the third academic function faculty are supposed to pursue — original scholarly research — has tended to remain less integrated within the service-learning movement.

As a form of service-learning, action research is a way of achieving an even higher synthesis, a way of uniting all three academic functions: service, teaching, and scholarship. Whereas the service-learning movement promotes community service as a form of teaching, the action research movement promotes scholarly research as a form of community service.[1] Thus, when action research is done with students, it becomes not only both service and scholarship but pedagogy as well.

As promising as that synthesis sounds, action research as a stage of service-learning is also a daunting endeavor, combining the difficulty of integrating service and pedagogy with the added difficulty of producing original scholarly research. Accordingly, the purpose of this essay is to examine not just the great potential that action research offers as a form of service-learning but the obstacles to it. For most of us who attempt it, action research will remain a stage of service-learning to which we may aspire, but a difficult stage to reach consistently.

What Is Action Research?

The concept of action research emerged as a reaction to the standard model of scholarly research that prevails in the academy. In the standard model, scholarship is the knowledge produced by the ongoing dialogue of a community of scholars. As that dialogue advances, like all dialogues, it leaves behind those not party to it. The scholarly dialogue develops its own categories and distinctions, issues and questions.

In empirical fields such as sociology, scholarly research proceeds from and for the academy. Scholarly research is undertaken to answer questions raised within an academic community of scholars, and, once the relevant observations are made, researchers return to the academy to present their findings to their peers. We sociologists may do ethnographies and other kinds of research that aim to serve the poor and oppressed by uncovering the causes of poverty and oppression. Even then, however, our standard scholarly research remains oriented toward the academy. It is from the academic community of sociologists that our research questions arise. It is, consequently, toward our academic community of sociologists that our research agendas are directed. Ultimately, it will be other sociologists who principally consume our research product. Indeed, what makes this whole enterprise not just research but scholarly research is precisely its addressing of the issues and questions debated by a scholarly community.

While it is now fashionable to do so, such purely scholarly activity should not be dismissed. The academy remains one of the few sites left where certain fundamental questions are even raised. Where else, for example, is there critical dialogue on the nature of capitalism? It is not enough, moreover, simply to raise such questions. For there to be any advance on the answers, thinking must be sustained and cumulative. That requires the kind of engagement with previous thought that is the essence of scholarship. Even as a purely scholarly community, sociology has developed substantive findings, research methodologies, and theories that, were anyone besides ourselves to listen, would serve to build a better future.

There has been, nevertheless, a growing dissatisfaction with the standard model of scholarly research, a dissatisfaction that has become particularly acute among sociologists. The question raised by Robert Lynd (1939) some 50 years ago is still relevant today. We sociologists may be producing knowledge, but "knowledge for what?" When Lynd first asked that question, his concern was to move sociologists away from the production of knowledge that serves society's elites and more toward the production of knowledge that might serve the downtrodden. To a considerable extent, sociology has made that shift. The dominant sociological discourses today treat of oppression, domination, and exploitation in all their many guises. Today, we attend to the voice not just of first-world subordinates but also of postcolonial "subalterns" (Spivak 1988). No longer can anyone accuse our discipline of favoring the rich and powerful.

Yet we sociologists still experience dissatisfaction. One reason is that Lynd's question still goes unsatisfactorily answered. This knowledge we are producing, we still may ask, is knowledge for what? If we are now producing knowledge that might be used to right social wrongs, it remains perfectly clear that this knowledge is not being so used. Despite the issues we sociologists talk about, we come to find that we largely are talking to ourselves. What is to be done?

It is no use fooling ourselves with some "trickle-down" theory of academics. Trickle-down academics is what we offer the people we study when they ask us how our research will benefit them. We tell our subjects that through us their voice will be heard, that other people will read about their situation and react to it. Something, somewhere eventually will be done. Results eventually will trickle down to affect our subjects' lives for the better. Perhaps we believe this. Perhaps it is true. The larger truth, however, is that the resulting trickle from trickle-down academics is generally no greater than what results from trickle-down economics.

Become public intellectuals, Russell Jacoby (1987) tells us. We should write in language accessible to the general public and on topics in which the general public is interested. Although this is sound advice, it is advice with definite limitations. First, even if we write accessibly and on topics aimed at a broad audience, the general reading public is small. According to educated estimates (Norman 1994), the readership for the serious fiction reviewed by *The New York Times* is well under a quarter million. The readership for serious nonfiction is presumably smaller. According to public opinion surveys, six is the median number of books read a year, and only two of the six tend to be nonfiction (Gallup 1993). The nonfiction reading is mostly "how to" books, biographies, spiritual guides, and manuals. There is a reason we sociologists write largely for ourselves.

A more fundamental problem is that even if we do determine to write for a broader audience, we may have no way to reach it. It is largely not our own decision whether we each become as public an intellectual as Russell Jacoby. Seemingly overlooked by Jacoby, there is a publishing industry out there with its own agenda and its own ideas about the marketability of what we have to say. In most cases, if we are not a brand name intellectual to begin with, we just are not destined to become one.

Action research is an alternative way to become a public intellectual. Instead of necessarily attempting to address a mass public, in action research sociologists become public co-partners in research with the local communities neighboring our academic institutions. Action research is not so much research done *on* a local community as research done *with* a local community. In contrast with the standard model of academic research, action research is research in which the community participates at all levels of the process. The community helps to design the study, the community helps to collect the data, and the community helps to analyze the results.

Because the community helps to design the study in the first place, the community has a share in the research agenda. That community voice ensures that the results of the research will be of consequence not just to the academic researcher's community of scholars but to the local community as well. What distinguishes action research, therefore, is its direct benefit to the community situated at the site of the study.

In the standard model of academic research — even in ethnographic research — community residents are relegated to objects of study. We, the academic researchers, are the active subjects. We observe; they get observed. In action research, by contrast, community residents become co-active subjects with the academic researcher. Community residents participate, which is why some variants of action research are explicitly labeled *participatory action research* (Brown and Tandon 1983).

What the Civic Community Receives From Action Research

The active participation of a community in research is empowering. It is one way in which even the marginalized can begin to exert control over their own lives. When a community undertakes a neighborhood needs assessment, for example, it begins to give public thought and public voice to its own situation. It begins publicly and collectively to recognize that it has needs, that those needs are unmet, that those needs could be met.

Such reflection is an occasion for "conscientization" (Ellacuria 1991a, 1991b). Once people arrive at the recognition that they have unmet needs, they begin to ask why those needs are unmet. They begin to raise questions that are not just sociological but political as well. What, for example, would it take to get those needs met?

It is not just political consciousness that may be raised by such a research process. One of the afflictions of powerlessness is what Lerner (1986) refers to as "surplus powerlessness," the experience of having even less power than one actually has. The powerless frequently lack self-confidence, particularly the self-confidence to take collective action. Confidence is built only by historical experience, the historical experience of success. By successfully completing the successive tasks of a research project, a micro-history of success is communally experienced.

Along with change in community consciousness comes change in community organization. As is well known (see, for example, Wilson 1987), one of the problems of marginalized communities, particularly in our inner cities, is the abandonment of community-organizing institutions such as churches and clubs. Yet cooperative, coordinated research activity is itself an organizing process. People brought together and organized for research may remain together and organized for action.

Sometimes, the conscientization and community organization resulting from action research can be quite dramatic. For her master's thesis at Lincoln University, for example, Josephine Hood helped the residents of a housing project in Chester, Pennsylvania, conduct a needs assessment. Empowered by that experience, the city's project residents eventually assumed administrative control of the city's housing authority.

Perhaps even more dramatic is the case of the University of Central America (UCA) in El Salvador. Founded by the Jesuits in 1965, the UCA is an entire institution committed to action research. In the case of the UCA, it is not just individual faculty members who partner with the oppressed but the university itself. Philosophy students are sent to help *campesinos* articulate their own conception of human rights. Psychology students document and explore the psychological effects of terrorism. Engineering students aid in the development of appropriate technologies. Sociology students discuss feminism with female factory workers (see Hassett and Lacey 1991).

Throughout El Salvador's long turmoil in the 1980s, the UCA was building an organic relationship with the country's poor, an organic relationship that had a mobilizing effect. That effect was so great that by 1989, the Salvadoran military took drastic measures to stifle it. In November of that year, the army surrounded the campus and murdered six of its Jesuit faculty, including Ignacio Ellacuria and Ignacio Martin-Baro, the rector and vice-rector of the school.

I happened to be in the city of San Salvador one year later, on the first anniversary of the martyrs' deaths. I was there as thousands of *campesinos* from across the country flooded into the capital for the commemoration ceremonies. I marched in their candlelight procession and joined them in singing, "Where, now, are the prophets?" I wondered how many of us North American academics would be so missed by even our neighboring communities.

Since action research is done in collaboration with a civic community that may develop a momentum of its own, there is no telling in advance just how politically dramatic will be the results of an action research project. Some of us may find that indeterminacy disconcerting, and, indeed, since most of us are not at places like the UCA, many of us may wonder just how politically dramatic our own institutions will tolerate our being. Even if our more conservative institutions will not murder us for our efforts, they may have other unpleasant ways to deal with us.

For better or worse, such worries probably need not concern us. While perhaps anything empowering is also political, action research need not be radical. Even when our own agenda is radical, dramatic effects will normally take a long time to incubate, long enough for us to ascertain our own comfort level with the direction events are taking. In the meantime, our successes, although real, will likely be small.[2]

Accordingly, at the more conservative of our institutions, administrations will hardly distinguish action research from service-learning in general, to which they accord attention only modestly beyond benign neglect. In such a context, our general worry will be not that we have become too visible but that we are not visible enough. Indeed, to the extent that our lives are governed by promotion and tenure decisions, a more pressing concern is the relationship between action research and scholarship.

Action Research and Scholarship

At the UCA in San Salvador, social research is not just observing. It is doing. Yet the question remains whether this doing, this action research, is also scholarship. Given the dissatisfaction with what currently passes for scholarship within the academy, some would argue that service research ought to count as scholarship too. Undertaken by sociologists, the argument goes, action research is a sophisticated endeavor that relies on sociological methods and insights, and yields a more efficacious result than most sociological research. Our understanding of sociological scholarship ought to be expanded to include it. While it certainly will not do simply to declare by fiat that service research is scholarship, we could theoretically stretch what we mean by scholarship to encompass it.

Alternatively, in keeping with the traditional notion of scholarship, we might simply recognize that some, but not all, service research is service scholarship. According to this alternative, which I tend to favor, to qualify as sociological scholarship, it is not sufficient that a research project draws on the theory, the methods, and the substantive insights of the scholarly community of sociologists. Instead, to be scholarship, the research must in some way give something back not just to the civic community we partner with but to our scholarly community as well. To be sociological scholarship, the research must in some way advance the ongoing scholarly dialogue of sociologists.

On this criterion, much of the service research I, myself, do with my students may be good service-learning, but it is not service scholarship. One course I teach, for example, is on computer-assisted data analysis, using SPSS. Whereas in the past my students would have analyzed an arbitrary data set, I have lately tried to make this offering into a service-learning course by having the students analyze data that local community organizations need to have evaluated. Usually, representatives from such organizations as the Red Cross or United Way come to the class with completed questionnaires. The students then code the questionnaires, enter the information into the computer, and analyze it statistically. The community organizations receive a final report.

Because my students now see themselves as directly serving the community, they consider the course much more meaningful than before. It happens that some students drop the class and forget to return the questionnaires they had been assigned. As this usually entails only a few lost cases, I normally do not worry about it. The remaining students, on the other hand, sometimes astonish me. It has happened that they have tracked down the dropouts, recovered the data assigned to them, and entered the information into the computer themselves. The community, those students have felt, needed all the data it had given us.

The community organizations are always grateful for the analyses they receive from this class. Yet while the data are always sociological, they have so far lacked broad sociological significance. Although I always look for it, the data have not yet offered any new substantive or theoretical insights to the academic community of sociologists. Accordingly, there has never been any call for me to approach our community partners about the possibility of publishing an article on the results.

What I do with this class may be good service research. Insofar as I also do the research with students, it may likewise occasion good service-learning. I do not think, however, that such research qualifies as service scholarship.

If that assessment is correct, we begin to see why scholarly action research is so daunting. It requires us simultaneously to meet two separate agendas of two separate communities. It requires us to do research in collaboration with a civic community that directly benefits that civic community, research that at the same time also addresses issues of concern to the scholarly community of academic sociologists. Those of us who undertake scholarly action research must, therefore, occupy a marginal position between two worlds.

The dilemma is that the research interests of the academic community will not automatically coincide with the research interests of the civic community. We already know that much of what interests the academic community is of little direct benefit to our civic communities. Conversely, much of the research that might benefit our civic community will be of little interest to our academic community.

The solution to the dilemma is not to discard one of its horns; the solution is not simply to say "damn the academic community." That would surrender the real potential of action research to be scholarship, even as the academic community currently understands that term. It would surrender as well the appeal of self-interest the academic community has in doing scholarship. At the University of Pennsylvania, Harkavy and his colleagues (Benson, Harkavy, and Puckett 1994; Harkavy and Puckett 1995) maintain that action research represents potentially better scholarship than we have been doing. The solution, then, is to prove it. The solution is to address the interests of the civic community and the academic community simultaneously.

Can that be done? Although such a dual objective is difficult to accomplish, it can be accomplished. We at Drexel University have accomplished it ourselves at least once — and accomplished it, moreover, as a form of service-learning. I had received a small grant from the national Campus Compact to do action research with my students. I placed them over three terms at a community center in a largely African-American neighborhood close to Drexel. One of the students, who happened to be from Japan, managed to build a strong relationship with the center's senior group, to whom she taught origami.

By the third term of the project, we began to explore research possibilities with the senior group. Although the senior group offered a great range of activities and services, its funding depended on its lunch program. Unfortunately, so few people were participating in the lunch program that the group's overall funding was endangered.

I referred my student to a gerontologist in our department, and together they developed a questionnaire in collaboration with the senior group to find out why more neighborhood seniors did not eat lunch at the center. The questionnaire was then broadened so as to offer as well a needs assessment of neighborhood seniors. The sample was generated snowball fashion by the participating members of the senior group, who, along with college-age VISTA volunteers, were trained to interview neighborhood seniors in their homes. The senior member of each two-person team put the interviewee at ease, and the VISTA volunteer administered the questionnaire.

The whole process served as a recruitment tool, and the lunch program gained enough new participants to preserve overall funding. At the same time, the study generated findings that were of interest not just to the neighborhood senior group but to academic social science as well. It turned out that there was a scholarly literature in gerontology on senior centers to which our findings spoke. Moreover, our study documented that, for various reasons, many neighborhood seniors were not receiving the government services or benefits to which they are entitled. That was an important sociological finding as well.

The entire study became our student's senior thesis, which won the department's senior thesis award. Revised versions of the paper were presented at the Eastern Sociological Society (Mizuno, Kutzik, and Porpora 1994) and the Gerontological Society of America (Kutzik, Mizuno, and Porpora 1995) meetings. We further expect some version of this paper eventually to be published. Here, then, is one example of an action research project that was arguably a success both as service and as scholarship.

It is one thing to do research as a service to the community. That will always remain an important part of our vocation. It is also important to do service research with our students so that it becomes a form of service-learning. When, however, we specifically undertake to do action research as a form of scholarship, we must choose our sites and projects with theoretical care. However much they may benefit the community, not all projects will be equally likely to contribute to the scholarly dialogue of our discipline. In advance, therefore, we need to bring to service scholarship a strong appreciation for theoretical and substantive issues and choose those projects most likely to address them.

The scholarship associated with action research may take many different forms. At this early stage, it may still be a scholarly contribution to our discipline just to undertake a project that illustrates how action research is done. As time goes on, however, there ought to be a deepening scholarly dialogue about action research itself. What are the variants of co-participation? Who exactly constitutes the civic community with whom we are to partner — community organizations or their clients? These are theoretical questions about action research that action researchers might address in a scholarly way. Action research poses methodological issues too, relating to such matters as diversity and voice. Such methodological issues may be likewise the subject of action research scholarship (see, for example, Kelly 1993).

Ultimately, however, if action research is not to be ghettoized as just another sectional interest within sociology, its scholarly results will have to speak to the broader discipline. If Harkavy and his colleagues are correct that action research represents a better form of research, then that will have to be evident from its yield independent of the participatory method employed. The writings of the UCA Jesuits (see Hassett and Lacey 1991; Petras and Porpora 1993) lay a theoretical foundation for the scholarly promise that action research offers, but eventually that promise to the discipline will need to be routinely fulfilled.[3]

Action Research as a Form of Service-Learning

As difficult as it is just to do scholarly action research, such research is even more difficult to do with students as a form of service-learning. When service scholarship is done with students, the students themselves will need to be academically prepared. They, too, will have to be alive to the disciplinary issues on which the unfolding research might touch.

Even to begin a scholarly action research project presupposes an ongoing relationship with a civic community. Those of us from the academy — whether professionals or students — cannot just arrive on site with an invitation to do research together. If the research is to be collaborative, the civic community and the academics need to develop a mutual understanding of what each other is about. Such relationship building is a long-term process with important implications for student involvement. The long-term nature of relationship building makes it difficult — although not impossible — to do action research with students in a single term. Ordinarily, at least a term will be needed to develop a relationship with a community partner. That may be accomplished by having students engage in service-learning at the community site.

Whatever methodology the specific action research project will ultimately employ, at the stage of relationship building, the process will share characteristics with ethnography. Ethnographers spend a long time with the group they are studying just getting acquainted. During that time, ethnographers may anxiously wonder whether what they are doing will lead to a scholarly result. The same worries will afflict action researchers at this stage.

The professors involved will themselves need to be patient. The students in turn will need to be reassured that they are not required to produce a research product. At this stage, they must be told, service-learning is all that is expected. If, however, some scholarly research is to eventuate, then the students must be sensitive to the research possibilities that might be suggested to the community partner. The students must become like ethnographers, knowing what to observe, what is of potential sociological significance and what is not. That in turn requires the students to receive some training in ethnographic methods.

If students are to be involved in action research over several terms, that possibility must be institutionally created in the curriculum. The solution my department has adopted may not work everywhere. Drexel University is on a quarter system, and students typically take between five and seven courses a term, an excessive course load for reflective thought. Yet that very course load has allowed us to open space for our students to participate in action research. Specifically, over their years with us, sociology majors are now required to take the equivalent of three to five courses in supervised field placements that begin as service-learning and potentially end with an action research proposal. Should students emerge from their service-learning experience with an action research proposal, they can pursue that research over another three terms as their senior thesis.

This arrangement works out well for the students but not necessarily for the faculty. While the students are now academically compensated for their service-learning/action research activity, the faculty are not. The teaching burden on the faculty supervising the field placements has, accordingly, risen. Ideally, such added faculty burden should also be institutionally addressed.

The arrangement also presents faculty with a pedagogical problem: continuity. If an action research project spans multiple terms, some students will continue with it and some will not. Each term, the supervising faculty member is confronted with the possibility of too few students to maintain project continuity or, at best, students at different levels of initiation. In the latter case, the faculty member must acquaint new students with both the community partner and the scholarly issues involved while maintaining the interest of continuing students. This is not an easy task.

In short, scholarly action research itself is not easy, and it is all the more difficult when it is done with students as a form of service-learning. There is, however, one consideration that makes it all less daunting than I have portrayed it. Instead of specifically setting out to do scholarly action research, we should perhaps see it as an ever-present possibility that may grow out of our ongoing service-learning relationships with our various community partners. If scholarly action research is a goal, then at least some of our community partners ought to be chosen for their potential to realize that end. Even then, however, since action research is participatory, we will have no advance certainty about what if any scholarly contribution will result. Students and faculty must both simply remain alert to the scholarly potential.

In the meantime, if both faculty and students remain oriented toward action research possibilities, students' service-learning experiences can be considerably enriched. Such an orientation pushes students further to connect their service experiences with the scholarly literature. It prompts them to begin asking themselves scholarly questions: How might this concrete experience of mine be expanded into a study that supports or challenges some aspect of the literature? How might such a study elaborate on or fill the gaps in what the literature has already discussed?

If we think of scholarly action research as always an inherent possibility in an ongoing service-learning relationship, then its ideal form need not be consistently reached. There are levels of scholarship. The standards that apply to a professional journal or scholarly conference need not be applied to an undergraduate senior thesis. Even if an action research project falls short of professional standards of scholarship, it still may constitute a very advanced form of service-learning.[4]

There are levels, too, of co-participation with a civic community. Ideally, perhaps, one and the same research question will be both academically interesting and of concern to the civic community. In that case, the interests of the academic and civic communities will be exactly aligned. At other times, however, we may apply the same research that serves a civic community to different, academic ends. Alternatively, we may simply piggyback academic research on research that serves a civic community. Sometimes, too, we may just use our service to the community as an occasion to do our own independent sociological research. There is much that might potentially fall under the label of co-participation.

In the end, if we faculty do not expect too much of ourselves, if we do not necessarily stake our entire scholarly careers on doing action research, then the ideal of scholarly action research will always remain a way for us to deepen our students' service-learning experience — and our own.

Notes

1. There is a large, interdisciplinary literature on action research. However, for those looking specifically for an introduction to the sociological literature, see the November and December 1993 issues of *The American Sociologist,* which, under the special editorship of Edna Bonicich and Randy Stoeker, were entirely devoted to the topic.

2. What happens to an activated, conscientized community when a professor decides things are getting too politically hot for him or her? One answer is that we should determine in advance the likely political outcomes of our projects and not undertake anything we are unwilling or unable to see through. This, however, is not a fully adequate answer. Even with advance visualization, we may still be overtaken by "the cunning of history."

3. Edward Zlotkowski (1996) makes a similar point about service-learning in general. Zlotkowski argues that service-learning educators need "to begin writing not just for publications targeted at a service-learning audience but also for professional journals in their field" (128). Whether action research is done as a form of service-learning or not, its results must eventually contribute a content interesting to sociological journals that do not have action research as their focus.

4. Academics, of course, should always be up front with their community partners if they see their involvement with the community as also a potential project for research scholarship. In an ongoing relationship between academic and community partners, it might be established initially that some projects will emphasize direct service to the community, while others will tend primarily to address a scholarly audience. As long as there is fair give-and-take in this regard, the relationship will be mutually beneficial.

   Students, too, should be acquainted early with a project's goal — whether that goal is primarily service to a community, primarily scholarly, or both simultaneously. Doing both simultaneously is clearly the most difficult undertaking. Students, consequently, have little difficulty shifting back from that ambitious goal to either pure community service or pure scholarship. In our program, one of the challenges we set for both our students and ourselves is to take an ongoing service-learning experience and eventually develop a project that is also of scholarly interest. That shift is difficult for our students and for us.

References

Benson, Lee, Ira Harkavy, and John Puckett. (1994). "Communal Participatory Action Research as a Strategy for Changing Universities and the Social Sciences: The University of Pennsylvania and West Philadelphia as a Case Study." Paper presented at the Invitational Conference on Improving Urban Schools: Better Strategies for the Dissemination and Utilization of Knowledge, sponsored by the National Center on Education in the Inner Cities, September 8-10, Alexandria, VA.

Brown, David L., and Rajesh Tandon. (1983). "Ideology and Political Economy in Inquiry: Action Research and Participatory Research." *Journal of Applied Behavioral Science* 19(3): 277-294.

Ellacuria, Ignacio. (1991a). "Is a Different University Possible?" In *Towards a Society That Serves Its People*, edited by John Hassett and Hugh Lacey, pp. 208-219. Washington, DC: Georgetown University Press.

————. (1991b). "The University, Human Rights, and the Poor Majority." In *Towards a Society That Serves Its People*, edited by John Hassett and Hugh Lacey, pp. 177-207. Washington, DC: Georgetown University Press.

Gallup Organization. (1993). Gallup poll conducted December 1990. (USGallup.922024, R31). *Public Opinion Online*: Roper Center at University of Connecticut.

Harkavy, Ira, and John L. Puckett. (1995). "The Action Research Tradition in American Social Science: Toward a Strategy for Revitalizing the Social Sciences, the University, and the American City." Trondheim, Norway, and Stockholm, Sweden: Scandinavian Action Research Development Program (ACRES).

Hassett, John, and Hugh Lacey, eds. (1991). *Towards a Society That Serves Its People*. Washington, DC: Georgetown University Press.

Jacoby, Russell. (1987). *The Last Intellectuals: American Culture in the Age of Academe*. New York, NY: Basic Books.

Kelly, Dierdre M. (1993). "Secondary Power Source: High School Students as Participatory Researchers." *American Sociologist* 24(1): 8-26.

Kutzik, David, Motoko Mizuno, and Douglas Porpora. (November 1995). "African-American Community Dwelling Elderly: The Results of a Participatory Research Project." Paper presented to the meeting of the Gerontological Society of America, Los Angeles, CA.

Lerner, Michael. (1986). *Surplus Powerlessness*. Oakland, CA: Institute for Labor and Mental Health.

Lynd, Robert S. (1939). *Knowledge for What?* Princeton, NJ: Princeton University Press.

Mizuno, Motoko, David Kutzik, and Douglas Porpora. (April 1994). "African-American Community Dwelling Elderly: Formal and Informal Supports, Service Access, and Health Needs." Paper presented to the meeting of the Eastern Sociological Society, Philadelphia, PA.

Norman, Michael. (January 30, 1994). "A Book in Search of a Buzz: The Marketing of a First Novel." *New York Times Book Review*: 3.

Petras, Elizabeth McLean, and Douglas V. Porpora. (1993). "Participatory Research: Three Models and an Analysis." *American Sociologist* 24(1): 107-124.

Spivak, Gayatri. (1988). "Can the Subaltern Speak?" In *Marxism and the Interpretation of Culture*, edited by Cary Nelson and Lawrence Grossberg, pp. 271-313. Urbana, IL: University of Illinois Press.

Wilson, William Julius. (1987). *The Truly Disadvantaged*. Chicago, IL: University of Chicago Press.

Zlotkowski, Edward. (1996). "Does Service-Learning Have a Future?" *Michigan Journal of Community Service-Learning* 2: 123-134.

Examining Communities and Urban Change: Service-Learning as Collaborative Research

by Garry Hesser

The thesis of this essay is quite simple: There is a remarkable and productive synergy that is created when the teaching and practice of sociological analysis are brought into conversation and dialogue with the cities and neighborhoods where our colleges and universities are located. An active collaboration with genuine reciprocity (Mintz and Hesser 1996) can benefit the community, engage our students in the development of the "sociological eye" (Derber 1996), and advance our understanding of local communities as well as the field of urban/community sociology. When this kind of collaborative research occurs, the outcome is both good sociology and good service-learning.

Historical and Conceptual Context

The founding and flourishing of American sociology is intricately and intimately tied to the study of cities and community. The Chicago School of sociology constructed theory in the context of locally based research, and most faculty members developed a close relationship with the community. In addition, early "Chicago sociologists, grounded in a philosophy of pragmatism, studied and intervened in the urban problems confronting their community . . . [including] progressive public education, the Hull House project, urban planning, crime and delinquency prevention programs, and other community activities through teaching, research, and service" (Pestello et al. 1996: 148; cf. Lyon 1987: 9-10).

Since the early days of sociology, Comte, Durkheim, Weber, and others have struggled with the central question: What makes community possible? Admittedly, the concept of "community" has been debated and is frequently blurred by its wide-ranging use by sociologists to include nonterritorial criteria, such as social groups and total institutions (cf. Bellah et al. 1985; Lyon 1987; Poplin 1979; Suttles 1972). However, Hiller (1941); Hillery (1955), Reiss (1959), and Warren (1978) initiated a process that has resulted in a general consensus that "territorial community" is indeed a critical unit of analysis and form of social organization. Hillary (1955) contended that communities "consist of persons in social interaction within a geographic area and having one or more additional common ties" (111). This definition provides us with a territorial variable (geographic area), a sociological variable (social interaction), and a psychosocial variable (common ties) that are at the heart of most ecological and social system approaches to the study of cities and communities (Flanagan 1993; Poplin 1979).

Following the "eclipse" of interest in community in the 1950s and 1960s, there was a strong revival that resulted in the reestablishment of the Community Section of the American Sociological Association. The section rapidly grew to more than 540, ranking in size and prestige with the other sections. Lyon (1987) explains this resurgent interest in the following way:

> The main reason for the revival of interest in community sociology lies in the development of a more circumscribed view of America as a mass society. It has become clear that significant ethnic and racial differences in values and behavior continue to exist. Perhaps more important for community sociology, we have discovered that significant differences in local politics, economics, and lifestyles exist between communities. . . . The community is obviously no longer a self-contained, self-sufficient, homogeneous village, but neither has it become an impotent group of unrelated, alienated, anonymous residents with little or no local ties. (15)

Today, community sociology is attempting to discover, describe, and understand the interaction between the mass society and the local community.

Several recent presidents of the American Sociological Association, e.g., Herbert Gans, Kai Erikson, James Coleman, William Gamson, and Amitai Etzioni, focused their theoretical and empirical research on issues related to community. They, like Richard Sennett (1997), have found that "the city [community] is such a fertile ground for sociologists like me." More recently, the voices of Gottdiener, Feagin, Keller, Logan, Molotch, Sassen, Castells, Giddens, Harvey, and others have joined the chorus of Simmel, Weber, Hawley, Addams, Wirth, Burgess, Park, Whyte, and others who also found the city community a compelling and "fertile ground," as Sennett puts it. As one synthesist suggests:

> The field of urban sociology acknowledges that cities are arenas of behavior, dynamic elements of social ecology, backdrops for the human search for meaningful social ties, gameboards on which powerful players compete for greater profits while the less powerful struggle to use the same space to make a living and raise families. Urban arenas are the modern battleground for the class struggle, and an incubator for social problems that provide the focus for a range of social movements. Cities constitute a socially defined environment that helps shape the choices that individuals make, choices that in turn continuously create and alter that environment. . . . [Any of these aspects] of urban issues is quite enough to provide a lifetime of study for any one individual. (Flanagan 1993: 3-4)

Flanagan's contention, underscored by Sennett's comment, is at the heart of this chapter, namely, that *the community as a unit of analysis, both as a dependent and as an independent variable, is one of the most interesting and critical forms of social organization upon which to focus one's "sociological eye."* Not only is it interesting to we who, like Sennett, already see ourselves as professional sociologists, but it is *both* a "fertile" and exciting entry point *and* an accessible focus for "capstone" research for our students as we try to help them discover and embrace the sociological imagination.

Experiential Education, Collaborative Community-Based Research, and Service-Learning

In the past decade, there has been a resurgence of interest in and commitment to community-based research that takes a more "participatory action research" approach (see Porpora's essay in this volume). The following describes a wide variety of ways in which sociologists are rediscovering and reaffirming the legacy of Jane Addams and the early Chicago School approach. Addams and others embraced a powerful pedagogy and quality of learning that results when students join with faculty and the community in a collaborative search for a deeper understanding of communities and how they work.

In his ASA presidential address, James Coleman strongly supported the need for sociology to demonstrate its essential contribution to the greater public by focusing on a rational reconstruction of society (Coleman 1993; cf. Gamson 1995). Decades earlier, Coleman was also an ardent and articulate spokesperson and theorist advancing experiential education (Coleman 1972a, 1972b, 1977). Coleman's two themes come together in community-based collaborative research that also embraces the objective of enhancing the quality of teaching and student learning. Although they don't always call it "service-learning," there is growing evidence that sociologists are increasingly embracing the synergy that comes from integrating participatory community-based research with the sociology curriculum, including specific courses, internships, and student research.

The following case descriptions illustrate how sociologists are engaging in mutually beneficial research with both communities and our students as partners in the research enterprise. The first example involves the reorganization of an entire sociology department at the University of Dayton around the concept of "community and the practice of sociology." Here the focus is clearly on sociology faculty as "citizen-scholars" who endeavor to engage both the community and their students in the teaching and research enterprise. Their focus has been upon developing a coherent, meaningful academic program that also supports and enables faculty to engage in a quality and quantity of research that is sustainable in a teaching institution. Throughout the program, majors engage in increasingly sophisticated forms of service-learning.

The second example focuses upon a reciprocal, expanding collaborative relationship between faculty and community at Loyola University of Chicago. The Policy Research and Action Group (PRAG) program provides students with the opportunity to engage in service and learning by participating in research projects largely controlled by the community and the faculty. There is indeed a strong interest in and commitment to the learning of sociology on the part of students, but this seems to be primarily a splendid by-product and not the central focus of PRAG.

The third example involves a consortium of eight colleges and universities in the Minneapolis–St. Paul area that has formed the Neighborhood Planning for Community Revitalization (NPCR) project. NPCR gives the community and the student higher priority. In this example, faculty are primarily mentors, with only two faculty per year funded for research, as compared with approximately 30 community-student collaborations per year. However, the main point of this essay is that all three models and approaches, though rarely referred to as "service-learning," come closer to the espoused principles of service-learning than do many other explicitly named programs, *and* all three are excellent opportunities for sociology students and faculty to engage in the kind of sociological inquiry that has long been at the heart of the "sociological imagination."

Community and the Practice of Sociology: University of Dayton

The sociology department at the University of Dayton has initiated an alternative approach to teaching, research, and service, a program that integrates the curriculum with research and service, using the Dayton metropolitan area as the sociological setting for its work. This approach to sociology involves taking the role of citizen-scholar as "[the department develops] community-based teaching and research programs that serve . . . students, the university, the community, and the profession" (Pestello et al. 1996: 148).

The department initiated its holistic approach in 1991, using the Chicago School of sociology as a model. From the latter it adopted two assumptions: (1) Theory is constructed in a context of locally based research; and (2) faculty members of the university can develop a close relationship with the community. The department notes that the founding fathers and mothers of this approach "contributed to progressive public education, the Hull House project, urban planning, crime and delinquency prevention programs, and other community activities through teaching, research, and service" (Pestello et al. 1996: 148).

Following the lead of Suzanne Keller (1988), the sociology department embraced the "community" as a vital concept for theory and research, a place where students (and faculty) can ground "abstract and overgeneralized statistics by locating them in meaningful social space . . . [where] good ethnographic accounts of evolving communities . . . [enable] students to learn and use sociological concepts and methods at both the pure and the applied level" (Pestello et al. 1996: 149). This citizen-scholar model asserts that understanding community stability and change requires empirical research on the local level employing the full range of research methodologies. Further, it posits that communities and regions invite and require "thick description of ongoing processes at the local level" that leads to deeper understanding of the "interrelationships of communication networks, demographic characteristics, power relations, local conventions and practices, local economic activities, government agencies, and historical circumstances" (Pestello et al. 1996: 150).

Dayton's four "defining dimensions" are instructive to those of us who seek to develop effective programs in comprehensive universities and liberal arts colleges where resources are increasingly limited even as teaching, research, and service expectations increase. First, nearly all communities are faced with difficult social problems that require in-depth sociological analysis. Second, a sociology department can be a "major source of sophisticated, empirical knowledge and quantitative and qualitative information about the community." Third, because "social processes and structures are mutable, [the department believes] that it is possible and reasonable to make intelligent interventions in these social processes and structures in order to improve the quality of community life." And, finally, it contends that "effective social intervention requires a thickly contextualized and complex understanding of local conditions, processes, and resources" (Pestello et al. 1996: 151).

Subsequently, this emphasis on "local knowledge" and "thick contextualization," concepts introduced by Clifford Geertz, has led to a holistic curricular revision that enables majors to explore the community in increasing depth, with first- and second-year students going into the community for study and/or service, moving on to internships, and culminating in "collaborative research projects." One such collaborative research project has focused upon how a sense of community can be maintained in inner-city neighborhoods in contemporary society. Faculty members and students conduct neighborhood surveys, with the analysis used by neighborhood committees and city officials as they develop strategic plans for neighborhoods. This collaborative action research model began in one particular neighborhood but has subsequently spread to numerous other Dayton neighborhoods.

Building Community: Sociology in Action

In the late 1980s, Philip Nyden, professor of sociology at Loyola University of Chicago, helped to establish the Policy Research and Action Group. PRAG consists of a group of Chicago-based community leaders and university-based researchers who have worked to build a collaborative network to bring community knowledge and perspectives to the research process.

Noting that community leaders and groups too often lack the appropriate resources to do quality research, the executive director of a Latino organization, for example, has found that universities have the resources for quality research that community groups lack. Reciprocally, the community provides the university with a fertile setting in which to do mutually meaningful research. PRAG provided a Latino housing advocacy group with graduate students as research assistants, enabling the group to document that of Chicago's 110,000 units of assisted housing, fewer than 3 percent housed Latino families even though Latinos make up 25 percent of the eligible population. This research has led to public policy assessment and changes in practice in Chicago and in the U.S. Department of Housing and Urban Development (Nyden et al. 1997: xxiv).

In a book consisting of 27 case studies of collaborative university-community research projects, Nyden and his colleagues emphasize that "adding chairs to the research table" involves accepting a new set of critics. "Research done *with* the community not *to* it" involves academics and nonacademics working "together in identifying the research issue, developing the research design, collecting the data, analyzing the data, writing up the results, and even working with policymakers and practitioners in designing programs and policies" (Nyden et al. 1997: 4). Like the sociology department at Dayton, Nyden and his sociology colleagues at Loyola stress both accountability to the neighborhood *and* maintaining rigorous research that is "an honest representation of the issue being studied."[1]

Of critical importance to service-learning are the opportunities for students that evolve over time from these carefully established collaborative relationships. These opportunities emerge where

> . . . a familiarity with each other's [college's and community's] working styles and a trust develops. . . . For faculty and students, this is an exciting and empowering process. You feel that you are part of something and not just on the sidelines watching the world go by. Collaborative research demystifies the political process by allowing faculty and students to understand how decisions are influenced and made. It reduces cynicism and apathy. . . . When collaborative research involves undergraduate and graduate students as part of the research team, it produces memorable experiences for students. After graduation they remember their involvement in that community survey or that report that was ultimately featured in the local newspaper. When students think about urban issues they no longer pull up some fuzzy abstract image in their mind; they see real communities and real faces. For professor and student, collaborative research provides

another method of learning. Practical experiences give everyone a real "hook" on which to hang theories and more abstract concepts. Practical experiences with all their complexities help faculty and students guard against oversimplification. (Nyden et al. 1997: 8-12)

Nyden and his sociology colleagues join Kretzmann and McKnight (1995) in asking sociologists and other academics to undergo a "paradigm shift" by approaching a community's "half-full" capacities, instead of our usual emphasis on "half-empty" social problems:

> *For decades the majority of U.S. sociology departments have taught a course entitled Social Problems. We have never heard of a course entitled Social Solutions. To map and analyze the dimensions of social problems — crime, inequities, racism, corporate control, and environmental hazards — is seen as scientific research. To discuss and describe alternative practices and develop solutions is seen as moving more toward politics and advocacy — areas that are perceived as a threat to the objectivity of research. We are not calling for the end to basic social research. . . . However, the traditional separation of social research from policy development and program design has produced a gap between research and practice. (Nyden et al. 1997: 240)*

Like the sociology department at Dayton, Loyola has found an intimate connection between community-based collaborative research and the learning goals of an undergraduate sociology curriculum. Nyden is also the director of Loyola's Center for Urban Research and Learning, where collaborative research and the fundamental educational goals of an undergraduate education are continually explored. Nyden and his sociology colleagues emphasize that they are

> *. . . not suggesting that collaborative research should be the research method within the social sciences, nor are [they] suggesting that involving students in community-based collaborative research is the only way of teaching. [They] are presenting a case for strengthening this area as an additional approach to research and an additional way of teaching in the university. (Nyden et al. 1997: 12)*

Although service-learning has permeated virtually all types of colleges and universities since 1986, collaborative community-based research seems to have taken hold more frequently in the "second tier of universities. . . . Elite universities are still very much wedded to discipline-defined and -generated research agendas; community social change is not what drives this research" (Nyden et al. 1997: 16). As sociologists explore the role of service-learning through the mode of collaborative research, we might well ponder the words of a New York University historian of university development:

> It is astonishing how few social scientists (outside of professional schools)
> at New York's two great research universities, NYU and Columbia, are
> studying the issues on everyone's minds — the delivery of health care,
> poverty and inequality, race relations, education, urban politics, the parties
> and the electoral system, the environment, and others one could name.
> (Bender 1996: 11-12)

Nyden and his colleagues, complemented by Pestello et al. at Dayton, Gaventa at Tennessee, Porpora at Drexel, Peter Park, and many other participatory action research practitioners in sociology, contend that the "flat-footedness of elite universities in responding to this new environment has left the door open to other universities [and colleges] who are ready to participate" (Nyden et al. 1997: 17).

As Porpora also emphasizes in his essay in this volume (see p. 135ff.), the assumption that traditional "academic-driven" research and its claims for objectivity result in more-accurate knowledge is contested and open for debate.[2] A fortunate group of us were introduced to participatory action research at an ASA Summer Institute at UCLA led by sociologists William Foote Whyte, Peter Park, Paulo Freire, and Paul Baker. Park, who is also president of the Center for Community Education and Action, makes the connection between community-based participatory action research and developing the "sociological imagination" when he explains that "participatory research provides a framework in which people seeking to overcome oppressive situations can come to understand the social forces in operation and gain strength through collective action" (Park 1993: 3).[3]

Neighborhood Planning and Community Revitalization

As the sociology departments at Loyola and Dayton have demonstrated, collaborative community-based research can involve students through research as part of courses, internships, independent study research projects, work-study assignments, and group research. The Center for Urban and Regional Affairs (CURA) at the University of Minnesota has been making it possible for graduate and undergraduate students to do collaborative research with neighborhood organizations for nearly 30 years. CURA was begun under the leadership of Fred Lukermann and John Borchert, who were chairs of Minnesota's nationally ranked geography department, and other leading social scientists at the university.

In 1996, CURA expanded its efforts to give urban neighborhoods more influence in determining their futures. In response to Minneapolis's neighborhood revitalization program, CURA sought and obtained federal funding from an Urban Community Service grant administered by the U.S. Department of Education. The program is patterned on three decades of linking University of Minnesota graduate students to the needs of community organizations and neighborhoods. The new initiative, Neighborhood Planning for Community Revitalization, has expanded that base and is a consortium of eight colleges and universities in the Twin Cities (Augsburg, St. Catherine, Hamline, Macalester, Metropolitan State, Minneapolis Community College, St. Thomas, University of Minnesota, and the Higher Education Consortium for Urban Affairs). "All members of the consortium have a commitment to urban revitalization through community service," reports the evaluator of their first three years (Gladchild 1996: ix).

Neighborhood Planning for Community Revitalization (NPCR) represents a "premier" form of service-learning when one examines it in the light of the "principles of good practice in service-learning" (Mintz and Hesser 1996). The community and students play central partnership roles in a way that "course-embedded" service-learning rarely does. Genuine collaboration and reciprocity, the hallmarks of quality service-learning, have become the centerpiece of NPCR. As its director, Kris Nelson, describes it:

> NPCR links the resources of Twin Cities universities to neighborhood organizations. The value of this linkage is evident not only in the [100] research projects supported by NPCR over the past three years but also in the relationships that endure beyond each project. Students earnestly engage in neighborhood work and gain a greater understanding of the power of private citizens working together for the common good of their community. . . . Students have given dedication, new energy, and knowledgeable insights. Faculty have made their time and expertise available to advise students. Community mentors have volunteered their time to support students and the neighborhoods. University staff have set up new systems and procedures to deploy students and faculty. And, most importantly, neighborhood organizations have welcomed university assistance and taught all participants. [emphasis added] (Gladchild 1996: vii)

The program's third-year evaluator describes NPCR as

> . . . applied research assistance to neighborhood organizations, usually in the form of a graduate or undergraduate student research assistant for a specified number of hours. . . . By and large, the process, though complex, works quite well when: (1) the control of the project and supervision of the student rests with the neighborhood organization, (2) each school supports its students, and (3) NPCR provides technical assistance to support each project. (Gladchild 1996: ix)

The evaluator noted that NPCR staff and the proposal review committee assist in the revising and clarifying of proposals from neighborhood organizations, serving as collaborators who are proactive in assisting the neighborhoods in their quest to obtain the research assistance they need.

Modeling quality service-learning practice, a neighborhood organization selects the best-qualified student from a pool of applicants. Then the NPCR project director meets with the student and the neighborhood project supervisor to develop a work plan. If communities are to be served and not exploited or subjected to additional stress by working with a student (or a faculty member, for that matter), it is essential that a work plan be developed that has clear roles, a common understanding of objectives and activities, and an understanding of possible resources available for the research. This process emulates the kind of preparation that increases the probability of quality participatory action research and a good service-learning experience for the student. In addition, it underscores principles put forth by Kretzmann and McKnight (1993) that are widely affirmed among members of the service-learning community: "The experience of conducting an NPCR research project builds the [neighborhood's/community's] capacity to define and address problems, then acquire and apply outside resources" (Gladchild 1996: x). In other words, the community's capacities are strengthened for its long-range and comprehensive revitalization efforts.[4]

The NPCR model places neighborhoods in the driver's seat, and undergraduate students become the researchers, supported by faculty mentors who offer advice and assistance. Each student researcher has two mentors with whom the student meets at least three times during the project's duration, which may or may not conform to academic terms. A faculty mentor offers advice on research design and methodology (something that I have done for six research projects). A community mentor directs the student to resources, contributes expertise on the issue being researched, and puts the project into perspective for the student. NPCR also provides technical assistance to the student researcher tailored to the goals of the project. For example, CURA staff often advise on computer and Geographic Information Systems (GIS) sources, and the Minnesota Center for Survey Research can be consulted about survey research design. As with the Dayton sociology department and the PRAG consortium (Loyola et al.), the faculty and their institutions bring sustained continuity and long-term commitment into the mix.

As in the cases of the sociology department at Dayton and the PRAG Chicago consortium, there is an opportunity here for two faculty-directed research projects each year

> ... as a means for both fostering community-based research and providing community groups with information useful to their work. The topics must have broad application across Minneapolis neighborhoods and address important public policy concerns or governmental practices that affect the ability of Minneapolis neighborhoods to successfully undertake revitalization activities. (Gladchild 1996: xi)

The largest local foundation has now funded NPCR to undertake similar collaborative research in the other twin city, St. Paul. This is a further indicator of the quality and value of this kind of community-based collaborative research.

A More Modest Approach

As a teacher of urban sociology and director of sociology internships, I have found that neighborhood organizations and students can mutually benefit from course-embedded, small-scale research projects. For example, one team of five students in a Community and Modern Metropolis course gathered the baseline data needed by a neighborhood community development corporation (CDC). These data and the students' report are being used by the neighborhood developer to assess and monitor the changes that have taken place in two high-rise apartments built by for-profit developers but recently converted to nonprofit, affordable housing under the management of the CDC. Drawing upon a 20-year relationship between Augsburg's sociology faculty and this particular neighborhood and CDC, students from future classes will continue to assist the CDC in the research and data needs that it identifies.

Another group of students from the same class has worked with the property committee of a neighborhood association as part of an ongoing study of a residential block that is zoned industrial. The neighborhood association was charged with the creation of a strategic plan and the setting of priorities for the expenditure of more than $5 million for neighborhood revitalization. A major debate took place concerning how much of the housing rehab portion should be invested in an industrially zoned and aging block of housing. The students designed a questionnaire and interviewed residents in order for the committee and staff to have a clearer idea of the attitudes and preferences of the residents of that block, who until then had largely played a passive and silent role in the neighborhood planning process.

Another ongoing service-learning option for our students is to do a sociology internship with one of the Minneapolis neighborhood organizations that are engaged in the city-wide "neighborhood revitalization program" in Minneapolis. As in the case of students who contract to do Neighborhood Planning for Community Revitalization research projects (as described above), our interns work with a particular neighborhood organization or the city-wide neighborhood revitalization program staff by undertaking research and projects identified in their learning agreements. Like the sociology faculty at Dayton and Loyola, I have found the quality of learning and the grounding of concepts to be greatly enhanced by this kind of active engagement through service-learning.

Conclusion

A strong case can be made that sociology is now playing a major role in shaping the future of service-learning. The recently published *Building Community: Social Science in Action* (Nyden et al. 1997) was written by sociologists who have been actively engaged in collaborative community-based research. Based upon their own experience and the 27 case studies that they present in their book, Nyden and his sociology colleagues offer a rationale for expanding their research to include their students in this form of service-learning:

> When collaborative research involves undergraduate and graduate students as part of the research team, it produces memorable experiences for students. After graduation they remember their involvement in that community survey or that report that was ultimately featured in the local newspaper. When students think about urban issues, they no longer pull up some fuzzy abstract image in their mind; they see real communities and real faces. For professor and student, collaborative research provides another method of learning. Practical experiences give everyone a real "hook" on which to hang theories and more abstract concepts. Practical experiences with all their complexities help faculty and students guard against oversimplification. . . . It provides a better grasp on the complexities of policy development. . . . Just as social science can "lift the veils" that obscure social processes, so too can collaborative research open windows on entirely new experiences for professors, students, and community activists. (Nyden et al. 1997: 12-13)

How will we know if sociologically oriented, community-based participatory action research merits our attention and support? Certainly one outcome that is recognized and emphasized by those involved in or assessing the programs described above is that communities and students are empowered with a "sociological imagination" as they engage in this form of service-learning. Furthermore, community-based collaborative research seems to enhance students' capacities to utilize the concepts and methods of sociology. And congruent with the writing and practice of Coleman, Gamson, Gans, Etzioni, and others, this approach enables our students — and us ourselves — to address the vital issues and questions that confront citizen-scholars who are called in a democracy to accept the challenge to build, as well as to understand, community.

As Porpora suggests in his essay in this volume, participatory action research may just be the "highest stage of service-learning." The three models described in this chapter underscore what is at the heart of the "principles of service-learning" (Mintz and Hesser 1996); namely, that sustained collaboration and reciprocity enhance the capacities of communities and students alike. This approach to sociological research and to the teaching of sociology taps a rediscovered synergy that involves faculty, students, and the community in a collaboration marked by "new opportunities for all involved. By putting our minds together, we can see new things from a fresh perspective and develop innovative applications" (Nyden et al. 1997: 13). If this is not what we mean by the "sociological imagination," then what is?

Notes

1. Other examples of community-based collaborative research centers include the Voorhees Neighborhood Center, which is part of the University of Illinois at Chicago's Center for Urban Economic Development in the College of Urban Planning and Public Affairs. The main goals of the Voorhees Center are (1) to provide technical assistance and research needs requested by community organizations and coalitions in the Chicago area and (2) to provide urban planning graduate students practical expertise in community development while they are studying for their master's degree. The Loka Institute is based in Amherst, Massachusetts, and has a focus upon making technology responsive to democratically decided social and environmental concerns. Through research and advocacy, the Loka Institute works with grass-roots public interest groups, everyday citizens, academics, and workers to create opportunities for all citizens' involvement in science and technology decision making. Nyden et al. (1997) identify 27 other similar collaborative efforts to "build community" through applied social science research. Their cases also include a number of examples where things did not work well, with analysis and reflection that should assist readers in not repeating their mistakes and make us more sensitive to the many issues that must be taken into account when engaging in this kind of collaborative research. The NPCR/CURA evaluation report by Gladchild (1996) also provides assessment feedback from the multiple participants and a framework for evaluating community-based collaborative research.

2. For an excellent discussion of participatory action research to complement Porpora's chapter elsewhere in this volume, the reader is encouraged to read Chapter 2 of *Building Community: Social Science in Action* (Nyden et al. 1997: 14-28).

3. Another sociologist and early member of the Invisible College (a national association of service-learning educators) who has "pioneered" participatory action research in Appalachia and nonurban settings is John Gaventa (1993).

4. Gladchild (1996) cites examples of student research projects of particular interest to sociologists, including "Single Parents Building Community in the Neighborhood"; "Lyndale Neighborhood: Health Indicators, Social Research, and the Civic Process"; "Neighborhood Housing Conditions: Survey Methodology"; "Neighborhood in Transition: An Analysis of Factors Influencing Property Value Change in the McKinley Neighborhood"; "Linden Hills Library Community Survey: Final Report"; "Providing Support for an Innovative Neighborhood Economic Development Strategy: A Survey of the Needs of Home-Based Business in the Marcy-Holmes Neighborhood"; "Jordan Neighborhood Crime Research"; "Livability in Minneapolis Neighborhoods: An Examination of Problem Rental Property"; "Community-Oriented Policing and Crime

Prevention"; "Telling Stories and Creating Jobs: Community Arts as a Tool for Social Change"; "Implementation Study of the Stevens Square–Loring Heights Social Services Plan"; and "There Goes the Neighborhood: The Impact of Subsidized Multifamily Housing on Urban Neighborhoods." (This last project was a faculty-directed undertaking that involved two students as research colleagues and coauthors of the final publication by CURA.)

References

Bellah, Robert, Richard Madsen, William Sullivan, Ann Swidler, and Steve Tipton. (1985). *Habits of the Heart: Individualism and Commitment.* Berkeley, CA: University of California Press.

Bender, Thomas. (March 1996). "Universities and the City: Scholarship, Local Life, and the Necessity of Worldliness." Paper presented at the Urban Universities and Their Cities conference, University of Amsterdam, Amsterdam, Netherlands.

Coleman, James. (February 1972a). "The Children Have Outgrown the Schools." *Psychology Today:* 72-82.

―――. (December 1972b). "How Do the Young Become Adults?" *Phi Delta Kappan* 54(4): 226-230.

―――. (1977). "Differences Between Experiential and Classroom Learning." In *Experiential Learning: Rationale, Characteristics, and Assessment,* edited by Morris Keeton, pp. 49-61. San Francisco, CA: Jossey-Bass.

―――. (1993). "The Rational Reconstruction of Society." *American Sociological Review* 58(1): 1-15.

Derber, Charles. (1996). *The Wilding of America.* New York, NY: St. Martin's Press.

Flanagan, William. (1993). *Contemporary Urban Sociology.* New York, NY: Cambridge University Press.

Gamson, William. (1995). "Hiroshima, the Holocaust, and the Politics of Exclusion." *American Sociological Review* 60(1): 1-20.

Gaventa, John. (1993). "The Powerful, the Powerless, and the Experts: Knowledge Struggles in an Information Age." In *Voices of Change: Participatory Research in the United States and Canada,* edited by Peter Park et al., pp. 20-38. Westport, CT: Bergin & Garvey.

Gladchild, Pat. (1996). *Bridging Two Worlds: NPCR Program Evaluation Final Report (1993-1996).* Minneapolis, MN: Center for Urban and Regional Affairs.

Hiller, E.T. (April 1941). "The Community as a Social Group." *American Sociological Review* 6: 189-203.

Hillery, George A. (1955). "Definitions of Community: Areas of Agreement." *Rural Sociology* 20(2): 111-123.

Keller, Suzanne. (1988). "The American Dream of Community: An Unfinished Agenda." *Sociological Forum* 3(2): 167-183.

Kretzmann, John, and John McKnight. (1993). *Building Communities From the Inside Out: A Path Toward Finding and Mobilizing a Community's Assets.* Evanston, IL: Center for Urban Affairs and Policy Research, Northwestern University.

Lyon, Larry. (1987). *The Community in Urban Society.* Chicago, IL: Dorsey Press.

Mintz, Suzanne, and Garry Hesser. (1996). "Principles of Good Practice in Service-Learning." In *Service-Learning in Higher Education,* edited by Barbara Jacoby, pp. 26-52. San Francisco, CA: Jossey-Bass.

Nyden, Philip, Anne Figert, Mark Shibley, and Darryl Burrows, eds. (1997). *Building Community: Social Science in Action.* Thousand Oaks, CA: Pine Forge Press.

Park, Peter. (1993). "What Is Participatory Research? A Theoretical and Methodological Perspective." In *Voices of Change: Participatory Research in the United States and Canada,* edited by Peter Park et al., pp. 1-19. Westport, CT: Bergin & Garvey.

Pestello, Frances, Dan Miller, Stanley Saxton, and Patrick Donnelly. (1996). "Community and the Practice of Sociology." *Teaching Sociology* 24: 148-156.

Poplin, Dennis. (1979). *Communities.* 2nd ed. New York, NY: Macmillan.

Reiss, Albert J. (June 1959). "The Sociological Study of Communities." *Rural Sociology* 24: 118-139.

Sennett, Richard. (February 1997). "The Virtues of the Center." Presentation at the Project Urban Europe Conference, University of Minnesota, Minneapolis, MN.

Suttles, Gerald. (1972). *The Social Construction of Communities.* Chicago, IL: University of Chicago Press.

Warren, Roland. (1978). *The Community in America.* 3rd ed. Chicago, IL: Rand McNally.

Afterword

Sociology, Service, and Learning, For a Stronger Discipline

by Carla B. Howery

Reading this book, and some of the literature cited in each chapter, I exclaim with enthusiasm, "Service-learning is back on the map in sociology!" Throughout this book, our colleagues challenge us to return to our roots as an applied discipline, to draw in the scholarship of teaching (and to contribute to it), and to offer "how to" (and "how not to") suggestions to spur us to plunge into service-learning.

Sitting at the national professional association, my perspective is slightly different from that of the sociology faculty who contributed the chapters in this volume. Often at the American Sociological Association (ASA), the professional staff call ourselves "the full-time eyes and ears of the discipline" and summarize our work as "field development" — helping sociology and its departments thrive and lead. From that vantage, I want to commend this volume and address two important issues. First, what can service-learning do for sociology, to strengthen and enrich our field? Second, how can sociology participate in the national conversation on service-learning in its various incarnations, especially in view of changes in higher education?

Service-Learning Can Enrich Sociology

The very roots of American sociology dovetail with service-learning. In 1906, Lester Frank Ward helped found ASA (then called the American Sociological Society) to bring scientific attention to social problems, and became its first president. Our field has always espoused the interplay of theory, research, application, and reformulation, as an ongoing and iterative process. And if we have embodied this process in our research scholarship, we can then ask how well it is anchored in our teaching.

One way in which sociology seems ripe for service-learning is that we are a field that emphasizes a *mode of thinking* as much as a *body of content*. Review a hundred sociology undergraduate curricula and you will find a

---

Carla B. Howery is the deputy executive officer of the American Sociological Association. She directs two of ASA's core programs: Academic and Professional Affairs, and the Spivack Program in Applied Social Research and Social Policy.

small common core, but considerable variation. The field is young and diverse, and sociologists hold to a noncanonic approach to their field. (The ASA's book *Liberal Learning and the Sociology Major* is an example.) As a result, asking sociology faculty about their primary goals for the major leads to a common refrain: to prepare students in the sociological perspective (methods, theory, and concepts), to engage them in a sociological imagination applicable to a range of social phenomena. In short, the field emphasizes a process or mode of critical thinking, which service-learning can stimulate.

Sociologists stand before campus curriculum committees and argue for the value of a critical thinking/social science research approach for all students, regardless of major. A basic sociological view should be part of most students' college educations, especially in such a psychologically oriented culture as ours! While I sing this same song with enthusiasm myself, I look over my shoulder to assess the extent to which this perspective is being made available, intentionally and successfully, to the average undergraduate. While we may have a way to go, the goal is worthy, and service-learning is a key part of the repertoire.

Although sociology may not have a canon of core courses, there are key ideas in the field that are woven in most courses. Those ideas center on social inequality and concepts of power, privilege, and role across dimensions such as race, class, and gender. Such a reduction of the field to a few ideas is possible (and palatable) only because of their import. Social structure cannot be seen, and thus students learning about it must experience directly or indirectly its dimensions. Service-learning provides that opportunity to see how social location shapes so much of what occurs in our individual and collective experiences.

Service-learning provides access to social worlds that students may not otherwise encounter. Most service-learning projects place students in socially or economically disadvantaged locations, since those are the sites where service is sought. In this volume, Kerry Strand and other contributors note that such experiences (for privileged students in particular) may reinforce stereotypes as much as dispell them. I remain optimistic that direct experiences coupled with scientific research and reasoning is a good combination. Even for students who are "of" the group receiving the service, coming into the group in a different role (as a service provider/student) can give a different frame to one's own experience.

Three other opportunities where sociology students can excel are these: (1) to see social organization (rules, roles, and relationships) in what *appears* to be a situation of social disorganization; (2) to critically examine (off-site, of course) the agency or group providing the service in order to understand how social problems are addressed, who are the stakeholders, unintended consequences, and so forth; and (3) to use the service-learning experience as a vehicle to discuss the ethics of social research. In her preface, Judith Blau notes some of these issues, such as confidentiality, and the imperative for honest presentation of one's identity in a research situation.

There are many studies that indicate how internships and service-learning help sociology students with job skills. "Sociologist" is not a common job title, even for Ph.D. holders, outside the academy. Students need to sell their skills and experiences. The service-learning (or internship) situation encourages an analysis of what the student has done, with what results, and how the academic enterprise is applicable to real-world issues. Having this experience with "client-driven work," responding to what is needed, is an important developmental exercise for students. Working in teams, meeting deadlines, holding to responsibilities — all are important skills to hone.

Furthermore, sociology is a field that lends itself to several levels of involvement in service-learning. For the beginning student, simply serving in a setting and observing social behavior is valuable. The skill of describing phenomena, prior to analysis, is an important step for a junior social scientist. Collecting data, as part of service-learning, is a more advanced stage. Can you count the number of children coming to a day-care center and do a breakout by race and gender? Finally, service-learning in the form of community action research engages the more sophisticated student sociologist. It is at this point where we see sociological service-learning as more than being a good citizen, more than charity, and more than leadership development. Working with community groups on their agenda, in the role of a junior sociologist, demands and engenders professional talent that cannot be found in just any reliable volunteer.

How Might Service-Learning Fit Into National Conversations and Trends in Higher Education?

From my national perch, or catbird seat, here are several key topics I wonder about, and to which I hope to engage sociologists' input.

How can we institutionalize service-learning into faculty rewards? As we move to a broader view of scholarly work, we need to take care to evaluate and reward this wider span. How do we know effective service-learning in sociology when we see it? Do students learn more, as Garry Hesser suggests? How can we identify skilled faculty, and develop faculty from beginners to more-skilled service-learners? Do faculty need to undertake service-learning themselves in order to be able to use it as a pedagogy in their repertoire?

Sociologists need to attend to the negotiation of "service" with "learning." Richard Kendrick notes that sometimes one side of the equation is emphasized more than the other, or we strive for balance. I would add that sometimes they are slightly incompatible. While the purpose of service-learning is to enhance learning through service, service and learning are not one and the same. Faculty need to provide careful attention to their overlap. Perhaps any kind of service produces learning, but the sociologists in this book aspire to identify service sites and stimulate particular experiences so that particular educational outcomes are more likely. But because students are serving or helping, neither they nor the faculty member fully calls the shots about what will occur. Will 10 days of service at a juvenile detention center present hundreds of random surprises for students to interpret and from which to learn? Will the 20th day of service at a nursing home show any new events or lessons that the first did not provide? Or is that monotony in itself the lesson?

Sometimes there needs to be negotiation between the needs of the service provider and the goals for student learning. For example, a sociologist wants students to understand the differences between service delivery to homeless individuals and families in different sections of a large metropolitan area. She asks whether students can help hand out food from a "soup wagon" one night. The service provider agrees, but only if he can count on 10 students each night for at least three months. The faculty member, trying to engage the students in comparative experiences, also agrees but wants the individual students to move from one facility to another, helping at a different one each week during the semester. The comparative approach will generate more experiences, more data — but perhaps less useful service.

How do we move, developmentally, from a course to a curriculum? If service-learning, like hands-on research, is a valued skill for all sociology students, how do we build it into our curriculum? We must move service-learning (or any other particular educational goal or pedagogy) *from the charismatic individual to the collective department.* How can we ensure that a sabbatical leave, a faculty retirement, or a switch in teaching assignments won't purge a department of service-learning?

Departments need to reflect on how to integrate the goals and means of service-learning into their curriculum. And further, if service-learning is seen as developmental — from simple observation and description, to data collection and analysis, to community action research — then students must move through mastery of those phases.

Finally, sociologists can take the lead in looking at some of the unintended consequences of service-learning. For example, Jose Calderon has noted that this approach has aided in the retention of minority students who undertake service-learning in their own communities. They are both experts to other students and yet are learners, coming to their community in the role of student. Does service-learning achieve certain substantive goals more effectively than others?

Service-learning is the right topic to help sociologists to rediscover their disciplinary roots, to engage in the scholarship of teaching, to constructively reform their majors, and to enhance their leadership role within academia. This full-time partisan for sociology believes that this book, *Cultivating the Sociological Imagination*, helps propel such an ambitious agenda.

Bibliography

Sociology and Service-Learning

by Garry Hesser

Ansley, Fran, and John Gaventa. (January/February 1997). "Researching for Democracy & Democratizing Research." *Change* 29: 46-53.

> Discusses the questions "Whose voices are strengthened by university research?" and "Who participates in research in the first place?" Linking their work to a longer history of community-based research and providing lists and addresses of many of the current university-based collaborative community research centers, the authors build a strong case for community-based research as a contribution to linking American democracy and higher education.

Baker, Paul. (1980). "Inquiry Into the Teaching-Learning Process." *Teaching Sociology* 7: 237-245.

> One of the key leaders in the formation of the Undergraduate Teaching Section of the American Sociological Association spells out his rationale for the development of the "teacher-scholar" role, in which faculty members become involved and collaborate with their students in the teaching and learning enterprise. Without discussing service-learning, Baker provides a framework that supports experiential education/service-learning.

Bellah, Robert, Richard Madsen, William Sullivan, Ann Swidler, and Steve Tipton. (1985). *Habits of the Heart: Individualism and Commitment.* Berkeley, CA: University of California Press.

> A landmark book that provides a critical sociological context for a reexamination of the issues that have given rise to the interest in service-learning, especially the college and university presidents who founded Campus Compact and issues that have been central to the past decade of AAHE's conferences and priorities. An excellent book, along with the subsequent publications by its authors, for service-learning internship seminars and sociology courses that focus on service-learning and/or individualism and community.

The author is indebted to earlier efforts by Janet Luce and her NSEE colleagues (1988), who identified sources that formed the early foundation for service-learning and its resurgence in the 1980s.

Boros, Alex, and Raymond Adamek. (1981). "Developing Applied Sociology Programs." *Teaching Sociology* 8: 387-399.

Offers a rationale for a community-based sociology program that integrates applied and theoretical sociology.

Boyer, Ernest. (1990). *Scholarship Reconsidered: Priorities of the Professoriate.* Princeton, NJ: Carnegie Foundation for the Advancement of Teaching.

A now classic book that expanded the definition of scholarship to areas beyond research ("discovery") to include "application," "integration," and teaching. Has become the basis for much of the dialogue and discussion of role of "the New American College."

―――― . (March 9, 1994). "Creating the New American College." *Chronicle of Higher Education*: A48.

An educational leader's articulate call for colleges and universities to celebrate teaching and selectively support research while also taking special pride in their capacity to connect thought to action, theory to practice.

Bradfield, C.D. (1992). "Introductory Sociology." In *Education and Action: A Guide to Integrating Classrooms and Communities,* edited by T.M. Lieberman and K. Connolly, pp. 198-203. St. Paul, MN: Campus Outreach Opportunity League.

Bradfield's syllabus represents one of the early efforts to integrate a service-learning component into an introductory sociology course at a major university. The entire book was produced by COOL staff, who had been student leaders in the effort to integrate community service into courses and the academic objectives of faculty.

Bryant, Bunyan. (1993). "Detroit Summer: A Model for Service-Learning." In *Praxis I: A Faculty Casebook on Community Service-Learning,* edited by J. Howard, pp. 67-74. Ann Arbor, MI: OCSL Press, University of Michigan.

Emphasizing "learning how to learn rather than facts and theories," this article describes an immersion program and the process of "extracting meaning from the experience," using seminar formats, critical questions, and journals.

Calderon, Jose, and Betty Farrell. (1996). "Doing Sociology: Connecting the Classroom Experience With a Multiethnic School District." *Teaching Sociology* 24: 46-53.

Describes an innovative undergraduate sociology course in which students assist in the development and teaching of a multicultural curriculum to high school students in a Los Angeles school district undergoing rapid demographic change. This engages students in participant observation research and provides one model for service-learning linking the community and the classroom. The authors describe the origin and organization of the Pitzer College project in the Alhambra School District, and address a number of structural and substantive challenges that emerge in teaching a community-based course.

Chesler, Mark. (1993). "Community Service-Learning as Innovation in the University." In *Praxis I: A Faculty Casebook on Community Service-Learning,* edited by J. Howard, pp. 27-40. Ann Arbor, MI: OCSL Press, University of Michigan.

Describes a 15-year relationship between the Michigan sociology department and the Office of Community Service-Learning, with a particular focus on Soc 389: Practicum in Sociology (Project Community), which combines student service in community institutions, experiential learning, and academic growth. Article describes the program and some of the problems encountered in its ongoing implementation.

Chickering, Arthur, and Associates. (1981). *The Modern American College: Responding to the New Realities of Diverse Students and a Changing Society.* San Francisco, CA: Jossey-Bass.

Describes the needs of today's students and implications for college curricula and instructional strategies, indirectly making a case for service-learning as a means for meeting curricular objectives and as a response to some of the needs of today's students.

Cohen, Lorraine. (1995). "Facilitating the Critique of Racism and Classism: An Experiential Model for Euro-American Middle-Class Students." *Teaching Sociology* 23: 87-93.

A course called Community Tutoring made visible and real the structural oppression affecting persons of color and women, who were often attacked and marginalized. The professor and a text by African-American scholars, building upon the four-hour-a-week tutoring of students deemed at risk by their teachers, enabled students to see and analyze their own privilege and critically reflect upon social justice and the impact of race and class.

Coleman, James. (February 1972). "The Children Have Outgrown the Schools." *Psychology Today*: 72-82.

Spells out how important experiential education was to Coleman and how carefully he had thought through its role in the educational process and the educational institution and its reform. Gives a context for his ASA Presidential Address (see Coleman 1993) and role on the Presidential Advisory Panel (see Coleman 1974).

————. (December 1972). "How Do the Young Become Adults?" *Phi Delta Kappan* 54(4): 226-230.

Delineates his understanding of the socialization process and its connection to epistemology, and the importance and validity of experiential learning to the overall educational enterprise.

————. (1977). "Differences Between Experiential and Classroom Learning." In *Experiential Learning: Rationale, Characteristics, and Assessment*, edited by Morris Keeton, pp. 49-61. San Francisco, CA: Jossey-Bass.

Most sociologists are unaware of Coleman's important role, along with Keeton, in articulating a theoretically and empirically supported rationale for experiential learning as a needed complement to classroom learning.

————. (1993). "The Rational Reconstruction of Society." *American Sociological Review* 58(1): 1-15.

Coleman's 1992 Presidential Address, focusing upon the "Great Transformation," which he characterizes by the decline of primordial institutions based on the family as the central element of social organization and the replacement of these institutions by purposively constructed organization. The latter has been accompanied by a loss of informal social capital on which social control depended. Coleman introduces an example, "bounties on children," to illustrate how sociology can contribute to the design of purposive organization.

————, et al. (1974). *Youth: Transition to Adulthood*. Chicago, IL: University of Chicago Press.

This report of the President's Advisory Committee addressing the question of "appropriate environments in which youth can best grow into adults" presents one of the strongest arguments for inclusion of service activities as a necessary element in the growth process, including specific proposals for public service for youth 16 or older.

Corwin, Patricia. (July 1996). "Using the Community as a Classroom for Large Introductory Sociology Classes." *Teaching Sociology* 24: 310-315.
Discusses how a student service program can be implemented without a large staff and without cost. Service-learning gives students a chance to explore sociological concepts in action and enables the instructor to use relevant examples, in lectures, from volunteer experiences shared by students. Explains how service experiences enhance classroom discussion, and fosters debate about social issues growing out of involvement in five sites.

Crawford, Isaiah, Anne Figert, Yolanda Suarez-Balcazar, Philip Nyden, and Jill Reich. (1996). "The Use of Research Participation for Mentoring Prospective Minority Graduate Students." *Teaching Sociology* 24: 256-263.
Forty undergraduate students of color were identified and recruited to participate in year-long research projects related to the quality of life in urban communities. Each participating faculty member had three to four students, with the summer stipend allowing students and faculty to fully engage in the research process, including weekly seminars together to discuss policy implications along with the literature and methodology of research.

Daly, Kathleen. (1993). "Field Research: A Complement for Service-Learning." In *Praxis I: A Faculty Casebook on Community Service-Learning*, edited by J. Howard, pp. 85-96. Ann Arbor, MI: OCSL Press, University of Michigan.
Before coming to Michigan, Daly taught sociology at SUNY-Albany and Yale. The article describes an upper-division criminology course involving firsthand observation of criminal court proceedings and learning how to systematically observe and collect information to be compared with literature in the field.

Dewey, John. (1963). *Experience and Education*. New York, NY: Collier.
The "elder statesman" of experiential education attacks the false dichotomy between thought and action, and recommends goal-directed activity as a continuous process of "reconstruction of experience." Dewey's theses should remind service-learning faculty that experiences can also be miseducative. Therefore, structures and methods for reflecting upon those service experiences are as important as the experience itself. This suggests that course-embedded service-learning and internship seminars are critical in order for the experience to be educative.

Divinski, R., A. Hubbard, J.R. Kendrick, and J. Noll. (1994). "Social Change as Applied Social Science: Obstacles to Integrating the Roles of Activist and Academic." *Peace and Change* 19: 3-24.

Examines the obstacles to reconciling the conflicting roles of academic and activist, arguing that the most difficult barriers to overcome exist in the academic world, but recognizing that there are barriers to integration in the domain of social movement organizations, too. The article concludes with ideas for how activist academics can further integrate their roles in order to create a social science of social change.

Ender, Morten, Brenda Kowalewski, David Cotter, Lee Martin, and JoAnn DeFiore, eds. (1996). *Service-Learning and Undergraduate Sociology: Syllabi and Instructional Materials*. Washington, DC: American Sociological Association.

Among ASA's "resource materials for teaching," the book contains syllabi from a wide variety of courses, articles on service-learning and sociology, sociology courses on service-learning itself, and a bibliography. Among its many strengths as a resource is its emphasis upon a wide continuum of service-learning in sociology, ranging from service experiences embedded in regular courses, sociology courses with service-learning as a focus, field study, and internships.

Etzioni, Amitai. (1993). *The Spirit of Community*. New York, NY: Random House.

Etzioni elaborates upon his understanding and advocacy of a "communitarian" approach to sociology and social policy.

Freire, Paulo. (1973). *Education for Critical Consciousness*. New York, NY: Seabury Press.

Rather than a "banking" method, in which instructors deposit knowledge and skills in students, Freire sees education as a dialogue through which teachers and students examine their life experience and develop reflective and literacy skills needed for such examination. Freire's philosophy and sociological perspective provoke service-learning practitioners to examine the outcomes and context of their practice, with a focus on making the experience empowering for the learner as well as those to be served.

————. (1985). *The Politics of Education: Culture, Power, and Liberation.* South Hadley, MA: Bergin & Garvey.

A theoretically and politically challenging work that incorporates the language of critique with the language of possibility. In the spirit of "structuration" and the sociological perspective, Freire views history as never foreclosed; just as the actions of persons are limited by the specific constraints in which they find themselves, they also make those constraints and the possibilities that they may follow by challenging them.

Furco, Andrew. (1996). "Service-Learning: A Balanced Approach to Experiential Education." In *Building Connections: Expanding Boundaries — Service and Learning,* edited by B. Taylor, pp. 2-6. Columbia, MD: Cooperative Education Association.

Builds on Sigmon's "SERVICE-LEARNING" typology to distinguish between a collection of various types of experiential education and their relationship to service-learning and each other.

Galura, Joe, and Jeffrey Howard, eds. (1995). *Praxis III: Voices in Dialogue.* Ann Arbor, MI: OCSL Press, University of Michigan.

Continuation of excellent series of faculty and community partners involved in the University of Michigan service-learning program, one of the best-established programs in a major research university involving the sociology department as a central keystone.

Galura, Joe, Rachel Meiland, Randy Ross, Mary Jo Callan, and Rick Smith, eds. (1993). *Praxis II: Service-Learning Resources for University Students, Staff, and Faculty.* Ann Arbor, MI: OCSL Press, University of Michigan.

As the title suggests, this volume is filled with curricular materials for use by faculty, including a major section by the senior editor and Mark Chesler, professor of sociology at Michigan (pp. 83-206), consisting of 14 curricular modules for the sociology department's practicum Project Community (Soc 389). Also includes a journal workshop, community-building exercises for classes, and other helpful teaching and learning materials. Another major section (pp. 207-340) discusses in detail service-learning projects affiliated with Michigan's Sociology 389 course.

Gamson, Zelda F. (January/February 1997). "Higher Education and Rebuilding Civic Life." *Change* 29: 10-13.

> As a sociologist who has played a key role in experiential education and service-learning, Gamson concludes that the commitment to community service on the part of colleges and universities is lip service. She concludes that the conditions that would encourage more than just the very committed faculty do not exist on most campuses, and argues that higher education needs to rebuild its own civic life and learn from communities that are doing just that.

Gaventa, John. (1993). "The Powerful, the Powerless, and the Experts: Knowledge Struggles in an Information Age." In *Voices of Change: Participatory Research in the United States and Canada,* edited by Peter Park et al., pp. 20-38. Westport, CT: Bergin & Garvey.

> Gaventa is a sociologist long associated with Myles Horton and the Highlander community and its community organizing and training efforts established by Horton. Gaventa is now teaching and continuing to do participatory action research in Tennessee. He is an active member of the Invisible College.

Giles, Dwight. (1994). "The Impact of a College Service Laboratory on Students' Personal, Social, and Cognitive Outcomes." *Journal of Adolescence* 17: 327-339.

> Examines the impact of a required service element of limited duration and scope on the social responsibility of college students. Found that student perceptions of clients were more empathetic after service and that they were more likely to attribute problems to circumstances beyond the control of clients. Self-reports revealed increased understanding of social problems (knowing), as well as the value of community service itself.

————, and Janet Eyler. (1994). "The Theoretical Roots of Service-Learning in John Dewey: Toward a Theory of Service-Learning." *Michigan Journal of Community Service-Learning* 1: 77-85.

> The authors link aspects of John Dewey's educational and social philosophy to the development of a theory of service-learning, including experiential learning, reflection, citizenship, community, and democracy.

Giles, Dwight, and J.B. Freed. (1985). *The Service-Learning Dimensions of Field Study: The Cornell Human Ecology Field Study Program.* Raleigh, NC: National Society for Experiential Education.

Presents four dimensions of service-learning and applies them to field study as a method of education. Emphasizes prefield courses as a starting point for developing field study that is fully integrated into the curriculum of the academic department.

Giles, Dwight, Ellen Porter Honnet, and Sally Migliore. (1991). *Research Agenda for Combining Service and Learning in the 1990s.* Raleigh, NC: National Society for Experiential Education.

Beginning with this collaboration with the Johnson Foundation (Wingspread), Giles and other sociologists have led the way in framing and articulating a research agenda for research on the many dimensions of service-learning.

Gizelokowski, K.P. (1986). "Merging the Theoretical and the Practical: A Community Action Learning Model." *Teaching Sociology* 14: 110-118.

Presents an alternative, integrated experiential model for introducing fieldwork to sociology students. This model challenges conventional sociology by merging sociology with community action for social change.

Gladchild, Pat. (1996). *Bridging Two Worlds: NPCR Program Evaluation Final Report (1993-1996).* Minneapolis, MN: Center for Urban and Regional Affairs.

The results of a three-year evaluation of Neighborhood Planning for Community Revitalization, which has engaged more than 100 students and a half-dozen faculty in community-based collaborative research. Provides an excellent overview of how the program has been structured and funded as a consortium, feedback on the first three years, and recommendations for sociology departments considering this form of service-learning.

Gondolf, Edward. (1980). "Learning in the Community." *Teaching Sociology* 7: 127-140.

Offers a rationale for a community-based sociology program that integrates applied and theoretical sociology.

Harkavy, Ira, and John Puckett. (1995). "The Action Research Tradition in American Social Science: Toward a Strategy for Revitalizing the Social Sciences, the University, and the American City." Trondheim, Norway, and Stockholm, Sweden: Scandinavian Action Research Development Program (ACRES).

Documents the long-standing, but often forgotten and/or denied, practice of research that has been done in active partnership and collaboration with neighborhood activists and public agencies. Their history reminds social scientists and historians of our roots and the powerful catalytic effect of "action research," as well as its validity. The authors explore the potential of action research for the rejuvenation of the academy in the service of the communities in which we are located.

Hassett, John, and Hugh Lacey, eds. (1991). *Towards a Society That Serves Its People*. Washington, DC: Georgetown University Press.

Celebrates the lives of Fathers Ignacio Ellacuria, Ignacio Martin-Baro, and Segundo Montes, who were killed in El Salvador during their quest for social justice grounded in a theology of liberation.

Hesser, Garry. (1990). *Experiential Education as a Liberating Art*. Raleigh, NC: National Society for Experiential Education.

Integrates the research on effective teaching and learning by Cross, Gamson, McKeachie, Kolb, and others, and builds a case for the value of redesigning undergraduate education to include service-learning and other forms of experiential, field-based education into the heart of the curriculum because of service-learning's intrinsic value to conceptual and overall learning outcomes.

——— . (Fall 1995). "Faculty Assessment of Student Learning: Outcomes Attributed to Service-Learning and Evidence of Changes in Faculty Attitudes About Experiential Education." *Michigan Journal of Community Service-Learning* 2: 33-42.

Study exploring faculty assessment of the quality of student learning associated with service-learning reveals that faculty find improved learning outcomes when they incorporated a service-learning component in traditional courses. Examines the evidence that might explain why faculty attitudes toward and practice of experiential education have changed so dramatically in the past decade.

Hondagneu-Sotelo, Pirette, and Sally Raskoff. (1994). "Community Service-Learning: Promises and Problems." *Teaching Sociology* 22: 248-254.

Offers a rationale for a community-based sociology program that integrates applied and theoretical sociology, with a service-learning dimension. Asserts that community service holds the potential to enhance the sociology curriculum, but also discusses the challenges and difficulties that arise when trying to integrate academic content with community experience.

Howard, Jeffrey, ed. (1993). *Praxis I: A Faculty Casebook on Community Service-Learning.* Ann Arbor, MI: OCSL Press, University of Michigan.

As the title suggests, this book includes principles of service-learning and 11 case studies of undergraduate courses across the disciplines, including two by sociologists and others by social scientists, plus four graduate courses, all in applied social science. Howard has played a major role in conceptualizing and disseminating service-learning among faculty while building an effective program at a major research institution.

Jacoby, Barbara, et al. (1996). *Service-Learning in Higher Education: Concepts and Practices.* San Francisco, CA: Jossey-Bass.

Jacoby and 15 higher education faculty, deans, and service-learning professionals spell out the most current theory and practice, with examples from many campuses. A comprehensive guide to developing quality experiences in curricular and student affairs programs. Describes and provides contact information for national organizations that support service-learning and resources that are useful in postcollege service and career choices.

Kelly, Dierdre M. (1993). "Secondary Power Source: High School Students as Participatory Researchers." *American Sociologist* 24(1): 8-26.

Discusses conditions that foster and hinder participatory research, using examples from a project aimed at dropout reduction among students in a "last-chance" California high school. Concludes that youths need to be taken seriously as knowers and potential agents of change, and that adults who work with adolescent researchers need to model democratic teaching and leadership.

Kendall, Jane, and Associates, eds. (1990). *Combining Service and Learning: A Resource Book for Community and Public Service.* 2 vols. Raleigh, NC: National Society for Experiential Education.

The single most useful service-learning resource published to date, with more than 1,000 pages and 200 articles and case descriptions concerning combining service and learning. The editors' assessment of programs and history leads to their conclusion that service-learning worthy of the label will be integrated into the central mission and goals of educational institutions, establish a balance of power between educational and community partners, and wed reflection to experience, including reflection utilizing the concepts and methods of the disciplines and a liberal education. Kendall was one of the most influential and effective leaders who contributed to and helped shape the current interest in service-learning, both as executive director of NSEE and editor of these volumes.

Kendall, Jane, John Duley, Thomas Little, Jane Permaul, and Sharon Rubin. (1986). *Strengthening Experiential Education Within Your Institution.* Raleigh, NC: National Society for Experiential Education.

Created out of an ongoing FIPSE project to provide institution building and organization development consulting to colleges and universities, this book represents a "theory-practice-theory" outcome from the dialogues and learning that took place during the collaboration's first three years. A source book for those seeking to institutionalize experiential education, it also introduces the reader to five of the most influential leaders and practitioners who shaped the resurgence of service-learning in the 1980s and 1990s.

Kendrick, J.R., Jr. (Fall 1996). "Outcomes of Service-Learning in an Introduction to Sociology Course." *Michigan Journal of Community Service-Learning* 3: 72-81.

Explores the effects of service-learning on Introduction to Sociology students by comparing students in a service-learning course with students in a more traditionally taught format. Concludes that students in the service-learning course showed greater improvement in measures of social responsibility and personal efficacy, and greater ability to apply course concepts to new situations.

Kolb, David. (1984). *Experiential Education: Experience as the Source of Learning and Development.* Englewood Cliffs, NJ: Prentice-Hall.

One of the first prominent organizational behavior scholars to theoretically and empirically document the evidence to support the theoretical assumptions of Dewey, Piaget, Lewin, and Freire regarding the claim that learning is the process whereby knowledge is created through the transformation of experience. Kolb's model is widely utilized by service-learning faculty in the design of service-learning and describes the sequence of experiential learning as a continuous cycle that includes experience, reflection, generalization, and application of theory to new practice.

Kretzmann, John, and John McKnight. (1993). *Building Communities From the Inside Out: A Path Toward Finding and Mobilizing a Community's Assets.* Evanston, IL: Center for Urban Affairs and Policy Research, Northwestern University.

Building upon their work at Northwestern University and the undergraduate urban studies program of the Associated Colleges of the Midwest in Chicago, Kretzmann and McKnight have become leading theorists informing service-learning practitioners. Their emphasis upon "finding and mobilizing a community's assets" has challenged the university's tendency to "invade" communities to document or fix problems. They have challenged service-learning to be collaborative and follow the lead of the community in supporting its assets, doing no harm, and not creating dependencies.

Kupiec, T., ed. (1993). *Rethinking Tradition: Integrating Service With Academic Study on College Campuses.* Denver, CO: Education Commission of the States and Campus Compact.

Edited collection focusing on the philosophy and practice of service-learning. Includes essays on the institutionalization of service-learning, pedagogy, program evaluation, assessment of student outcomes, and other topics. The volume features a collection of syllabi from courses in sociology and other disciplines.

Lena, Hugh. (Winter 1995). "How Can Sociology Contribute to Integrating Service-Learning Into Academic Curricula?" *American Sociologist* 26: 107-117.

> Argues that sociology can make a unique contribution to the integration of service experiences into the academic content of courses across the curriculum. By virtue of its theoretical, conceptual, methodological, and pedagogical legacies, sociology contributes to an understanding of the potential and promise of community service for academic inquiry. The article describes a unique venture in which an interdisciplinary team of faculty and students designed a major and a minor in Public and Community Service Studies making extensive use of sociological concepts and methodology.

Luce, Janet, Jennifer Anderson, Jane Permaul, Robert Shumer, Timothy Stanton, and Sally Migliore. (1988). *Service-Learning: An Annotated Bibliography Linking Public Service With the Curriculum.* Raleigh, NC: National Society for Experiential Education.

> A useful reference source for materials that formed the intellectual and research base for the resurgence of interest in and commitment to service-learning in the 1980s.

Lynd, Helen. (1945). *Field Work in College Education.* New York, NY: Columbia University Press.

> This "lost" book by a prominent sociologist is an in-depth analysis of the contribution of field experience education in the liberal arts curriculum of Sarah Lawrence College. Field studies were a large component of that curriculum in the late 1930s. The entire college was committed to involving students directly in the practice of the social sciences and to dealing with the social needs of its immediate environment in Yonkers. Lynd names seven purposes of liberal arts education that are well served by field education, and documents her claims with data from case studies of courses and individuals. She also reports on the importance of field experience in helping students develop skills in higher levels of cognitive thinking, observation, and generalizing from field study, and the overall skills of acquiring and using knowledge. Lynd's research documents what a new generation of researchers are finding, namely, that enabling students to test their theoretical knowledge and relate it to actual situations through fieldwork fosters intellectual integrity and strengthens students intellectually.

Markus, Gregory, Jeffrey Howard, and David King. (1993). "Integrating Community Service and Classroom Instruction Enhances Learning: Results From an Experiment." *Educational Evaluation and Policy Analysis* 15(4): 410-419.

An empirical assessment using an experimental design to measure the differential learning that can be attributed to a service-learning component in a social science class (political science) at the University of Michigan. Evidence supports the claim that conceptual as well as other positive outcomes result from a service-learning approach to teaching and learning.

Marullo, Sam. (1996). "The Service-Learning Movement in Higher Education: An Academic Response to Troubled Times." *Sociological Imagination* 33(2): 117-137.

Service-learning movement frames, resource mobilization, and the emergence of the movement are analyzed. The role of sociology is examined in the movement's mobilization and emergence. Argues that service-learning should be critical of the status quo, challenge unjust structures and oppressive institutional operations, and provide an opportunity for institutionalizing social justice activism on college campuses.

McGowan, Thomas, and Sara Blankenship. (1994). "Intergenerational Experience and Ontological Change." *Educational Gerontology* 20: 589-604.

Uses the phenomenological concept of change in self-understanding to structure an analysis of the experiential impact of college-based intergenerational service-learning project. Content analysis of students' journals indicated that students participated in a variety of experiences, with phenomenological theory providing insight and a framework for assessing the impact of program participation.

Mintz, Suzanne, and Garry Hesser. (1996). "Principles of Good Practice in Service-Learning." In *Service-Learning in Higher Education*, edited by Barbara Jacoby, pp. 26-52. San Francisco, CA: Jossey-Bass.

A sociologist and colleague with a background in student affairs review and synthesize the major "principles of good practice in service-learning." They emphasize collaboration, reciprocity, and diversity as "lenses" of a kaleidoscope by which to design and through which to assess and revise our practices in combining service and learning in higher education.

Nyden, Phil, Joanne Adams, and Kim Zalent. (1997). "Creating and Sustaining Racially and Ethnically Diverse Communities." In *Building Community: Social Science in Action*, edited by Philip Nyden, Anne Figert, Mark Shibley, and Darryl Burrows, pp. 32-41. Thousand Oaks, CA: Pine Forge Press.

> Discusses a six-year partnership of community organizers and university-based researchers working side by side in seeking ways to strengthen links across different racial, ethnic, and income groups in two of the most diverse communities in the United States. Reports from this project have focused on housing, business development, interreligious cooperation, and the needs of youth, often influencing local social services and local and national public policy.

Nyden, Philip, Anne Figert, Mark Shibley, and Darryl Burrows, eds. (1997). *Building Community: Social Science in Action.* Thousand Oaks, CA: Pine Forge Press.

> Four sociologists have outlined and discussed a rationale and effective models for "university-community collaborative research," including significant attention to the value and importance of including undergraduate sociology students through classes, internships, and research colleagues as part of Loyola's Center for Urban Research and Learning. Includes 27 case studies of community-based collaborative research.

Ostrow, James. (1994). "Sticking to Our Principles in Research." *NSEE Quarterly* 19: 4-5, 28-29.

> The author defends the scientific strength of an interpretive focus on immediate experience in educational research. He argues that the focus on measurement in many methods of inquiry sacrifices opportunities to understand and formulate more clearly what is allegedly measured.

———. (1995). "Self-Consciousness and Social Position: On College Students Changing Their Minds About the Homeless." *Qualitative Sociology* 18(3): 359-377.

> The author locates certain patterns of experience lying at the heart of students' claims to have changed their minds about the homeless after visiting homeless shelters and meal programs. He analyzes these patterns through an exploration of the relationship between self-consciousness and social position.

Palmer, Parker. (September/October 1987). "Community, Conflict, and Ways of Knowing: Ways to Deepen Our Educational Agendas." *Change* 19: 20-25.

Originally an address delivered at the 1987 AAHE National Conference on Higher Education, in which this sociologist and educational theorist argues that if the academy is to contribute to the reweaving of community, then objectivism — the dominant epistemology in higher education — must be countered/balanced in a way that emphasizes the generation and transmission of knowledge through ways of knowing that form an inward capacity for relatedness, which objectivism tends to destroy. Palmer has also become an articulate spokesperson and supportive critic of service-learning in higher education.

Parilla, Peter, and Garry Hesser. (1998). "The Value of Internships for Student Development." In *The Internship Handbook: Development and Administration of Internship Programs in Sociology,* edited by Richard Salem and Barbara Altman, pp. 45-64. Washington, DC: American Sociological Association.

Outlines the educational and developmental outcomes and advantages to sociology students and curriculum from field experience and experiential education, including service-learning internships. A complement to the authors' 1998 publication "Internships and the Sociological Perspective: Applying Principles of Experiential Education" (*Teaching Sociology* 26[4]: 310-329).

Park, Peter. (1993). "What Is Participatory Research? A Theoretical and Methodological Perspective." In *Voices of Change: Participatory Research in the United States and Canada,* edited by Peter Park et al., pp. 1-19. Westport, CT: Bergin & Garvey.

A leading sociologist spells out a conceptual framework and methodological rationale for participatory action research in the introduction to a volume containing articles and essays by leading practitioners of participatory research.

Parker-Gwin, Rachel. (1996). "Connecting Service to Learning: How Students and Communities Matter." *Teaching Sociology* 24: 97-101.

Explores and underscores the importance of collaboration and reciprocity in the design of service-learning as part of the sociology curriculum.

Pestello, Frances, Dan Miller, Stanley Saxton, and Patrick Donnelly. (1996). "Community and the Practice of Sociology." *Teaching Sociology* 24: 148-156.
>Presents a community-based model for undergraduate sociology education that employs the concept of "citizen-scholar." Citizen-scholars integrate their academic activities of teaching, research, and service into a coordinated whole. Includes reflections on how this model has affected the teaching, research, and service activities at the University of Dayton.

Petras, Elizabeth M., and Douglas Porpora. (1993). "Research: Three Models and an Analysis." *American Sociologist* 24(1): 107-124.
>Examines three models of participatory research: parallel process, mutual engagement, and the University of Central America (UCA) model. Tensions that may arise between service and scholarship are discussed. It is concluded that participatory research must provide a spectrum of theory, methods, and substance that sociologists find of importance, independent of the way that such contributions are generated.

Porter, Judith, and Lisa Schwartz. (1993). "Experiential Service-Based Learning: An Integrated HIV/AIDS Education Model for College Campuses." *Teaching Sociology* 21: 409-415.
>Describes and evaluates an innovative combined experiential and classroom learning approach to teaching the sociology of AIDS at Bryn Mawr College. Sociological theories for explaining aspects of epidemiology and other dimensions are tested and demonstrated.
>Volunteering, in conjunction with formal coursework, promotes a visceral learning experience, stimulates research, and reveals limitations of health belief models.

Reardon, Kenneth. (1989). "Public Markets and Urban Social Life." In *Contemporary Readings in Sociology*, edited by Judith DeSena, pp. 135-145. Dubuque, IA: Kendall-Hall.
>Describes the use of field research (participatory action research) done in New York City as part of Cornell University's Urban Studies semester program. This particular study was done in collaboration with the vendors at the Essex Street Market and is one of the most powerful examples of community-based collaborative service-learning research.

————. (Fall 1994). "Undergraduate Research in Distressed Urban Communities: An Undervalued Form of Service-Learning." *Michigan Journal of Community Service-Learning* 1: 44-54.

Describes two participatory action research projects completed by undergraduates for community-based organizations in New York City that dramatically affected municipal economic development and affordable housing policies in two low-income minority communities.

————. (1997). "Participatory Action Research and Real Community-Based Planning in East St. Louis, Illinois." In *Building Community: Social Science in Action*, edited by Philip Nyden, Anne Figert, Mark Shibley, and Darryl Burrows, pp. 233-239. Thousand Oaks, CA: Pine Forge Press.

Describes an elaborate university-community partnership that leveraged significant university resources to assist one of the poorest communities in the Midwest. With the blessing of the university president, faculty and students forged relationships with community organizations. Stung by past false promises from the university, community leaders took time to become involved in this new process. A comprehensive planning process, the development of a curriculum for community leaders, and implementation of the process are described and discussed.

Rice, R. Eugene. (1991). "The New American Scholar: Scholarship and the Purposes of the University." *Metropolitan Universities* 1: 7-18.

A leading sociologist and educational leader links the work that he and Boyer did to rethink the various types of scholarship to the process of reexamining the role of faculty and the university/college in its
· engagement with the wider community and society. Rice has also played an important role in faculty workshops on combining service and learning.

Schön, Donald. (1983). *The Reflective Practitioner*. New York, NY: Basic Books.

Schön examines varied professions to illustrate how professionals go about solving problems, and suggests that effective problem solving relies less on formal education and more on improvisation learned in practice, "reflection in practice." This becomes an excellent theory and description of an approach to the sociological practice of service-learning.

———. (1987). *Educating the Reflective Practitioner*. San Francisco, CA: Jossey-Bass.

By a professor of city and urban planning, this and the previous volume, though not specifically concerned with service-learning, provide an excellent linkage between grounded theory and the theory espoused in disciplines. An early and influential theorist in the faculty development emphasis upon experiential education and promoting engagement in learning, Schön focuses on how to combine the higher knowledge of research-based, scientific rationality with the "mired" knowledge of working in the professional world. Schön calls for a "reflective practicum" aimed at helping students acquire the kinds of "artistry essential to competence in the indeterminate zones of practice."

Schultz, Steven. (1990). "Learning by Heart: The Role of Action in Civic Education." In *Combining Service and Learning: A Resource Book for Community and Public Service*, Vol. 1, edited by J. Kendall and Associates, pp. 210-224. Raleigh, NC: National Society for Experiential Education.

Internships, field experiences, and other action learning directed toward helping students become active and effective participants in public life are the author's preferred forms of service-learning. Schultz suggests that in order to fulfill its civic purposes, education must bring together both the classical and experiential modes of learning, and must begin by renewing civic community within the academy itself.

Sigmon, Robert. (1973). "North Carolina: Early Leader in Service-Learning." In *Service-Learning in the South: Higher Education and Public Service*, edited by Robert Sigmon, pp. 23-30. Atlanta, GA: Southern Regional Education Board.

This essay should remind readers of the earlier histories of service-learning, particularly the statewide internship programs, urban corps, and urban studies programs that arose in the late 1960s and early 1970s. Sociology faculty across the nation played key roles in supporting students in programs such as these, as well as the 1972 University Year of Action.

———. (1979). "Service-Learning: Three Principles." *Synergist* 8: 9-11.

Perhaps no practitioner of service-learning has contributed more to the field than the author of this "early" essay, which discusses three fundamental principles and strategies to put them into practice. The principles stress that those being served control the services provided, that those being served become better able to serve and be served by their own actions, and that those who serve also are learners and have significant control over what is expected to be learned.

Stanton, Timothy. (1990). *Integrating Public Service With Academic Study: The Faculty Role.* Providence, RI: Campus Compact.

One of the most important documents by one of the most influential leaders in the service-learning field. Stanton's work at Cornell in the College of Human Ecology, with the National Society for Experiential Learning, and at Stanford gave credence to the wisdom of this publication, which many think shaped the direction and strategy of Campus Compact and the entire field of service-learning.

Stoecker, Randy. (1997). "The Imperfect Practice of Collaborative Research: The 'Working Group on Neighborhoods' in Toledo, Ohio." In *Building Community: Social Science in Action,* edited by Philip Nyden, Anne Figert, Mark Shibley, and Darryl Burrows, pp. 219-225. Thousand Oaks, CA: Pine Forge Press.

A sociologist discusses what happens when an initially cooperative project turns adversarial and factionalized. Helpful lessons in what to avoid when engaged in collaborative community-university research projects.

Appendix

Three Sample Syllabi

Sociology 380   Workshop in Sociology
Wednesday 4:00 - 6:50   Professor Enos
sweetfern@ids.net   456-8026

This course will provide students with an opportunity to apply social research
skills in the context of performing community service. We will explore issues
related to homelessness, family violence and criminal justice combining field
experience and scholarly work in these areas. Objectives here are to gain
familiarity with social problems and social responses, to learn about their
communities as social scientists and to examine relationships among individuals,
families, organizations and the state.

Requirements and grading

Final Paper	30%	
Site visit reports		10%
Final product		20%
Special reports	30%	
Communities & higher education		10%
Civic arts		10%
Community study		10%
Journaling/field notes	10%	
Class presentations	10%	
Class participation	10%	
Final reflection essay	10%	

Students are required in this course to be involved in field work, preferably work
that involves service to the community. Community here is broadly defined. The
final paper will provide the student with an opportunity to examine and present
what has been learned in the field. This final project will link field knowledge to
an appropriate literature in sociology.

Materials - Purchase a three ring binder to hold articles and other handouts.
You will need to purchase a separate notebook or create a system to take field
notes. These will be collected and responded to three times over the semester.
**Also, at the end of the semester, you will submit all the work you have done
over the semester as a collection.**

Articles on reserve Articles will be on reserve at the library. Please obtain a
picture ID so you may take these out.

E-mail and the internet I will be providing a list of helpful and interesting
internet resources so you can learn what other students are doing in these sorts
of courses nationwide.

Class participation is required. We have limited enrollment to 20 in this class so that we can employ a seminar design. This means that success of the learning opportunity depends on you and your fellow students. This course has been designed to surface some important and controversial topics. I do not expect or desire universal agreement by all students. I do expect respect of each others' opinions, positions and rights to learn and grow. You should come to class having read all the assigned material.

Required texts:
Nyden, Philip et al. 1997. Building a Community: Social Science in Action. Thousand Oaks CA: Pine Forge Press.

Coles, Robert. 1993. The Call of Service. Boston: Houghton Mifflin Company.

Jorgenson, Danny L. 1989. Participant Observation: A methodology for Human Studies

On Reserve
Fisher, Nadler and Alagna. "Recipient Reactions to Aid." Psychological Bulletin 91(1) 27-54.

Putnam, Robert. "Bowling Alone: America's Declining Social Capital." Journal of Democracy Volume 6, No. 1 January 1995.

Ramos, Francisco Martins. "My American Glasses." In Philip DeVita and James D. Armstrong Distant Mirrors: America as a Foreign Culture. Belmont, CA: Wadsworth Publishing.

Bunis, William K., Angela Yancik, and David A. Snow. 1996. "The Cultural Patterning of Sympathy Toward the Homeless and Other Victims of Misfortune." Social Problems, 43:4, 387-402.

Hursh, Barbara. 1981. "Learning Through Questioning in Field Programs." In Lenore Borzak (Editor) Field Study: A Sourcebook for Experiential Education. Thousand Oaks, CA: Sage Publications.

Steele, Shelby. 1990. "I'm Black, You're White, Who's Innocent? The Content of Our Character." New York: St., Martin's Press.

Bellah, Robert. 1985. Habits of the Heart. Los Angeles CA: University of California Press.

Anspach, Renee R. 1991. "Everyday Methods for Assessing Organizational Effectiveness." Social Problems 38(1), 1-19.

Walker, Alice. 1997. <u>Anything We Love Can Be Saved: A Writer's Activism</u>. New York: Ballantine Books. Introduction, xxi-xxv.

Special Reports
Community and College Lecture and discussion; the role of the college and university in the larger society; What is the purpose of higher education? How is RIC involved in the community? What community service is provided by departments, faculty, clubs, administration, programs etc.? Is this a formal arrangement?

Assignment: Prepare a report no longer than three pages in length describing a program or highlighting an individual at RIC that serves the community in some manner. In this report, identify the program, describe projects, leadership, include a brief discussion of history and learn/analyze motivations. Should activities like this be expanded? What rewards accrue to the community? to those involved as providers? What does the community teach? These will be compiled into a report produced by the class for the office of the president or another official at the college. Because we want to get as broad as possible span of community involvement and service, we will avoid duplication by informing each other what we will be investigating. **10 points   Due date: October 29**

Civic arts Responsibilities of citizenship; what does this mean? what are the links between the social and the political? what are obligations as members of the civil society?

Assignment: One of the obligations of citizenship is keeping informed about issues or letting elected representatives know about our opinions about public policy. The assignment here is to prepare a letter to the editor, to an elected official, to a director of a nonprofit organization to inform them about an issue important to you. You also have the option of attending a public meeting and sending a follow-up letter to the organizers. These letters will be discussed in class.   **10 points   Due date: October 15**

Community study In most communities, individuals and organizations are working to solve problems. These efforts may be taken up by individuals, nonprofit organizations, churches and publicly-funded organizations. Select one of the following issues (homelessness, hunger, youth violence, teen pregnancy) and find out what your community is doing to help address the problem. You will need to contact individuals in your community to research this issue gathering at least 3 sources of information on this. It is important to remember here that addressing a problem includes direct service. advocacy, lobbying and so on and that social problems are complex and involve a great many efforts.
                                    10 points   Due date: November 19

Field notes Field notes are the basis of qualitative research. In some instances, these can be taken right on the scene where the observer is unobtrusive and not part of the action. In other instances, the observer must make mental notes and then get these on paper, as soon as possible. There are a number of guides for taking field notes and we will use a combination of approaches. Later in the semester I will distribute some field notes from my research in a women's prison.

Finding a placement During the first class, we will be discussing possible placements for service. We will brainstorm as many as we can. Three factors should go into your selection of a service site. 1] Practical- can you get there and back? do their needs mesh with your availability? 2] Personal - do you have a particular interest in this issue? the population? 3] Course related concerns -is the placement one that conforms to the aims of the course? Check these with the instructor. Last summer, you completed a survey to identify your interests and talents so that we can make a good match between community needs and what you have to offer. There are many organizations that can help you find a volunteer/service activity. You are expected to do community an average of 10 hours per week over the course of the semester. I will be checking in with agency staff to follow your progress in these assignments. There are many organizations that can help you locate service/volunteer placements. One of the major one is Volunteers in Action (VIA). Contact them at 421-6547. Also refer to the class handout on local opportunities for service. Speakers will be addressing the class over the course of the semester and this will provide some ideas as well.

Site visit reports
On September 24th, we will make our first site visit to the Women's Division at the ACI in Cranston. In this 4-5 page essay, you should cover at least some of the following points.

- Description of the site and the population
- Expectations and reality
- Goals of institution and goal displacement
- Balancing custody and rehabilitation
- What is the problem that this institution is supposed to address?
- Helping in this setting-what are the barriers to 'helping' this population?
- What are some ways that college students could get involved here? In Nyden et al (1997), the authors advocate community-college relationships. What sort of partnerships and projects might be developed at the Women's Division?
- There are a number of programs here that are directed to individually changing or treating women. What are some structural sociological systemic changes that might address the problem?

Site visit reports will follow this general format. Where appropriate, these should be tied to assigned reading and class discussions.

Assignments   **Materials with asterisk are on reserve***

Class one   Sept. 3
Overview of course
Introduction to service learning
Models and opportunities
Reflection guides: Introduction to field work
Starting field notes and journaling
Assignment essays
Coles Handout; Boyer Handout; Walker Introduduction*

Class two   Sept. 10
Jorgensen Ch. 1: Hursh*
Qualitative research
Nyden Chapter one: Coles Ch. 1

Class three   Sept. 17
Jorgensen Ch. 2
Selecting a site
Finding literature about the setting
Two page report due 10 points
Nyden Chapter two: Coles Ch. 2

Class four   September 24
The helping relationship
Fisher, Nadler and Whitcher-Alagna*
Jorgensen Ch. 3: Coles Ch. 5

Class five   October 1
Jorgensen Ch. 4
Steele*; Bellah*
Community and gender

Class six   October 8
Jorgensen Ch. 5
Nyden Case Study 1: Coles Ch. 4

Class seven   October 15
Jorgensen Ch. 6
Bunis *
Nyden Case Study 11
Civic arts project due (10 points)

Class eight   October 22
Anspach*
Jorgensen Ch. 7
Nyden Case Study 12

Class nine   October 29
Jorgensen Ch. 8
Community and college (10 points)
Coding and interpreting

Class ten   Nov. 5
Grounded theory
Jane Wagner-Handout□
Nyden Ch. 6: Coles Ch. 3

Class eleven   Nov. 12
Nyden Case Study 13
Putman*

Class twelve   Nov. 19
Jorgensen Ch. 9
Nonprofits: Community foundations
Community study due (10 points)

Class thirteen   Nov. 26
Martins Ramos*: Coles Ch. 8
Class presentations
Nyden Case Study 17
Final Paper due (20 points)

Class fourteen   Final project due Dec. 3 & 10
Class presentations
Nyden Conclusion: Coles Epilogue
Final reflection essay (in class 10 points)

Additional readings may be assigned. Because we are covering topics that are
newsworthy and the subject of considerable debate, I may add items to our
readings that are found in the popular media and academic press.

In class essays and questions for reflection

Some of the following will become the basis of questions that should be addressed in field notes. We will also address some of these in class.

What are some of the responsibilities of citizens?
When you think of citizenship what comes to mind?
Where do social problems come from?
What are the reasons for poverty, homelessness, violence, etc.?
When you consider these problems, do you usually examine the individuals involved and try to figure out how specific behaviors and attitudes have contributed to the problem or do you usually examine larger factors? What are the pros and cons of each approach?

Why is poverty defined as a social problem? Playing a thought experiment, imagine what our society would be like if excess wealth was a social problem. What values would underlie the definition of 'too much money' as a social problem? What sorts of programs might be in place to solve this problem?

Who is responsible for solving social problems? Should families be the primary providers of care? If families fail, should extended families be the next layer of care? When should we rely on formal organizations? When should the state step in?

Think of one social problem and pose one question you would like to know more about in order to begin solving it. This does not have to be a problem that is widely recognized or that affects a majority of the population. First, describe the problem; then suggest some questions; finally, suggest some ways to learn more about this in an effort to do something about it.

Journal essays 1. What are the possible connections between service and learning? Or experience and learning? As sociologists, how do we connect what we learn from texts and professors to what we see in the 'real world'? What is closer to the truth?

2. Identify two sociological lessons you have learned and review what is was that you found so true or compelling? What did these theories or concepts tell you or explain?

3. Have you ever volunteered in the past? Do you remember how that experience was?

4. If you are thinking about volunteering or doing service in this course, what do you think you would anticipate your experience being if you were to go to a different setting from one you are accustomed to? For example, if you had the

opportunity to work as a tutor in a school different from that you attended, let's say a school for the physically handicapped or a school with students who are primarily another race or ethnic group, how would you prepare yourself for these experiences?

5. After your first visit to the field site, what questions have come up? We will be discussing these visits in class. What is the most significant thing you noticed about the site? Did it meet your expectations? What questions are in the back of your mind? What do you want to observe closely the next time?

6. How does your organization work with others in the community? Does it have a particular niche? How does it get clients? How do clients get better? What is provided to them? What does the agency need to support itself?

7. The helping relationship is generally thought of as positive. What are some of the negative aspects? Some argue for a dismantling of social programs because they disable people and communities. Present this position. Others argue that professionals are able to diagnose and treat problems. Argue this position as well. Chose one social problem and discuss how each position might treat the issue, identify clients, suggest blame and propose fixing the problem.

8. Write an essay that incorporates different perspectives on a social situation. For example, in an intake situation, write from the different perspectives of the client giving information, the person taking the information and the entity requesting such data. What are some of the rules governing interaction here? What could be better? What is at stake?

READING A COMMUNITY: THE CITY AS A TEXT
A "3M"/TRIANGULATION APPROACH

METHODS & TECHNIQUES
(KA & AW)
-EXISTING INFORMATION/DATA
-OBSERVATION
-INTERVIEWS

MODELS: LENSES/FRAMEWORKS
(THEORIES AND CONCEPTS)
-POETS Ecosystem
-Social Systems/LRF's
-Vertical and Horizontal Patterns
-Political Economy/New Urbanism
-Agency and Structuration
-Conflict/Competition

REGION-COMMUNITY-CITY-NEIGHBORHOOD
(E.G., MPLS NHD, MPLS, REGION)

MILIEU: CONTEXT AND COMPARISONS
POLIS, METROPOLIS, METROPOLIS
PLURIBUS VERSUS UNUM: GROWING SEPARATION
STRATIFICATION AND THE RULES OF THE GAME
WHO RUNS THIS TOWN: POLITICS AND POWER
SPACE AND PLACE: ECONOMY AND RACE
BALANCING BUDGETS AND PAYING THE WAY

READING THE CITY-COMMUNITY-REGION AS A TEXT: ASSUMPTIONS

1) You and I can discover and explore that "invisible" highway called social organization [social structure, culture, & institutions].

2) Communities, like all social organization, are the result of social-economic forces and human activism ["agency"].

3) Reading and understanding communities [and all social organizations and institutions] can liberate and empower people for effective citizenship and community building.

4) Reading and understanding communities is significantly enhanced by developing skills in research methodology, theories and concepts, and comparative knowledge and information, enabling us to understand:
-What is happening?
-Why is it happening?
-Who benefits the most and the least from the way things are?
-Why it that the case?
-If one wanted to change things to improve the quality of life for more residents
of the community, what public policies and actions would be required?

5) Healthy people [and communities] are growing and helping others to grow.

Garry Hesser, Augsburg College
Mpls, MN 55454 [hesser@augsburg.edu]

SOCIOLOGY 211: HUMAN COMMUNITY AND MODERN METROPOLIS
or
THE CITY AS TEXT: READING AND UNDERSTANDING COMMUNITIES AND NEIGHBORHOODS IN THE TWIN CITIES AND U.S.

I. "READING" A COMMUNITY THROUGH A "3M" LENS: METHODS, MODELS AND MILIEU

A. METHODS AND TECHNIQUES OF INVESTIGATION AND INQUIRY: SOCIOLOGY AS A SOCIAL SCIENCE/EMPIRICAL

1. Gathering Relevant, Existing Information (Data)
2. Observation (often as a Participant)
3. Interviewing and Asking Good Questions
4. "Knowledge About" and "Acquaintance With" Continuum

B. MODELS: LENSES OR FRAMEWORKS (Theories and Concepts)
1. SOCIOLOGICAL PERSPECTIVE: Where the Individual [Agent] and Social Forces/History Converge
2. POETS Ecosystem
3. FUNCTIONAL FRAMEWORK: Theory for Community Systems
4. Horizontal and Vertical Relationship: Within and Between Open Systems (Warren)
5. Locality Relevant Functions: Social Systems and Social Organizations (Warren)
6. "New Urban Sociology: Political Economy and Agency

C. MILIEU: CONTEXT AND COMPARISON FOR READING A CITY:

1. POLIS, METROPOLIS, METROPOLIS
2. PLURIBUS VERSUS UNUM: GROWING SEPARATION
3. STRATIFICATION AND THE RULES OF THE GAME
4. WHO RUNS THIS TOWN: POLITICS AND POWER
5. SPACE AND PLACE: ECONOMY AND RACE
6. BALANCING BUDGETS AND PAYING THE WAY
7. REBUILDING CITIES IN THE U.S.

II. THE COMMUNITY AS TEXT: PRACTICE MAKES PERFECT [or better]

A. SEWARD-MILWAUKEE AVENUE: CASE STUDY OF CHANGE
B. TRIANGULATING: OBSERVING, POETS, INTERVIEWING AND CONVERSING
   1. FIELD STUDY NGHD: CEDAR-RIVERSIDE, PHILLIPS, SEWARD, WHITTIER, POWDERHORN
   2. MINNEAPOLIS
   3. TWIN CITIES REGION
C. LOCALITY RELEVANT FUNCTIONS
   1. Met by your field site organization
   2. Other organizations meeting L-R-F's
D. PARTICIPANT OBSERVATION AND CRITICAL ANALYSIS [DIE]
E. CONNECTING THE TEXT [the community] TO THE TEXT [City Lights]
F. COMMUNITY LEADERS AND "AGENTS"

III. APPLICATION & INTEGRATION OF FIELD STUDY AND COURSE CONCEPTS AND CONTENT

Hesser, Augsburg College, Mpls

Human Community and Modern Metropolis
Sociology 211 [City Perspective]

Fall, 1998

Have you ever wondered if you would be the same "you" if you had been born into another family or grown up in another community? Well, sociologists contend that you would probably be a quite different person. Do you agree? Why do you think we come to that conclusion?

All of us live out our lives in communities. But, like fish in water, we take communities for granted, seldom taking the time or developing the tools to understand how to "read a community" and learn how the institutions around us create and mold us into the persons we are becoming.

This class will ask you to make use of your own experiences as you question and enlarge your understanding of the human community and social institutions. The objectives for this class include
-learning how to read a community using basic concepts and methods of sociology;
-learning how to understand communities as social systems which are a part of larger systems;
-learning to be a "participant observer" and gather important in formation helpful in "reading a community";
-improving your ability to learn from other persons, including your classmates;
-learning how to utilize existing information from organizational and government materials;
-applying the concepts and ideas of urban and community sociology to better understand what you are learning about Mpls, the Twin Cities and other major metropolitan areas; and
-enhancing your understanding and practice of citizenship and community service skills.

To begin this journey, I would like for you to think about what some sociologists have written:

"...to begin to solve the daunting problems [facing our times],
let alone the problems of emptiness and meaninglessness in our personal lives,
requires that we greatly improve our capacity to think about our institutions.
We need to understand how much of our lives is lived in and through institutions,
and how better institutions are essential if we are to lead better lives....
One of the greatest challenges, especially for individualistic Americans,
is to understand what institutions are--how we form them and how they in turn form us--
and to imagine that we can actually alter them for the better. [p.5]...

"Americans often think of individuals pitted against institutions.
It is hard for us to think of institutions as affording the necessary context within which we become individuals;
of institutions as not just restraining but enabling us; of institutions not
as an arena of hostility within which our character is tested but an
indispensable source from which character is formed. [p.6]...

Indeed, the great classic criteria of a good society--peace, prosperity, freedom, justice--
all depend today on a new experiment in democracy,
a newly extended and enhanced set of democratic institutions,
within which we citizens can better discern what we really want and what we ought to want
to sustain a good life on this planet for ourselves and the generations to come." [p. 9]

[Robert Bellah, et al, The Good Society, 1992]

Garry Hesser, Ph.D.
Augsburg College, Mpls, MN 55454
Murphy Place 112 [330-1664; PO # 83]
hesser@augsburg.edu [330-1784--FAX]
Office Hours: M-F, 8:00-10:15 a.m. & by appointment

TEXTS AND READINGS FOR COURSE:

Phillips, City Lights, 2nd Edition [required]
Warren, "The Community as a Social System" [Reserve]
Gist and Fava, "POETS" [Reserve]
Grams, "Learning by Participating" [Reserve]
State of City, 1994 [Reserve and loaner copies]
Neighborhood Profiles, Reports, Newpapers, KTCA-ch 2 and Local TV News, KNOW-FM [91.1].
The Face of the Twin Cities: Another Look, United Way Report [Reserve]
"Growth Options for the Twin Cities," Metropolitan Council [Reserve]
"Sprawl: Its Nature, Consequences, Causes", Henry Richmond [Reserve]

GRADING AND EVALUATION

Midterm Exam [10/22]	20%
Final Exam [12/17]	20%
Field Study Journal/Written Assignments	60%
Cumulative Monday Assignments [averaged]	20%
Cumulative Friday Journal Applications "	20%
Field Study Application-Integration Paper [12/10]	10%
Class Presentation on Neighborhood [12/3-10]	10%

CRITERIA FOR GRADING

1) See college catalogue for what a 4:0, 3.0, 2.0, 1.0, etc. mean at Augsburg; but, basically, students who achieve the basic requirements should expect to receive a passing grade of a 2.0. Grades above that will require "going the extra mile" in some or all elements of the course.
   Note: Review College Catalogue for meaning of 4.0 [consistent excellence], 2.0 [demonstrates basic competence]; 3.0 has elements of excellence, etc.

2) Expectation of what is required to perform satisfactorily in this class:
In general, being a full time student means that you devote at least 40 hours a week to your courses, i.e., 10 hours a week to this particular course. Students who receive grades of 4.0 on particularly assignments and the course itself will almost always spend that much time on the course and will demonstrate a thorough understanding of each of the elements of the course, including how they relate to each other. Students receiving a 4.0 will be able to use the course content to offer reasonable explanations of why cities and communities are the way they are and how communities affect their residents the way they do. They will be able to demonstrate their understanding in the various written and oral opportunities for evaluation, including the collaborative efforts of the group(s) in which they work. They will demonstrate a full familiarity and understanding of the materials covered in readings, class presentations/discussions, and field study.

3) On the first day of class we will discuss and decide upon other expectations and criteria for evaluation and course grading.

4) Attendance and active participation are essential for this course.
If is necessary to miss class, you are responsible for finding out what you missed and for any information provided on that day, including collaborative work which your group is expecting.

5) Late assignments will be lowered one grade for each day they are late,e.g., 4.0 to 3.5; 3.0 to 2.0,etc.

6) The college policy on Honesty and Plagiarism [see Student Guide] is the norm for this course. Each student must sign a statement at the beginning of the class promising to adhere to the policy. You are expected to do your own work where the assignment indicates, but collaboration and mutual assistance are also expected in conjunction with many assignments. If unsure, ask instructor.

7) If you have any special needs or challenges, please discuss them with me as soon as is possible so that accomodations can be made to enable you to be successful in this course.

Garry Hesser, Augsburg College

MONDAYS: Field Study Hours & brief assignments involving participant observation, interviews, analysis of existing data and reports on neighborhood/city, newspaper accounts, etc.

WEDNESDAYS: Text Reading Assignments, coming prepared with questions and ready to discuss

FRIDAYS: Review assigned readings, Reflective Journal entries connecting the Readings to what you are learning about your neighborhood, Minneapolis, the Twin Cities, and U.S. cities in general

WEEK #1--9/3ff

Wed
    A: none
    C: Field Trip to Milwaukee Avenue: What can be learned by observation?

Fri
    A: Read syllabus carefully
       Complete biographical sheet
       Meet for 15 minutes with professor [Murphy 112]-"Getting acquainted"
          - "What surprised you about Milwaukee Avenue?"
          - "What interests you most about Minneapolis and the Twin Cities?"
          - "What do you hope to be doing ten years from now?"
       "Field Study Journal #1: Reflect on why Milwaukee Avenue is the way it is; revisit (?)
    C: Group Reflection on Milwaukee Avenue: What can you learn from observations/data?
          -What did you and other classmates see and observe on the field trip?
          -Why do you and your classmates think that Milwaukee Avenue is the way it is?
       Lecture: Milwaukee Avenue as a Case Study for course--Intro to "analytical concepts"
       Introduction to Field Study Options
       Monday Field assignment

WEEK #2: LEARNING FROM EXPERIENCE/TRIANGULATION: YOURS & OTHERS

Mon 9/8
    A: Explore one of four quadrants of Cedar Riverside [*as assigned* and, if possible, with
       another classmate (or friend), stopping in at least one business/"busy place"
          - Complete "Field Study Observations" in Field Study Journal: I [Mondays]
          - Read-reflect on "PROJECTS" (p.23): How do they compare to this assignment?
    C: Reading a City: Four Quadrants of Cedar-Riverside
          - What can you learn from the observations of others [same and different quadrants]
          - Cf. CL, p. 23, "Understanding...", An Eye-Ear Tour...", "Varieties of Experience"

Wed
    A: City Lights, ch 1-"The Knowing Eye and Ear"
    C: Knowledge About and Acquaintance With: Overlapping Pathways to Knowledge
          - Introduction to "Triangulation": Theories, Disciplines, Observers, "KA" & "AW" to
            expand KK, KDK, & DKDK
          - Field Study Through Service-Learning: Reciprocity and Experiential Education
            Alternatives described and explained: Q & A

Fri
    A: Journal entry reflecting on how chapter 1 relates to your exploration of Cedar-Riverside [cf. p. 23,
       "PROJECTS"]
       Preliminary decision about Field Site [complete 1st, 2nd, 3rd choice form]
    C: Exchanging journals in small groups and learning more from each other
       Class discussion about "epistemology" and ways of knowing: KK, KDK, DKDK
          - "You have to DIE in order to learn"-Description, Interpretation(s), Evaluation
       Decide on Field Site: Negotiate locations [1st or 2nd choice]

WEEK #3 - 9/15ff: INTERDISCLIPLINARY APPROACHES TO UNDERSTANDING CITIES
Mon   A: Walking [plus busing, driving...] tour of Field Site Neighborhood
                  - Two hours of exploring, including 30 minutes in a restaurant(s), business
                      [Note: CL, p. 23, "Eye-Ear Tour", "Varieties of Experience"]
                - Preliminary observations and assessment based upon your observations
      C: Exchange Field Study Journal [I] and create a "fuller" [better?] one with core group
                - Enlarge your understanding by "triangulating" with data from others
                - KK, KDK, DKDK about the POETS Ecosystem, V/H, etc. of your neighborhood
                - Triangulating with different academic disciplines
      7:00 p.m. Michael Roan, "Listening Across Differences: World Religions & World Peace"
      [An opportunity to expand your understanding of the "S, P, & O" parts of POETS]
Tues
      Opportunity: _Christensen Symposium,_ cont. [Triangulating with "S"]
      11:00 Convocation: Roland Miller, "Listening Across Differences: What I Have Learned From Different Faiths"
Wed
      A: CL, ch. 2-"Thinking About Cities: Triangulating and Interdisciplinary Approaches"
      C: Orientation and Background information by Site Supervisors: Bring Questions
Fri
      A: Review ch. 2 and write Journal entry discussing how Sociology and one other discipline can expand your
          understanding of the neighborhood site you have chosen
      C: Exchange journals with your "secondary" group [classmates from other neighborhoods]
                - "Triangulating using Sociological Perspective [and other disciplines]"

WEEK #4 - 9/22ff: POSING THE QUESTIONS AND SEEKING "THICKER" UNDERSTANDING
Mon
      A: Begin/continue Field Study Service-Learning involvement
                - Read Neighborhood Profile on your Neighborhood [on Reserve in library]
                - Review information from orientation, neighborhood newspapers, available info
                - Utilizing this new data <u>and</u> your observations, identify <u>at least two</u> new KK [formerly DKDK] in
                  each section of the Monday Journal [I], expanding your previous insights
      C: Meet with core group to compare POETS understanding: KK, KDK, DKDK
            Overview of "Posing the Questions" and Objectives of the Course
Wed
      A: CL, ch. 3
      C: "If Sociologists and other Social Scientists often disagree, what can I understand?"
           How can we understand cause and effect when it comes to urban change & challenges?
                - Case studies that focus on "agency" as an independent variable
Fri
      A: Journal reflections using elements of POETS or other "theories" as possible "independent variables"/causes to
          explain or interpret what you have described
      C: Exchange journals with "core" group; discuss and expand your KK, KDK, DKDK
          Class discussion on "Doing Science" and the "causes of poverty" and how that relates to the _"operating theory" of_
          the organization where you are doing service-learning
          "Neighbors: Conservation and Change"

WEEK #5 - 9/29ff - DEEPER UNDERSTANDING BY "DISCOVERING THE RULES/NORMS"
Mon - "MICRO ANALYSIS": "UP CLOSE AND PERSONAL" INTERACTION
      A: Participant Observation through Service-Learning
          Grams, "Learning By Participation" [Reserve]-Read Grams and identify an interaction
          from your field study that could be analyzed using status, role, def'n of situation
          Write a one page entry [I] using _status, role, def'n of situation_ to explain an interaction
          N.B. _Go beyond the obvious since "social reality is rarely what it first seems..."_
      C: - Exchange essay with colleague(s)
                - Discuss "participant observation" as a research technique for "discovering rules"
                - Introduction to "Discovering the Rules"
Wed
      A: CL, ch. 11
      C: Lecture-Discussion of "Discovering the Rules": Understanding Residents of Nhds
          "Groupthink" video

Fri

    A: Review ch. 11; Friday Journal entry

    C: Journal sharing with core group
        Identify critical issues that your organization is trying to address/solve <u>and</u> their
        "Theory(s) in practice", i.e., why they do what they do

WEEK #6 - 10/6ff--" Thicker Analysis" Through Participant Observation and Service-Learning
Mon - "MICRO ANALYSIS: DIFFERENTIAL PERCEPTIONS & PERSONAL SPACE" [Cont]

    A: Repeat the Participant Observation assignment using concepts and ideas from ch 11 to explain and interpret what
        you have described, "going beyond the obvious" by giving some attention to the idea that "reality is socially
        constructed" and that most explanations require combining MICRO and MACRO ANALYSIS for a "thick"
        understanding
        <u>Suggestion</u>: You could adapt Project #1, p. 319f, formulating two hypotheses about some typical neighborhood
        behavior that you have observed.

    C: Share your written assignment and hypotheses with core group and report to entire class what you think are some
        of the most important "rules of behavior" in your neighborhood, including your best explanations as to why
        people behave as they do

Wed

    A: <u>CL</u>, ch. 16, pp. 451-471 [stop at "Environmental Psychology"]

    C: How Do Different People Experience a Sense of Place? And Why? Where Does PO<u>ET</u>S Fit Into This? What
        Difference Does that Make to You? Others? Residents of Your Nhd?

Fri

    A: Journal applying ideas of chapter to neighborhood; review ch 16 [pp. 451-471a]

    C: Exchange in secondary groups and compare and learn from each other

WEEK #7 - 10/13ff
Mon - AN HISTORICAL CONTEXT: U.S. CITIES IN THE PAST, PRESENT AND FUTURE

    A: Field Study
        Make use of the Reference Section of Lindell Library to identify major changes in Mpls & St. Paul from 1950 to
        present: 1hour search, reported in POETS format REF HA 202 A36 1949-1994; REF HA 203 C68 1995--<u>County</u>
        <u>& City Data Book</u> and ...<u>Extra:</u> REF G 1429 M51 M5 1978-1996 [<u>State of the City, Mpls</u>]--also on Reserve

    C: Minneapolis and St. Paul Histories: Vignettes from the Past
Wed - HOW WE GOT TO WHERE WE ARE [AND WHERE ARE WE GOING?]

    A: <u>CL</u>, ch. 4, pp. 94-109 [beginning with "Manchester, England..."]
        <u>CL</u>, ch. 15, pp. 422-423 [to "The Internal Structure..."]; 434-435 ["The Multinucleated Metropolitan Region" to
        "Where People Live"]
        <u>CL</u>, ch. 16, pp. 477-482 [Beginning with "Grand Designers" to "Megastructures..."]

    C: What Can We Learn From History?
        How do the Twin Cities compare to other metropolitan areas in the U.S.?

Fri

    A: Journal connecting the ideas of chapters to Mpls, St. Paul & nhd: DKDK, KK, KDK

    C: Journal exchange with secondary group

WEEK #8 - 10/20
Mon

    A: Review readings and exercises to date & "Take-Home" Midterm questions
        Review "Key Terms" from each assigned reading for matching part of exam

    C: Discuss the "take-home" essay questions for Mid-Term
        Work together in core group to assist each other in preparing for mid-term exam
        Questions and Answers

Wed 10/22

    A: Review and prepare for Midterm Exam: Essay and Matching

    C: Mid-Term Exam [essay test with questions selected from take-home questions]
        Blue Books provided; Honor Code in effect [sign name on blue book cover]

Fri

    A: MID-TERM BREAK

    C: NO CLASS

WEEK #9 - 10/27ff
Mon - CAN THERE BE A SENSE OF COMMUNITY IN A MODERN METROPOLIS?
    A: Service-Learning Participant Observation
        Using the POETS framework, consult the <u>City and County Data Book</u> and the <u>State of the City</u> reports and
        compare and contrast your neighborhood, the city as a whole, the suburbs and Hennepin County as a whole using
        the Field Study #8.
            <u>Note:</u> Other existing information/conversations with informed persons is welcome.
    C: Exchange essays with core group; discuss
        Rotate to "secondary" group; read essays; discuss similarities and differences and why?
Wed

    A: <u>CL</u>, ch 5, pp. 117-123 [stop at "Classical Urban Theory"]
        <u>CL</u>, ch. 6
        <u>CL</u>, ch. 15, pp. 434-435 [from "The Multinucleated.." to "Where People Live"]
    C: CAN THERE BE A SENSE OF COMMUNITY IN THE METROPOLITAN COMMUNITY?
Fri

    A: Journal Reflections applying chapter 6 to the changes in your neighborhood & Mpls
    C: Exchange with core group; discuss
        Rotate and compare with classmates from other neighborhoods

WEEK #10 - 11/3ff
Mon - SEARCHING FOR COMMUNITY: THE CHALLENGE/PROBLEM OF SUBURBIA
    A: Service-Learning Participant Observation
        Drive from Seven Corners to 180th Street in Apple Valley/Lakeville on <u>Cedar Avenue,</u>
        a similar route, or take the #7 bus from 22nd and Riverside to Mall of America
        Complete the journal assignment [# 9] reflecting/speculating on what this kind of development means to the city
        of Minneapolis and to your neighborhood
    C: Exchange essays within secondary group; discuss in small group
        Discuss "conclusions" with entire class
        Introduction to chapter 7
Wed

    A: <u>CL</u>, ch. 7; "Sprawl: Its Nature, Consequences, Causes" [On Reserve]
    C: The Costs and Benefits of Suburbanization

Fri   A: Review ch 7
        Journal connecting the ideas of chapter 7 & the Richmond article to the changes and challenges faced by
        Minneapolis and your neighborhood [and other central cities]
    C: Exchange journals; discuss and report back to class

WEEK #11 - 11/10ff--IMMIGRATION AND THE CITY: PAST AND PRESENT
Mon   A: Field Study
        Interview 2 "oldtimers" about the changes in the population in the neighborhood, the city and the metropolitan
        region during the past "decade"/few years.
           - write one page summary of key changes, strengths, good things, & challenges
    C: Exchange findings in core group
Wed

    A: <u>CL</u>, ch. 8--"Movin' On"
    C: "Give Me Your Tired, Your Poor" or Pluribus vs. Unum
        What Is It Like to Migrate to the Twin Cities in the 1990's?
Fri

    A: Journal connections: DKDK, KK, KDK
    C: Exchange and learn from each other; class discussion

WEEK #12 - 11/17ff--IDENTITY CRISIS: HOW MUCH DO RACE AND ETHNICITY MATTER?
Mon

    A: Service-Learning Field Study
        Re-visit the <u>State of the City</u> [G1429 M51] & <u>City and County Data Book</u> [REF HA202 A36; HA203]--see Journal
        I #11
        Complete the Monday Journal with as much comparative data as you can in one hour
    C: Exchange discoveries and compare to what "old timers" remembered [last week]

Wed

    A: <u>CL</u>, ch. 9; Ch 15, pp. 435-441[from"Where People Live" to "Economic Activities..."]

    C: Can American cities and society survive and/or transcend our "Identity Crisis"?

Fri

    A: Journal connections between chapter and Mpls/your neighborhood: DKDK, KK, KDK

    C: Exchange journals, discuss and learn from each other; begin planning "final" report

WEEK #13 - ll/24ff

Mon - SOME OF US CAN BE MORE THANKFUL THAN OTHERS: POVERTY & CITIES

    A: Service-Learning Field Study

    C: Examining the Distribution of Wealth in the Twin Cities: Another Face of the Twin Cities
        [United Way Report]
        Core Group Planning for Final Paper/Report/Division of Labor

Wed

    A: <u>CL</u>, ch. 10, pp. 278-290 [beginning with "A final note on class structure..."]
        <u>CL</u>, ch. 18, pp. 535-546 [beginning with "Local Occupational Structures..."]

    C: Affordable Housing: Is the Issue Class or Race or What?

Fri

    A & C: THANKSGIVING HOLIDAY

WEEK #14--GETTING THINGS DONE: AGENCY THROUGH AND ALONGSIDE GOV'T

Mon 12/1

    A: Service-Learning Field Study
        Final Paper-Presentation Preparation

    C: Creating Coalitions: People Who Are Making a Difference [Guest speaker]
        Introduction to Theories about "community power"

Wed - "The Skeleton of Power" as a Framework/Context for "Getting Things Done"

    A: <u>CL</u>, ch. 12, pp. 343-358 [beginning with "The Context of Local Government"]
        <u>CL</u>, ch. 14, pp. 387-392; 402-408 [beginning with "To conclude..."]

    C: Social Forces and Agency: Efficacy for You and Me [and our Neighborhood]
        First Neighborhood Group: Oral Report on Neighborhood [cf. paper format]

Fri

    A: Journal connections with DKDK, KK, KDK

    C: Second Neighborhood Group: Oral Report on Neighborhood [cf. paper format]

WEEK #15--REBUILDING THE U.S. CITY: ARE THERE OPTIONS FOR THE FUTURE?

Mon 12/8

    A: <u>CL</u>, pp. 504-508 [from "An Emerging Vocabulary" to "Identifying Basic..."]
        pp. 511-515 [from "Case Study: Caliente"]
        "Growth Options for the Twin Cities Metropolitan Area" [On Reserve]

    C: 3rd & 4th Neighborhood Group: Oral Report on Neighborhood [cf. paper format]
        Portland and Chattanooga Revisited

Wed

    A: Complete Group Paper: One paper for each neighborhood group/collaboration

    C: Fifth Neighborhood Group: Oral Report on Neighborhood [cf. paper format]
        Discuss Conclusions reached in papers and Final Exam Questions

Fri

    A: Review <u>City Lights</u> and course; Organize Answers for Final Exam

    C: Work in core groups on Final Exam questions; general class discussion

FINAL EXAM: Wednesday, December 17--10:15-12:15 p.m.

Dear Colleague,

Thanks for assisting me in finding places for my students to serve and learn. I often think of the "service" part of service-learning as one way to give something back to the community or the privilege of being a part of the community for the semester, a small return for the opportunity to observe and interact with you, your colleagues and those with whom you work.

In order for them to achieve the objectives identified on the attached handout from their syllabus, it would be very helpful if you would provide the following:

Orientation on Wednesday, September 18th from 11:00-12:00 [in Room 111 in Murphy Place: 2222--7 1/2 Street; see map; parking permit enclosed; stay and be my guest for lunch if you can after class]

- Mission and general scope of operations
- History of the organization, including key staff and volunteers over the years
- Primary accomplishments
- Staffing and "organization chart", with particular attention to where what they will be doing fits into the larger picture and objectives of the organiation
- General and important information about the neighborhood itself, including its strengths/resources and particular challenges faced by the neighborhood and city overall, major changes, etc.
- Annual reports, brochures, etc.
- Composition of the Board, how it is selected and budget
- Any other information [including videos or PR material] you think would be valuable

Opportunities over the course of the semester to ask questions and talk with you and those associated with the neighborhood and organization about

- what it is like to live and/or work in the neighborhood;
- the changes you have seen in the neighborhood;
- your understanding of what is causing some of those changes and some of the consequences you see;
- what you and/or your colleagues would like to see happen in the neighborhood;
- other organizations and persons contributing to the good things [and the not so good things] that you see;

Feedback on their effectiveness in assisting you

Encouragement for them to increasingly expand their involvement in public and community service, ranging from citizenship and political participation, community service, and career exporation in the kind of work that you do.

My overall objective is for students to understand the social forces and realities that are impacting urban neighborhoods and the impact that organizations and persons like yourself and your colleagues can and do have as we try to improve the quality of life for all our citizens.

With your neighborhood as a "case study", complemented by reading, lectures, media, and other resources, I want the students to help each other to develop a reasonably accurate picture of the critical elements of the neighborhood, Minneapolis, and the Twin Cities. Then, I want us to grapple with "why things are this way," "who seems to benefit the most and the least from the way things are", and "some of the things that might be done to change the way things are", if that were desirable.

It is my hope that each organization/neighborhood will have 4-6 students working together on a common project, if possible, or "independently" on a project or tasks that are useful to you and those you serve. In addition, to their weekly journals connecting the reading and their experiences-observations, they will do a number of excercises to enhance their understanding and learning. I also hope that it will be possible for you or a colleague to visit the class on one Friday during the semester to discuss what you see as some of the greatest challenges and opportunities facing the neighborhood and what you and your organization are doing to bring about changes in the quality of life for individuals and the neighborhood.

Thank you again. I look forward to working together with you and my students on this aspect of the course.

Sincerely,

Garry Hesser [330-1664]
Professor of Sociology and Director, Experiential Education
Augsburg College, Box 83

FIELD STUDY THROUGH SERVICE-LEARNING

Assignment:
Every student in Human Community and Modern Metropolis [Soc 211] is expected to do field work in one of the neighborhoods surrounding Augsburg.* This entails assisting in a neighborhood oriented organization, in active collaboration with 4-5 other students from the class, and will involve you in a minimum of 15 hours during the semester. The actual distribution of these hours is to be worked out with our contact at the agency in ways that are mutually acceptable to you and the needs of the agency.

Assumptions:
-Understanding and knowledge requires personal experience, as well as factual information and abstract reflection and generalization, i.e., research and theories;
-In order to achieve this level of understanding of contemporary urban realities, it is necessary to experience first hand some of the every day realities of persons and social organizations that make up the city;
-In addition, the personal experience is enhanced by preparation and a growing knowledge about the neighborhood and larger urban context, including the changes that are taking place;
-Such a field experience, which necessarily involves the personal and professional lives of other people, is a privilege that requires:
- *Reciprocity*
- *Collaboration,* and
- *Appreciation for diversity*, including gender, race, ethnicity, social class, values and life styles

OBJECTIVES AND DESIRED OUTCOMES

As the semester procedes, it is my hope that all of us involved in this course will achieve the following:
1. A thorough and accurate knowledge of the social, organizational and physical make-up of "your" neighborhood [city and region];
2. A knowledge of the major trends and changes that have taken place in "your" neighborhood, city and region since 1950;
3. A growing appreciation for the internal and external factors that help to explain why this neighborhood [and the city] are the way they are, including the impact that these social realities have upon the people, families and social organizations that live and operate within their "boundaries";
4. A knowledge of the history and structure of the organization you are helping, including a growing awareness of how the organization interacts with and affects other organizations and realities in the neighborhood, city and region;
5. A growing awareness and appreciation for professionals and organizations that are having a positive impact on the quality of life and the public issues and challenges facing the community; and
6. An understanding of how this particular neighborhood compares to other neighborhoods in the Twin Cities, the nation and the world.
7. A growing understanding of what is happening in most urban areas across the United States, why these trends are occuring, who benefits the most, and what alternatives are possible or desirable.

Summary: The provision of assistance to the organization makes it possible for students to assume a legitimate role in the everyday life of the organization. In addition, this service enables the student to give something back to the neighborhood and organization for the opportunity to be a "participant observer". The combination of first-hand experience and factual knowledge about one neighborhood [and an organization within it] will be the basis for learning about the trends and challenges facing U.S. cities and communities.

*Talk with me by 9/12 if you need an alternative to field study.

Garry Hesser, Augsburg College
Mpls, MN 55454 [hesser@augsburg.edu]

MAKING CONNECTIONS BETWEEN THE FIELD STUDY AND THE TEXT
City Lights, ch 1 (#1)

I. DESCRIPTION: <u>Describe</u> an experience, observation or conversation from your neighborhood or Mpls
> (Note: it might occasionally be a newspaper/TV coverage of an urban event or issue) which illustrates or is *related to this weeks reading* (approx 100 words):

II. <u>INTERPRET</u>/explain what you described above, using the key ideas and concepts from the chapter:
> (Note: <u>*Underline*</u> concepts and phrases from text to highlight the application; 200-300 words.)

III. WHAT NEW INSIGHTS HAVE YOU GOTTEN FROM THE FIELD AND TEXT?
-DKDK?

-KK?

-KDK?

MAKING CONNECTIONS BETWEEN THE FIELD STUDY AND THE TEXT
City Lights, ch 2 (#2)

I. DESCRIPTION: Describe an experience, observation or conversation from your neighborhood or Mpls

> (Note: it might occasionally be a newspaper/TV coverage of an event or issue) which illustrates or is related to this weeks reading (approx 100 words):

II. INTERPRET/explain what you described above, using the key ideas and concepts from the chapter:
> (Note: Underline concepts and phrases from text to highlight the application; 200-300 words.)

III. WHAT NEW INSIGHTS HAVE YOU GOTTEN FROM THE FIELD AND TEXT?
-DKDK?

-KK?

-KDK?

MAKING CONNECTIONS BETWEEN THE FIELD STUDY AND THE TEXT
City Lights, chs 12 & 14 (#12; _"time sheet" must be completed and all hours completed_)

I. DESCRIPTION: <u>Describe</u> an experience, observation or conversation from your neighborhood or Mpls
        (Note: it might occasionally be a newspaper/TV coverage of an event or issue) which illustrates or is related to this weeks reading (approx 100 words):

II. <u>INTERPRET</u>/explain what you described above, using the key ideas and concepts from the chapter: (Suggestion: In preparation for the final paper, focus on what you find in these chapters that helps you understand and answer items III and IV, i.e., vertical influences and publc policies and "agency")

III. WHAT NEW INSIGHTS AND UNDERSTANDING HAVE YOU GOTTEN FROM THE FIELD AND TEXT?
    -DKDK?

    -KK?

    -KDK?

HUMAN COMMUNITY AND MODERN METROPOLIS
SOCIOLOGY 211

PARTICIPANT OBSERVATION

SERVICE-LEARNING FIELD STUDY

JOURNAL
I. MONDAY: FIELD RESEARCH
FROM NEIGHBORHOOD TO REGION

FALL, 1998

Name_____

Campus P.O.#_____

Phone#_____Email_____Field Site:_____

FIELD STUDY NOTES FROM OBSERVATIONS
Milwaukee Avenue Neighborhood [due 9/5; #1]

1. <u>What</u> do/did you see [hear, smell, etc., i.e.,"empirical" evidence]? <u>People</u> [numbers, varieties, etc.]

<u>Organizations</u> [schools, businesses, churches, etc.]

<u>Physical Environment</u>
a) Natural

b) Person-made

<u>Technology</u> [means created to accomplish a goal, both physical and social]

<u>Culture [Values, beliefs, attitudes--often inferred from other evidence]</u>

2) Evidence of "vertical/external" influence [realities/forces outside community]:

3) Evidence of "horizontal" collaboration/connectedness within neighborhood:

4) Evidence of "agency"--"individual"/collective efforts to change/stabilize things:

5) Evidence of conflict over scarce resources:

6) Questions arising from inquiry [KDK]:

7) Surprises which "thickened" your understanding [DKDK]:

FIELD STUDY OBSERVATIONS:*What can you learn in 2 hours?*
Cedar-Riverside Neighborhood: One (1) Quadrant

1. <u>What</u> do/did you see [hear, smell, etc., i.e.,"empirical" evidence]? <u>People</u> [numbers, varieties, etc.]

<u>Organizations</u> [schools, businesses, churches, etc.]

<u>Physical Environment</u>
a) **Natural**

b) **Person-made**

<u>Technology</u> [means created to accomplish a goal, both physical and social]

<u>Culture [Values, beliefs, attitudes--often inferred from other evidence]</u>

2) Evidence of "vertical/external" influence [realities/forces outside community]:

3) Evidence of "horizontal" collaboration/connectedness within neighborhood:

4) Evidence of "agency"--"individual"/collective efforts to change/stabilize things:

5) Evidence of conflict over scarce resources:

6) Questions arising from your inquiry [KDK]:

7) Surprises that "thickened" your understanding [DKDK]:

FIELD STUDY OBSERVATIONS: *What can you learn in 2 hours?*

Your Field Site Neighborhood:_____[Day & time:_____]

1. <u>What</u> do/did you see [hear, smell, etc., i.e.,"empirical" evidence]? <u>People</u> [numbers, varieties, etc.]

<u>Organizations</u> [schools, businesses, churches, etc.]

<u>Physical Environment</u>
a) Natural

b) Person-made

<u>Technology</u> [means created to accomplish a goal, both physical and social]

<u>Culture [Values, beliefs, attitudes--often inferred from other evidence]</u>

2) Evidence of "vertical/external" influence [realities/forces outside community]:

3) Evidence of "horizontal" collaboration/connectedness within neighborhood:

4) Evidence of "agency"--"individual"/collective efforts to change/stabilize things:

5) Evidence of conflict over scarce resources:

6) Questions arising from exercise [KDK]:

7) Surprises that "thicken" my understanding [DKDK]:

**TRIANGULATING ON MY NEIGHBORHOOD AND ITS PLANNING DISTRICT:
EXISTING RESOURCES [9/22; #4]**

Minimally use: 1) Neighborhood Profile on Reserve; 2) 1994, 1995 or 1996 State of City, Mpls Plus Neighborhood newspapers, reports, and information provided in orientation, etc.

1. What do/did you find, i.e.,"empirical" evidence? People [numbers, varieties, etc.]

Organizations [schools, businesses, churches, block clubs, informal groups, clubs]

Physical Environment
a) Natural

b) Person-made

Technology [means created to accomplish a goal, both physical and social]

Culture [Values, beliefs, attitudes--often inferred from other evidence]

2) Evidence of "vertical/external" influence [realities/forces outside community]:

3) Evidence of "horizontal" collaboration/connectedness within neighborhood:

4) Evidence of "agency"--"individual"/collective efforts to change/stabilize things:

5) Evidence of conflict over scarce resources:

6) Questions:

7) Surprises:

LEARNING BY PARTICIPATING [due 9/29; #5]

1. DESCRIPTION OF A SITUATION IN WHICH YOU PARTICIPATED, i.e., what is/was the situation <u>and</u> how did the people within it behave:

2. EXPLAIN THE BEHAVIOR by reference to the way each person defines the situation and how particular statuses and role expectations might explain their differing definitions of the situation:

Questions growing out of this "micro-analysis"[KDK]:

Surprises the "thickened" my understanding[DKDK]:

LEARNING BY PARTICIPATING [#6]

1. DESCRIPTION OF A SITUATION IN WHICH YOU PARTICIPATED, i.e., what is/was the situation <u>and</u> how did the people within it behave:

2. EXPLAIN THE BEHAVIOR by reference to as many concepts and ideas from chapter 11 ["Discovering the Rules"] as you can to "go beyond the obvious" and "thicken your understanding":

Questions growing out of this "micro-analysis"[KDK]:

Surprises the "thickened" my understanding[DKDK]:

HOW MPLS HAS CHANGED: Learning from existing data [#7]

[Minimally make use of the City and County Data Books, State of City books; add other resources]

1. What did you find, i.e. factual evidence of changes in Mpls & St. Paul, 1950-97? People [numbers, varieties, etc.]

Organizations [suggestion: look at employers, type of employment, maps, histories

Physical Environment [pictures; newspapers; histories; dedications of buildings, roads, campuses, etc]
a) Natural, e.g., altered by nature, floods, weather

b) Person-made, e.g., Norwest Bank Building, IS 94, locks and dams, ...

Technology [means created to accomplish a goal, both physical and social]

Culture [Values, beliefs, attitudes--often inferred from other evidence]

6) Questions [KDK]:

7) Surprises that "thickened" my understanding [DKDK]:

HOW DO MPLS AND YOUR NEIGHBORHOOD COMPARE TO THE SURROUNDING COMMUNITIES? [10/27; # 8]

[Minimally make use of the City and County Data Books, State of City books; see 10/13 syllabus]

1. Use these sources to *compare* and *contrast* your nhd with Mpls & surroundings
People [incomes, diversity, growth rates, general demographics...]

"Your" Nhd   Mpls   *One* Suburb [your choice]   Hennepin County

Organizations [suggestion: use the Metro Section of newspaper, TV news, observe]

Physical Environment [pictures; newspapers; histories; maps; observations; informal conversations]
a) Natural, e.g., lakes, parks, lawns...

b) Person-made, e.g., look for different kinds of buildings, multinucleated...., mix of houses, etc

Technology [do you find any patterns that mark the differences?]

Culture [Values, beliefs, attitudes--be specific about your evidence]

6) Questions that this raises in my mind in the light of the course [KDK]:

7) Surprises that "thickened" my understanding [DKDK]:

TRIANGULATING ON THE SUBURBS: OBSERVING MORE CLOSELY[10/27; #9]

ASSIGNMENT: Drive or take a bus on one of the following trips:
- From Seven Corners down Cedar Avenue to 180th Street in Apple Valley/Lakeville;
- From downtown Mpls to "exurbia" on any major artery, e.g., Highway 7, 55, 5, 36, 35, 94, 394
- Drive from downtown Mpls to IS494 or 694 and then all around at least half the circumference

1. What do/did you find, i.e.,"empirical" evidence that *contrasts suburbs and city?*

People [numbers, varieties, patterns, trends as you travel out of city/into the city]

Organizations [schools, businesses, churches, employment opportunities, dining]

Physical Environment
a) Natural

b) Person-made

Technology [means created to accomplish a goal, both physical and social]

Culture [Values, beliefs, attitudes--often inferred from other evidence]

2) Evidence of "vertical/external" influence [realities/forces outside the suburb]?:

3) Evidence of "horizontal" collaboration/connectedness within suburb/region:

4) Evidence of "agency"--"individual"/collective efforts to change/stabilize things:

5) Evidence of conflict over scarce resources in the suburb:

6) Questions that come to mind *about suburbanization* doing this exercise [KDK]:

7) Surprises about suburbs and suburbanization[DKDK]:

LEARNING FROM OTHERS: INTERVIEWING "INFORMANTS" [11/10; #10]

ASSIGNMENT: While you are at your field placement site, giving plenty of time for busy schedules of community residents and staff, arrange for a 15 minute interview/focused conversation with someone who has lived/worked in neighborhood for at least 2 years, longer if possible, asking them their perceptions [cf. ch. 16 and "definition of the situation"] about changes in
1) Minneapolis; 2) their neighborhood; and 3) the Twin Cities overall.
N.B. Consult with your core group so that you are not interviewing the same people.

Person #1   Person #2

1. What major changes have you seen in the neighborhood during the past decade?

-major changes in the city?

-major changes in the Twin Cities region?

2) What are some of the greatest strengths of this neighborhood?

-of the city of Mpls?

-of the Twin Cities region?

3) What are some of the good things that are happening in this neighborhood now?

-in the city of Mpls?

-in the Twin Cities region?

4) What are some of the biggest challenges that we face in this neighborhood?

-in the city of Mpls?

-in the Twin Cities region?

Summarize and highlight what you learned, especially "new" information and insights [dkdk] and questions that stand out in your mind from all your accumulated KA & AW to date [on the back].

Learning More About Your Nhd & Minneapolis: *COMPARISONS* [11/17; #11]

Assignment: Spend an hour on this project, with an extra hour to spend at your field placement site.
-Peruse/scan the Neighborhood File [reserve] and State of the City book [1994]--Reference Section G 1429 M51 M5; "loaner" from class
-Look through the material, focusing upon the major trends *and how your neighborhood/its planning district COMPARE & CONTRAST WITH THE REST OF THE CITY OF MINNEAPOLIS* as captured in charts, graphs and summaries.
-In other words, *try to learn as much as you can in 1 hour,* taking advantage of having all this information collected for you and readily available. Be a sponge, learning as much new information ["KA"] and as much as you can to complement your previous experiences, reading, and field study assignments ["AW" & "KA"]. Complete the following before coming to class, including as much new information about the city as you can below [legibly], but at least two (2) new KK, focusing on: *COMPARISONS BETWEEN YOUR NEIGHBORHOOD AND THE REST OF THE CITY [other neighborhoods and the city as a whole* [DKDK before you perused the State of the City] in each category below. *Note: Be precise and as factual as you can, e.g., exact population, changes, etc., using a modified POETS assessment of the dispersion of race, ethnicity and poverty:*

1. Making use of the State of the City, 1994 you can make use of pp. *3-10,* 14-17, 20, 23, 24-29, 32-49, 51, 52,128-145, 154, 157, 160, 177 and other pages and sections, identify at least two significant *COMPARISONS BETWEEN*

          YOUR NHD   CITY [MPLS] with reference to:

a. POPULATION [P]
-Income/poverty

-Race and ethnicity

-Household characteristics

b. HOUSING [E]
      -Types and condition

c. PUBLIC AND PRIVATE INSTITUTIONS/ORGANIZATIONS ["O"]
-Schools, libraries, etc.

-Businesses, industries

d. PHYSICAL ENVIRONMENT [E]
-NATURAL "E", e.g., lakes, creeks...

-PERSON-MADE "E", e.g., highways, public parks,

2. What might explain these variations and why there are such differences within the city itself?
-Evidence of "vertical/external" EXPLANATIONS FOR THESE VARIATIONS/SIMILARITY:

-Evidence of VARIATIONS in "horizontal" collaboration/connectedness that might explain variations:

-Evidence of VARIATION in "agency"--"individual"/collective efforts to change/stabilize community:

-Other elements of "POETS":

SOCIAL LADDERS IN THE TWIN CITIES: ANOTHER LOOK
United Way Report and Update [due 11/24; # 12]

I. WHAT SURPRISED YOU [DKDK]?

II. MOST IMPORTANT NEW "KA" FOR UNDERSTANDING "HUMAN COMMUNITY IN A METROPOLIS" [KK]

III. QUESTIONS I HAVE AS A RESULT OF READING THIS REPORT [KDK]:

IV. KNOWING WHAT YOU KNOW NOW ABOUT CITIES AND METRO-POLITAN REALITIES, WHAT PUBLIC POLICY ACTIONS MIGHT BE TAKEN TO CHANGE THE TRENDS THAT ARE IDENTIFIED ["AGENCY"]?

Bentley College

SO 300 - Community Involvement

Spring 1998 Mondays (3:35 - 6:15)

<hr>

SYLLABUS

Professors:

> Jim Ostrow, Behavioral Sciences Department; Service-Learning Center
> Office: Morison 101A, ph 891-2920
> Maureen Goldman, English Department; Undergraduate Dean
> Office: Morison 386

Readings:

> Packet under course name sold in bookstore:
> Jonathan Kozol, Amazing Grace (New York: Crown, 1995)
> David Bollier, Aiming Higher (Washington, D.C.: American Management Association, 1996)
> Additional readings TBA

Course Description:

> In this course, students engage in public service within agencies or organizations in the Greater Boston area. In their written work and class discussions, they will reflect on both the purposes of that work as well as on its limits as a response to specific needs within the community and more general problems of social justice. Students will also explore issues of social responsibility and citizenship in the professions and business world in relation to the social problems that they become acquainted with through their community work.

Community Service Component:

> Students spend approximately two hours a week (more if they like) at their community service sites. The sites are located in Waltham and the Greater Boston area, with lots of options including multicultural youth clubs and public schools, day care centers, emergency adolescent shelters, homeless shelters and food programs, centers for low-income elderly citizens, addiction treatment centers, community youth groups, programs for the mentally challenged, local food pantries, drop in centers for HIV positive individuals, and involvement in Bentley's Immigrant Assistance Program

Fourth Credit Option:

> You may elect to register for an extra one-credit course that attaches to SO300. The basic requirement for the 4th credit is an *additional* two hours a week (minimum) community service and additional field note and analytical writing. The specifics are worked out independently with each student.

Grading Procedures:

Full attendance, completion of assigned readings, and active class participation are basic requirements for this course. Course work consists of written reflections completed each week during the term, with the final weeks of the semester devoted to producing an essay that is based on examples from your experiences and observations "in the field" plus relevant points from readings. The written reflections will be graded and returned every other week. The final grade is based on your written work, with active class participation being an important consideration. Our class discussions and your participation in them will center largely on your weekly written reflections, so it is necessary for all work to be submitted on time.

Late Work:

You are responsible for keeping up with the assignments announced during the course. If for some very, very good reason you miss a class, call or Email one of us **on that day** if you are unable to get the next meeting's work from another student. Again, because of the nature of this course, work must be submitted on time. If class is missed due to illness, work should be submitted as soon after as possible.

Rewrites:

Rewrites of papers are welcome and may be handed in at anytime, excluding the final two weeks of the semester. You **must** speak with one of us prior to doing a rewrite, particularly because some of the work, direct field descriptions, for instance, does not lend itself to rewriting. We recommend that you meet with one of us during the rewriting process, if for no other reason than we do the grading. When handing in a rewrite, attach the corrected original. Rewrites of late papers are graded as such.

Staying in Contact:

Speaking of Email, a requirement in this course is that you **check it every day** for messages from us or your classmates. Please come to our office as often as you like in order to continue discussing topics of interest, clear up any confusion about course requirements, assignments, ideas, or anything else. We are free at various times during the week, but you need to make an appointment - even during office hours. Bentley College gets (real big) money from you and gives (a very, very small bit of) it to us: You're owed our time; cash in.

Written Reflections:

The written reflections consist of assigned tasks in description and analysis. They are integral to each week's class discussion. Your written reflections will always have something to do with (1) the course readings, revealing your thoughts about authors' arguments, including relevant personal observations or experiences, and (2) your on-site work in the community. The reflections should be composed carefully and in complete sentences. All work should be typed on computer. Remember to save repeatedly as you are working, and always save work on both the hard drive and a floppy disc; never save work in only one place, because if something goes wrong you'll have to rewrite everything. Be prepared to type 3 or more pages each week.

Grading Criteria for Written Reflections:

There are different "levels" of analytical sophistication that you can adopt for the written reflections, and we will assign grades accordingly. We have tried to spell out the different criteria below; whenever you feel something is unclear, you should speak up - you should always know where you stand and why.

"A"   We will give this grade to well-composed, thorough treatments of assigned themes. These entries will include clearly developed, creative discussion of chosen points from the readings and chosen examples from your community service experiences and observations.

"A-"   The same criteria as above apply to this grade. Here, there were only scattered ambiguities in the development of specific points.

"B+"   In this case, the entry is sometimes awkwardly composed; but these are generally clear reflections with some creative criticism and examples.

"B"   Here, the entry is sometimes difficult to follow, but it includes plenty of creative criticism and examples. On the other hand, if the entry is a well-argued, straightforward discussion of specific points in the readings, but is weak in either reflection on/criticism of these points or in developed examples from the community site, it is at this level.

"B-"   The same criteria for a "B" apply here, with somewhat less development or clarity in the discussion.

"C+"   Here, the entry may be well-developed as far as it goes, but it is an abbreviated version of what was assigned. On the other hand, things may be thorough, if often hard to follow for the reader.

"C"   In this case, it is clear that the readings were completed, but the discussion of them and one's community service read more as a summary than developed reflection; also, often hard to follow.

"C-   As we go down in grade from here, it appears to us that the entry is produced very quickly just to "get it in." As you can see; if it is relatively cogent, it will pass.

Schedule of Readings:

1/26   Introduction

2/2   **Differences, Connections, and Perspective**
Agee, "Near a Church"; Geertz, "The Raid"; Selzer, "Imelda"

2/9   **Differences, Connections, and Perspective**
Chambliss, "The Saints and the Roughnecks"; Mansfield, "The Garden Party"

2/16   NO CLASS (Presidents' Day)

2/23   **What is "Community?"**
        Kozol, Amazing Grace

3/2   **What is "Community?"**
        Kozol, Amazing Grace

3/9   NO CLASS (Spring Break)

3/16   **What is "Community?"**
        Kozol, Amazing Grace

3/23   **Building "Community"; the Reach and Limits of "Service"**
        McNight, "Redefining Community"; Walker, "Everyday Use"

3/30   **Discovery and Idealism**
        Carver, "Cathedral," "A Small Good Thing"

4/6   **Social Responsibility and the Professions**
        Bollier, Aiming Higher

4/13   **Social Responsibility and the Professions**
        Bollier, Aiming Higher

4/20   NO CLASS (Patriots' Day)

4/27   **Service," Self, and Career**
        Selzer, "Imelda" (reread); "Toenails"; "Chatterbox"
        Handouts
        Discussion of final essays

SO 300 - Community Involvement
Sample Reflection Assignments

Written Assignment
Written Reflection #1
Perspectives and Relations With Others

In this course, we focus on the phenomenon of "perspective," and we will pay special attention to how our relations with others are framed by our perspectives. The stories by Agee, Selzer, and Geertz are actual accounts of the authors' experiences in unfamiliar cultures, where inhabitants' perspectives differ from their own. The authors are involved in various struggles in their relations with others as they deal with these differences. For this reflection, record your reactions to each of the three stories, referring to them in specific terms. Include one or more examples of related incidents from your own experience or observations in your discussion. Feel free to concentrate more on the stories that grab you. Any examples from your first efforts to enter/experiences in your community placements are welcome.

Written Reflection #3
[Double entry]

You have three separate tasks for this assignment, which covers two weeks and counts as a double entry. Each part should yield 1-3 pages; the total entry should be at least five pages in length - We're sure some of you will want to produce more; up to you. You have the option of completing only 1 of the first 2 tasks; you must do the third, since it is essential to the next class meeting. In any case, the completed entry should be at least a solid five pages in length.

(1) Produce a set of reflections on your experiences in and observations of the "To Tell the Truth" exercise and discussion. One way of defining the phenomenon of "belief" is the perception of what is true or false; The term "value" can be defined as the perception of "worth" - including such distinctions as "right vs. wrong" or "good vs. bad." Using these definitions, how would you characterize your (and others'?) beliefs and values as revealed during this event (protect others' identify by not naming them in your reflections)? What did you learn from the event? What is your view of "the homeless," and how was it influenced, if at all, by this event?

(2) Choose an event(s) from your first or second visit (or, if continuing, a current visit) to your community placements and describe it (them) in detail. Construct a moment-by-moment narrative that catches both the details of the social environment as well as your actual experiences - what you were doing, thinking, and feeling at the time of the instance(s) being described. Include in your descriptions what <u>others</u> appeared to be experiencing as you observed them at the time. Others names should be changed in order to protect

confidentiality. Try to choose event(s) that seem to really capture how you and others are viewing one another.

(3) For this final task, first identify a "community" that you have experienced. It is entirely your choice what counts as "a community" for you in this discussion, but you have to identify why you believe what you have chosen counts as a "community." On the back of this page, there is a fairly extensive list of key issues regarding the meaning of "community" as viewed from a sociological perspective. Each of these could be the topic of an extensive study. Look through the list; some of these issues will resonate with your understanding of the community that you have identified; others will not. Take one or more of these issues and reflect for a couple of pages on your experience of this "community."

Themes for exploring the meaning of "community"

- In what respects is community a part of a person's life?
- How do people express feelings of attachment to or detachment from their communities? What do these expressed feelings reveal about the characteristics of a community? Can the way one describes one's community be viewed as an expression of one's social values?
- What is the relationship between the physical meaning of community - its boundaries, central markers, etc. - and the subjective meanings of community - how it's perceived and felt about?
- How are the factors of population, density, or heterogeneity relevant to the experience of aspects of community life?
- How is one's social role or status a factor in one's perspective of one's community?
- What do differences between persons' characterizations of the same community indicate about the places being discussed or about their social positions within these places?
- Is the location of the people one associates with on various levels - friendship, familial relations, fellow workers, etc. - a significant factor in one's perception of one's community?
- What are the circumstances under which various members of a community associate with one another, and how is this indicative of the type of community one lives in?
- What are the social circumstances under which one feels that one does or doesn't "belong" to a community?
- What are different forms of community "involvement," and how is this a way of understanding the phenomenon of "community" and its significance in a person's everyday life?
- How do members of communities define and discuss "community issues," and how is this significant for our understanding of types of community?
- How does community change influence one's life and relations with others?

Written Reflection #4
Reactions to Amazing Grace

In this entry, please produce a set of reflections on the first four chapters of Kozol's Amazing Grace. Focus your attention on what "grabs" you in the book, and how what you read may relate to what we have read about or discussed in the course thus far. For each of the four chapters, organize at least part of your reflections around (1) what "shocked" you the most, (2) what acts or persons did you particularly admire, and (3) how would you tackle the problems that are revealed in the chapter if you had the resources [what resources would you need]?

Also in this entry, either as a separate section or integrated (if you desire), you should include a set of descriptive reflections on you experience in the community service setting thus far - focusing on initial impressions, perceptions, concerns, and relationship-beginnings - all of the sort of things that Kozol is focusing on also vis-a-vis his own experience in his setting.

Try to produce a solid three pages for the entire entry - more if you like!

Written Assignment
Reflection #8
Discoveries

In the readings by Raymond Carver, "A Small Good Thing" and "Cathedral," individuals have experiences that stir certain kinds of "discovery," "awakening," and sometimes transformations in personal perspective. "Big" moments are described in these texts, but it is worth noting that sometimes, the "smaller," seemingly trivial events can stir feelings of discovery and new awareness in our experience.

Please produce some reflections on the two readings by Carver that focus on the theme of discovery and change through experience. Include examples from your community service experiences in your discussion. We are not saying that you have been profoundly effected or transformed by these experiences (of course, we're not saying that you haven't). But these are new settings and experiences, so you've learned things; also, your own perspective has evolved vis-a-vis the setting and its inhabitants as you've become more familiar with things each week. Recount these changes and growth, think about how your views of particular things have developed, and try to draw direct or indirect connections to what you say about the readings.

Assignment #10
Final Essay

We want your final essay to be based upon an investigation of a topic or issue that is related to the general subjects of community and community involvement. We are open to any suggestions in class: we recommend the two alternatives of either conducting one or more interview, or conducting library research. When you go to write the essay, use examples from your "data," community service experience, experiences in class, and, of course, course or outside readings to develop your points. The essay should be 4 1/2 or more pages in length.

Some possibilities:

- Explore the topic of social responsibility in a profession or type of business by (1) interviewing one or more persons on the issue [perhaps a professional in a selected field; or an adminstrator at your site] or (2) investigating the topic through library research.

- Explore the topic of individuals' sense of belonging to a "community" through (1) interviews - perhaps using the interview schedule that was introduced in class (would be interesting to do this with folks at your community site) or (2) library research on the topic of community.

- Explore the topic of "community service" through (1) interviews - perhaps interviewing different persons' sense of you at your site (another idea would be to design a questionnaire on the topic and selecting a group to administer it to - you could run a "focus group" as well), or (2) library research on the topic of community service. This general topic could break down in several ways - e.g., the debate over Clinton's national service legislation, the views of members of a specific "community" on the topic of service, different views on the concept of "service," etc.

Final Essay: Suggested Guidelines

I.   Introduction (approximately 1/2 - 1 page)

  A)   You should begin with a clear introduction to the theoretical focus of your paper. What specific issue will this paper address?

  B)   After you establish your theoretical problem for the reader, go on to describe the primary subject matter of our analyses - which means the kinds of examples that you will be discussing.

II. Main Analysis (approximately 3 pages)

  In this section you are presenting and interpreting examples from your investigations. In your analysis you are expected to make creative use of ideas and examples from course or outside readings - and, of course, feel free to include examples from your community service experience.

III. Conclusion (approximately 1 page)

  What have your analyses contributed to our understanding of the topic? Discuss ways to further explore some of your ideas. Can you think of ways to research the points made in the paper? Your paper should end on a fresh note: opening up further lines of inquiry.

Appendix

Contributors to This Volume

Volume Editors

James Ostrow is director of academic affairs and associate professor of sociology at the Pennsylvania State University-Fayette. Prior to his appointment at Penn State, he served as director of the Bentley Service-Learning Center and chair of behavioral sciences at Bentley College. He is the author of *Social Sensitivity: A Study of Habit and Experience,* and his research on educational practice and human experience explores the intersection of social theory, continental philosophy, and American pragmatist philosophy.

Garry Hesser is professor of sociology at Augsburg College and the recipient of Campus Compact's 1998 Thomas Ehrlich Award for faculty achievement in service-learning. He is the past president of the National Society for Experiential Education and of the Higher Education Consortium for Urban Affairs. He is the author of *Experiential Education as a Liberating Art,* and his current research focuses on service-learning as well as the area of housing and neighborhood revitalization.

Sandra Enos is assistant professor of sociology and justice studies at Rhode Island College. She previously served as project director of the Integrating Service With Academic Study program at Campus Compact. She has published in the area of curricular options in service-learning.

Other Contributors

Martha Bergin is assistant professor of communication at GateWay Community College. Her scholarship focuses on intercultural communication and performance.

Judith R. Blau is professor of sociology at the University of North Carolina-Chapel Hill. Her books include *The Shape of Culture* and *Social Contracts and Economic Markets,* and she is completing a book on 19th-century America, *In Print: Papering Over Diversity.*

J. Richard Kendrick, Jr., is assistant professor of sociology-anthropology at the State University of New York College at Cortland. He conducts research on recruitment and participation in social movements, and integration of academics and activism.

Hugh F. Lena is professor of sociology and an instructional faculty member of the Feinstein Institute for Public Service at Providence College. His research interests are in medical sociology and organizational theory, with recent publications in the areas of service-learning basic needs provision in developing nations, and occupational stratification.

Sam Marullo is associate professor and undergraduate program director of sociology at Georgetown University. His research focuses on the causes of violence and efforts to reduce or prevent violence through conflict resolution and peer mediation.

Susan McAleavey is a member of the sociology and social work faculty at Mesa Community College. She has conducted numerous workshops and has published extensively on the subject of service-learning.

Douglas V. Porpora is associate professor of sociology at Drexel University. He is the author of *The Concept of Social Structure* and *How Holocausts Happen: The U.S. in Central America,* and he is completing a book on moral purpose and identity at the end of the millennium.

Kerry J. Strand is professor of sociology at Hood College. Her current research interests include women's reproductive health care and women in higher education, particularly factors that influence college women's persistence and achievement in mathematics.

Barbara H. Vann is associate professor of sociology and faculty associate in the Center for Values and Service at Loyola College in Maryland. She conducts research on the effects of poverty legislation, particularly welfare reform, on women.

Series Editor

Edward Zlotkowski is professor of English at Bentley College. Founding director of the Bentley Service-Learning Project, he has published and spoken on a wide variety of service-learning topics. Currently, he is senior associate at the American Association for Higher Education.